New Mediums, Better Messages?

New Mediums, Better Messages?

How Innovations in Translation, Engagement, and Advocacy are Changing International Development

Edited by

DAVID LEWIS
DENNIS RODGERS
MICHAEL WOOLCOCK

Great Clarendon Street, Oxford, OX2 6DP,
United Kingdom

Oxford University Press is a department of the University of Oxford.
It furthers the University's objective of excellence in research, scholarship,
and education by publishing worldwide. Oxford is a registered trade mark of
Oxford University Press in the UK and in certain other countries

Impression: 2

Published in the United States of America by Oxford University Press
198 Madison Avenue, New York, NY 10016, United States of America

British Library Cataloguing in Publication Data
Data available

Library of Congress Control Number: 2022930872

ISBN 978–0–19–885875–1 (hbk)
ISBN 978–0–19–885876–8 (pbk)

DOI: 10.1093/oso/9780198858751.001.0001

Printed and bound by
CPI Group (UK) Ltd, Croydon, CR0 4YY

Contents

PART III. ENGAGEMENT

Contributors

Maria Faciolince is a multimedia communicator, researcher, and ecofeminist activist focusing on shifting narratives around gender, and economic and environmental justice. She has an MA in Psychology and Anthropology from the University of St Andrews, and an MSc in Anthropology and Development from the London School of Economics and Political Science.

Jolene Fisher is Assistant Professor in Advertising, Public Relations, and Media Design at the University of Colorado, Boulder. Her research explores intersections of new media, gender, and strategic communication for development and social change.

Duncan Green is Senior Strategic Adviser at Oxfam GB and Professor in Practice in International Development at the London School of Economics and Political Science. He is author of *How Change Happens* (Oxford University Press, 2016). His daily development blog can is available at www.oxfamblogs.org/fp2p/.

Sophie Harman is Professor of International Politics at Queen Mary University of London where she teaches and conducts research into global health politics, Africa and International Relations, and global governance. She is the author of *Global Health Governance* (Routledge, 2012), and the *World Bank and HIV/AIDS* (Routledge, 2010), and produced her first feature film *Pili* in 2016.

Danny Hoffman is an anthropologist and the Bartley-Dobb Professor for the Study and Prevention of Violence at the Jackson School of International Studies, University of Washington (Seattle). He is the author of two ethnographies on West Africa's Mano River War and its aftermath, *The War Machines: Young Men and Violence in Sierra Leone and Liberia* (Duke University Press, 2011) and *Monrovia Modern: Urban Form and Political Imagination in Liberia* (Duke University Press, 2017).

Ben Jones is Senior Lecturer in Development Studies at the University of East Anglia. He is the author of *Beyond the State in Rural Uganda* (Edinburgh University Press, 2008).

Patrick Kabanda is a Juilliard-trained organist and a Fletcher-trained scholar of international affairs. Besides concertizing and lecturing worldwide, he has taught at Phillips Academy, and consulted for the World Bank's Office of the Senior Vice President and Chief Economist. He is the author of *The Creative Wealth of Nations: Can the Arts Advance Development?* (Cambridge University Press, 2018).

Emily Le Roux-Rutledge is Senior Lecturer in Social Psychology at the University of the West of England (Bristol). Her research examines the identities of marginalized groups in global contexts, and more specifically, how people interpret media, construct narratives about themselves, and negotiate their identities in the face of local and global public narratives about who they are and should be.

David Lewis is Professor of Anthropology and Development at the London School of Economics and Political Science. He is co-editor with Dennis Rodgers and Michael Woolcock of the volume *Popular Representations of Development* (Routledge, 2014). Since the 1990s he has released five albums as a singer-songwriter, some of which are available at https://davidlewis3.bandcamp.com.

Mark Ralph-Bowman has worked in education, journalism, and theatre in Uganda, Nigeria, and the UK. Currently he divides his time between creative writing and voluntary work with the Youth Justice system and supporting refugees.

Dennis Rodgers is Research Professor of Anthropology and Sociology at the Graduate Institute of International and Development Studies, Geneva (Switzerland), and the PI of the ERC Advanced Grant-funded project 'Gangs, Gangsters, and Ganglands: Towards a Global Comparative Ethnography' (GANGS). He is co-editor with David Lewis and Michael Woolcock of the volume *Popular Representations of Development* (Routledge, 2014).

Caroline Sage is a Senior Social Development Specialist in the World Bank, currently based in Nepal. Previously she was based in Nigeria with the bank, where she also ran monthly arts events to promote and engage with local contemporary artists. Caroline believes that the arts play a crucial role a community's development and sense of identity and connection. Attending contemporary arts festivals is one of her favourite things to do.

Shahpar Selim has a PhD from the London School of Economics and Political Science and is author of *Ecological Modernisation and Environmental Compliance: The Garments Industry in Bangladesh* (Routledge, 2011). She was recently a visiting researcher at the International Centre for Climate Change and Development (ICCCAD) working on green growth for Bangladeshi industries. She is currently working in development in Dhaka, Bangladesh.

Hilary Standing is Emeritus Fellow at the Institute of Development Studies, University of Sussex. She is a social anthropologist specializing in health systems development and reproductive and sexual health. In 2015, she published *The Inheritance Powder*, a novel based on a real-life development tragedy, the slow poisoning of millions of people in Bangladesh by arsenic in their drinking water thanks to a well-meant but disastrous international aid intervention.

Michael Woolcock is Lead Social Scientist in the World Bank's Development Research Group, and an Adjunct Lecturer in Public Policy at Harvard University's Kennedy School of Government. He is co-editor with David Lewis and Dennis Rodgers of the volume *Popular Representations of Development* (Routledge, 2014).

Introduction

Innovations in Translation, Advocacy, and Engagement in Global Development

David Lewis, Dennis Rodgers, and Michael Woolcock

Introduction

Academic social science or policy-oriented research documents have generally been the predominant modes of communication for engaging with the complex and contentious set of processes known as 'global development'. For the purposes of conducting serious empirical analysis that informs policymaking, implementation strategies, and evaluation protocols—much of it concerned with discerning the optimal use of public money for public purposes—this is perhaps as it should be. But it has long been recognized that development influences and is influenced by all aspects of human life, and that, as such, social science is but one representational option among many for conveying the myriad ways in which development is conceived, encountered, experienced, justified, courted, and/or resisted by different groups at particular times and places. In an earlier edited volume, *Popular Representations of Development*,[1] we brought together authors exploring the ways in which various genres within popular culture—novels, films, television, social media—had portrayed the phenomenon of development, comparing and contrasting the particular insights these media convey vis-à-vis mainstream social science. It was an original, instructive, and well-received venture, which generated strong sales, numerous citations, favourable reviews, and many seminar invitations.

Encouraged by this response, we considered the merits of a follow-up effort, and what its distinctive contribution would entail. Our deliberations led us to a conviction that there was both an intellectual and a practical rationale for a new volume on the topic. First, the intellectual context, extending the themes explored in our earlier book. As mainstream social science (including global development) has once again become strongly quantitative and economics centred, there is nonetheless an enduring sense that what is measured (and thus 'valued', 'managed', and

[1] Lewis et al. (2014).

David Lewis, Dennis Rodgers, and Michael Woolcock, *Introduction*. In: *New Mediums, Better Messages?*.
Edited by David Lewis, Dennis Rodgers, and Michael Woolcock, Oxford University Press.
 DOI: 10.1093/oso/9780198858751.003.0001

prioritized) may have become too narrow, that the powers of prediction claimed by some areas of economics and management may have overreached, and that the human dimension is in danger of being lost. Reflecting this concern, there is currently renewed interest in conversations between science, social science, and the humanities around the roles of different kinds of knowledge, stories, and data in apprehending the human condition, and how they might be more fruitfully integrated.[2]

For example, Morson and Schapiro (2017: 9, 13) argue that the humanities have something useful to offer economics to get it back on track; as they rightly assert, 'to understand people one must tell stories about them. There is no way to grasp most of what individuals and groups do by deductive logic'. More positively, 'the humanities could supplement economics: with stories, a better understanding of the role of culture, and a healthy respect for ethics in all its complexity'. For economist Thomas Piketty (2013), most prominently in his famous study of capitalism and inequality, nineteenth-century novels provide useful illustrations of processes and trends to which, he argues, mainstream economists need to pay closer attention. Similarly, innovative game theorists have explicitly argued that novelists such as Jane Austen effectively pioneered the field, in the sense that Austen 'theorized choice and preferences, prized strategic thinking, and analyzed why superiors are often strategically clueless about inferiors' (see Chwe, 2013). In South Africa, soap operas embedded with financial management messages have also been shown to positively alter viewers' debt and gambling behaviours (Berg and Zia, 2017).

In the reverse direction, Greenblatt (2018) deftly assesses the full corpus of Shakespeare's plays to derive a careful, mechanisms-based account of tyranny—of how those clearly unfit for political leadership nonetheless rise to and retain their hold on power, despite amply displaying 'infantile psychology and unquenchable narcissistic appetites'. More than 400 years have passed since *Richard III* and *Macbeth* (for example) were penned, but it is hard to imagine that the most comprehensive contemporary social scientific or historical inquiry into the dynamics of tyranny—or, for that matter, the passage of another 400 years—would yield qualitatively different conclusions from those Greenblatt discerns in Shakespeare. And classically, of course, 'the theatre' has been deftly deployed as a metaphor for understanding the necessary performativity of politicians (Geertz, 1980) and lawyers (Balkin, 2018).[3]

[2] Even on economic grounds alone, the arts and humanities themselves make an important material contribution to society. Kabanda (2018) makes a compelling case for the performing arts as both an important (if 'largely invisible') tradeable 'commodity' and a universal realm in which rich and poor alike find and express meaning.

[3] Numerous authors have also weighed in on the various rendering of complex legal matters in Shakespeare (e.g. Yoshino, 2012).

Such exchanges between seemingly contrasting epistemological modes of inquiry and representation are far from new. We see this recent trend as a continuation of earlier traditions of spirited conversations between the humanities, sciences, and social sciences—exemplified in discussions about relations between 'two cultures' (Snow, 1993), rhetoric and economics (Hirschman, 1991; McCloskey, 1998), literature and law (Posner, 2009), and literature and social science (Coser, 1972; Spradley and McDonough, 1973; Berger, 1977)—a tradition we were interested in extending and applying to the world of global development through our previous volume.[4] Our first aim with this new volume is therefore to continue to contribute to and sustain this intellectual debate, but taking it further, in particular extending the range of representational forms considered in our first volume to include theatre, music, photography, video games, radio, and journalism, among others, as well as offering new insights in relation to novels and blogs.[5]

The second dimension of this new volume is its engagement with development policy and practice. At the level of general public policy, there is new enthusiasm for behavioural science, 'big data', 'nudges', 'artificial intelligence', and randomized control trials.[6] Such approaches enable policy professionals to make bold new claims about how to engage with complexity, but at the risk of compounding the problem by over-relying on technical and instrumental approaches to problem solving. For example, at the time of writing, the Covid-19 pandemic is highlighting these kinds of tensions between expert researchers, policymakers, and citizens in finding supportable and implementable solutions. Epidemiologists are on a steep learning curve as they study the new (and mutating) virus, and in this complex and rapidly evolving field there is inherently a diverse range of expert views about what practitioners and politicians should be doing to protect populations. The necessarily 'unsettled' nature of current scientific advice has lead certain politicians for their part to selectively appropriate and instrumentalize advice that suits their own purposes, even as many expert models have been accurate enough in conveying risk and generating policy advice that, when heeded by political leaders and citizens, has helped save lives.[7] Faced with advice that can be experienced as confused and confusing, it is perhaps not surprising that many citizens are dismissing scientific advice altogether or complying only when it is consistent with what they already planned to do. Citizens might be better placed to adhere to prevailing scientific advice—or, more ambitiously, to appreciate the necessary

[4] See also Jasonoff (2017: 9), who uses four major novels by Joseph Conrad as the anchor for both a new biography of Conrad and 'a history of globalization seen from the inside out'.

[5] A wide range of new work continues to emerge on these topics, including Cooke and Soria-Donlan (2020), Bailey (2021), and Marsh (2021), suggesting that interest in our broad theme is intensifying.

[6] See, among many others, Leigh (2018).

[7] Available at https://www.theguardian.com/commentisfree/2020/apr/09/deadly-virus-britain-failed-prepare-mers-sars-ebola-coronavirus.

uncertainty that accompanies policy advice based on science that itself is learning as it goes about the problem it is confronting; but that they should comply with the advice anyway!—if it was conveyed to them in mediums and by people they find more compelling. We argue that our approach to 'broadening the canvas' is increasingly important as a constructive complement to high-stakes policy deliberation, in no small part because artistic mediums may resonate far more directly with how marginalized communities—e.g. migrants, refugees, those who are illiterate—convey their experiences to themselves and others,[8] and because a defining feature of the most complex problems is that they do not lend themselves to technical solutions.[9]

When it comes to the specific world of global development, we suggest that there is an increasing need to think in new ways about policy and practice. The concept of 'development' has expanded from an earlier emphasis on economic/technical concerns, from narrow Cold War geographies of the 'Third World', and from an emphasis on wealthy countries helping poor ones, to become one of the central organizing ideas of our age. Today, the idea of development speaks increasingly inclusively about how the world is changing more broadly, and to questions of who wins and who loses from such change (Gardner and Lewis, 2015), as well as to broader, philosophical questions of social justice and the 'good life' (not just in relation to people but also nature and the planet more generally). For example, the UN's Sustainable Development Goals (SDGs) now apply to all countries; thinking about poverty has widened to embrace 'quality of life' issues; and more nuanced conceptualizations have evolved with regard to democratization, poverty, and governance. As such, the ways we go about 'doing' development must also be expanded, going beyond the conventional modalities to include the role of culture, narrative, and emotion, responding to critics of development who point to continuing problems of 'solution driven aid'—i.e. aid that pays insufficient attention to local histories, diversity, cultures, contexts, and practices (Booth, 2018).

Development, as an intensely public space, is ideal ground on which to pursue these bigger questions of epistemology—to weigh up the merits of different logics of enquiry and new measures of experience. At the same time, however, this volume also explicitly aims to highlight and investigate how newer areas of development practice actively draw on unconventional and innovative modes of engagement such as the use of video games, theatre, or photography in order to reach new audiences or bring new messages, and/or to reflect changing realities and ideas. A critical exploration of these new frontiers of practice connects with our first aim but also takes the agenda initially developed in our *Popular Representations of Development* volume a significant step further, moving from simply

[8] For two recent highly acclaimed illustrations, see the graphic novels by Bui (2017) and Gharib (2019).

[9] On this issue, see, among others Andrews et al. (2017).

considering alternative representations of development to thinking about more transformative forms of 'doing development differently'. As such, we hope this volume will help push the debates beyond the epistemological towards the more practical, in the process engaging broader professional audiences and everyday citizens beyond academic social science.

The Structure of This Volume

In the conclusion to our *Popular Representations of Development* volume, we identified three broad issues that we felt were important for future research agendas to consider in relation to the existence of alternative forms of knowledge about development. These were:

(1) How popular representations of development can successfully compete with or (in some cases) even supersede social scientific representations from the perspective of both conceptual and empirical representation;
(2) The political economy of popular representations of development, including the differences between 'independent' vs 'mainstream' media, and the way that popular media productions shape debates;
(3) The extent to which popular representations of development represent alternative critiques that allow for the articulation of views that would be unacceptable in more orthodox mediums or forums.

This volume explicitly follows up on this agenda. We propose that the three above issues can be thought of more simply as respectively corresponding to processes of 'translation', 'advocacy', and 'engagement', and have organized this volume into three eponymous parts each presenting four contributions illustrating the key topics pertaining to each of these issues.

Translation

The first, translation, can be viewed from both the perspective of content and audience. One of the issues that clearly emerged from our previous exploration of more popular representations of development processes is that media such as novels, films, TV series, or blogs generally have a much greater reach than standard academic or policy outputs. This in itself is a reason for taking them seriously, whether with regards to their positive impact—e.g. influencing and mobilizing public opinion to act in relation to a crisis—or negative consequences—e.g. stereotyping, promulgating 'fake news', etc. On the other hand, a particular medium can also influence the nature of content, intrinsically offering or stressing different viewpoints and interpretations, as well as allowing for different forms of connection to an audience. This is something that is less considered, and is the focus of the four 'Translation' contributions to this volume.

We open with our own contribution on the way that the experience of development, as well as understandings of and responses to it, can be uniquely rendered via music. This has been a medium of choice through which marginalized populations all over the world convey their (frequently critical) views, while in the Global North music has also long played a prominent (if notorious) role in portraying the plight of the South's 'starving millions' as an emotional pretext for soliciting funds for international aid. We discuss the overlap between music and development in five specific domains: the tradition of western 'protest' music; musical resistance in the Global South; music-based development interventions; commodification and appropriation; and, finally, music as a globalized development vernacular. In doing so, we highlight the way that music offers different communicative modalities in and through which development debates are conducted, and how this, in turn, may lead to key stakeholders of development, such as the poor, finding said debates decidedly more open, authentic and compelling.

Chapter 2's contribution, by Danny Hoffman—himself a former professional photographer turned academic—contrasts the work of two photographers who take up, in very different ways, the subject of African dumping grounds. Dakar-based photographer Fabrice Monteiro and South Africa's Pieter Hugo have each produced well known and critically acclaimed bodies of work on the subject of accumulating African waste. In doing so, they build on a longer tradition of trash as trope in African image production, a tradition that uses the visual iconography of garbage to educate publics and to make political claims. Both artists employ an activist camera, seeking to use their work to catalyse action around environmental issues on the continent. But the different approaches to visualizing trash in Monteiro's *The Prophecy* and Hugo's *Permanent Error* reflect a broader divide over how photography communicates urgent issues in global development and what photography has to offer in the particular discourses of African environmental and economic futures. The two projects point towards different interpretations of the environmental and social politics of waste, and each calls for a different response from the audiences of their work.

The third and fourth contributions are in many ways mirror-images of each other. Chapter 3 is an account written by playwright Mark Ralph-Bowman of his experience writing and producing a play called *With You Always* which he had based on an academic book that he had copy-edited—an academic volume titled *Aid, NGOs and the Realities of Women's Lives: A Perfect Storm*. Contributions to the latter volume explored the difficult-to-unravel intersection between the real, lived experiences of women on the ground in the Global South involved either as recipients or distributors of 'aid' and 'development', and the rhetoric describing that reality to and in the North. It fundamentally challenged his (widely held) notion that 'doing no harm' with overseas aid was easy considering the clear visibility of poverty and underdevelopment, and the seemingly straightforward possibilities linked to food and material distribution. These experiences inspired him to write a play that also drew on his own experiences living in Uganda and Nigeria in the 1970s, insofar as the dynamics described in *Aid, NGOs and the Realities of Women's Lives* seemed to imply that very little had changed since then.

Chapter 4's contribution, by Hilary Standing, explores the dilemmas, challenges, and pitfalls that she encountered as an academic writing a novel, *The Inheritance Powder*, that drew on her real-life research, as well as the novel's subsequent journey into publication and reception. She particularly considers the broader representational questions that arose in this process, including her choice of a particular style of representation and the conventions that went with it, her politics and positionality as writer and how these differed from her work as an academic, and her relation to narrative viewpoints, the 'audience', and the role of commercial publishing as a gatekeeper of representations. She is especially concerned with the role of research and adherence to some kinds of empirical truth, exploring what novels 'do' differently—considering for example the role of humour, the 'irrelevant', the individual, and the particular (expanding on the idea of the freedom of fabrication), as well as what an academic has to learn about storytelling and audience.

Advocacy

In Part II of this volume, we are less interested in advocacy as it relates to instrumentally choosing a particular form of representation in order to seek to influence more efficiently, but rather to the potential reasons underlying said efficacy. The first of the four contributions to this part of the book, Chapter 5 by Duncan Green and Maria Faciolince, considers the nature and reasons for the popularity of the former's 'From Poverty to Power' (FP2P) blog. One of the world's most read global development blogs, with an annual readership of over 300,000, it is cited by government officials, academics, students, and aid workers all over the world. The chapter analyses the FP2P story, including its readership, the most read (and most controversial) blog posts, and the use of reader polls and guest posts, before then exploring some of the challenges of blogging within a large bureaucratic institution (Oxfam), and drawing potential lessons for academic and non-governmental organization (NGO) blogging.

Chapter 6, the second in this part, by Jolene Fisher, begins by describing the story behind the first development-oriented video game, 'Food Force', launched by the United Nations World Food Programme (WFP) in 2005. The downloadable

PC game, which was aimed at children aged eight to thirteen, took players to a fictitious island to teach them about the challenges of addressing hunger crises through six different emergency aid missions. The game, which was downloaded over six million times and played by approximately ten million people, was considered a hit and significantly conscientized people to the issue of hunger. Since then, almost forty digital games have been created specifically as tools for global development, including one called 'Half the Sky Movement: The Game',[10] which has been played by over one million players. Fisher explores how the narrative of this game reinforces a mainstream, neoliberal approach to development by framing poor women as responsible for overcoming social, cultural, and economic obstacles in order to change their lives for the better, arguing that such a narrative increases the burden placed on these women, while erasing the root causes of women's poverty and the expectation of state-based support. As such, Fisher highlights the potentially problematic nature of the content of popular forms of representation such as role-playing video games which rely on a number of non-explicit presuppositions.

Chapter 7, by Emily Le Roux-Rutledge, explores new forms of advocating for and representing women's empowerment, one of the key development issues of the last two decades. More specifically, her chapter seeks to understand some of the popular representations of women and development that are made available through the medium of radio, doing so by examining the BBC's *100 Women* series. Launched in 2013, following the infamous gang rape of a female student on a Delhi bus, the BBC's *100 Women* series tells the stories of 100 women each year, during what is called the BBC's 'women season'. Content goes out on various platforms, including the BBC World Service, which reaches a weekly global audience of 269 million—75 million of whom listen in English. In 2015 and 2016 half of the content featured women who came from the world's lowest income or least developed countries; Le Roux-Rutledge analyzes this content, drawing conclusions about how such stories shape understandings of women, empowerment, and development.

In Chapter 8, Ben Jones explores the *The Guardian*'s 'Katine' project, funded by the newspaper's readers. This involved collaboration between journalists, academics, and an NGO to carry out and document a range of development initiatives in Katine village, Uganda. This chapter draws on his experience as an involved academic, and points to some of the ways in which Katine offers an alternative way into thinking about and 'doing' development, but also the potential pitfalls of such novel forms of advocacy. He particularly highlights how the public scrutiny appearing on the website was a difficult experience for the NGO, and pushed it in directions it was not always comfortable with. This was partly due to the fact that, since *The Guardian* was funding the project, the pieces produced by Guardian

[10] See also the book by Kristoff and WuDunn (2010) with the same title, and companion children's edition.

journalists pushed the project in different directions. Both the NGO and the newspaper struggled to discuss their complex relationship in project documents, or on the project website, which Jones suggests was due to the fact that their relationship transgressed ideals of NGO expertise and journalistic values of objectivity and autonomy.

Engagement

Finally, we conceive the third issue, engagement, particularly from a perspective that explores how certain artistic mediums and representations can challenge more dominant, technocratic ones and the issues that they obscure, but also how the these can also facilitate new and better forms of engagement with stakeholders of development, including in particular the recipients of development aid, whose voices are frequently ignored or discounted.

In the first contribution to this part, Shahpar Selim engages with wider discussions about the neglect of the arts in engaging with climate change, focusing on the role of cultural resources in informing climate struggles and local initiatives to mitigate the phenomenon in Bangladesh. She begins by pointing out how Bangladesh's climate strategy has generally been to build institutional strength and capacity in climate change, to mainstream climate thinking across sectors, and to reach out to the most climate vulnerable populations with climate adaptive solutions. Structural and non-structural responses have been designed in ways that are mindful of local cultural contexts, but technical specialist knowledge has always held priority. She then goes on to argue for considering the importance of culture within climate change policymaking and programme design, and more specifically, enhancing the space for including putative 'non-expert' cultural resources in the form of paintings, theatre, poetry, songs, and literature, which she contends are a repository of local knowledge and practices. As such, she maintains that in order to build implementable and measurable progress towards adaptation or mitigation there is a need for policymakers and technical experts to engage with the broadest possible understanding of climate change, with culture being a powerful tool in advocacy that, if heeded, could multiply programme results and outcomes.

Chapter 10's contribution, by Caroline Sage, explores the ways in which contemporary arts festivals in Nigeria and Nepal not only encourage alternative representations and narratives of development, but also provide spaces for contestation and the deliberation of ideas about the country's future development. In particular, such festivals provide alternative narratives—to the seemingly dystopian visions of the future prevalent in Nigeria, to the 'lost Shangri-la' trope so often associated with Nepal—with many in fact overtly seeking to enhance their respective citizens' 'capacity to aspire' to something better. In so doing, the creative arts scene in both countries establishes itself as an important driver of change and development. Sage contends that despite the fact that attendees to such festivals are mainly the cosmopolitan intellectual class and the political elite, the contemporary arts festivals in which she has participated actually draw as much on hybrid combinations of local as well as global ideas and influences; by characterizing them solely as representative of an elite cosmopolitan ecumene, we miss how they also constitute spaces that help to define a national image and ultimately a 'more developed' imagined community.

Sophie Harman's Chapter 11 deals with a specific popular representation, the feature film *Pili*, about the everyday risk of HIV/AIDS in Tanzania, which she was involved in producing. The film was based on the stories of the cast of women who acted in the film, and Harman explores how the film impacted them as well as audiences more broadly. While 'impact' is more often than not conceived in educational terms or through the promotion of change, Harman argues that an underexplored aspect is affect: the emotions, thoughts, or experiences of the audience engaging in such representations. She reflects on the feedback she received on this from a range of audiences who watched *Pili*, including policymakers in the UK and global health hubs in Geneva and New York, everyday film audiences in the UK and Tanzania where the film is set, as well as those who participated in the production of the film itself in Tanzania, including those who were the subject of its representation. In so doing, she highlights how the impact and affect of popular representations can overlap and differ across a range of audiences, arguing that it is critical to take this into account when thinking about the universal appeal, authenticity, and impact of popular representations of development.

Finally, we close the volume with Chapter 12 by Patrick Kabanda, which considers 'the arts in the economy and the economy in the arts'. A powerful voice against integrating more artistic forms of expression within the realm of development is one contending that such endeavours represent something of a luxury, and in a field where decisions and investments frequently have literally life and death consequences, it is neither efficient nor ethical to devote resources to them. (Indeed, in 2016 such an argument was invoked when the UK government's Department of International Development, under pressure from coverage in the popular press, withdrew its financial support for a women's music initiative in Ethiopia, as we discuss in our contribution to this volume.) Through a set of contemporary cases from Zambia, Colombia, and the Philippines, however, Kabanda shows not only the value-added of less technocratic development initiatives, but also how they can in fact constitute the basis for significant economic gain, and that ultimately much of what we consider to be stone-cold economic transactions are in fact grounded in more artistic human expressions. Taking such expressions seriously suggests that in turning to less conventional forms of 'doing development' we are not facing potentially negative cost–benefit transactions but rather the possibility of engaging in more holistic, inclusive, and locally legitimate development practices.

Concluding Reflections, Future Directions

In putting this volume together, our aim was to further the agenda that we laid out in our previous book on *Popular Representations of Development*—that is to say, to try to frame and open up popular representation as an important new field of study that has to date been largely neglected by those engaged in research on global development. We do not claim to bring specialist knowledge to the subject that those more versed in media studies, literary theory, film studies, or post-colonial studies can bring (although of course some of our contributors are certainly able to do so). However, we very much hope that this collection will contribute to the opening up of new avenues for investigation and pose new questions across these boundaries and disciplines.

We believe this to be essential, as the current moment has seen an explosion in communication that is not only more frequent and intense, but also more diverse in form and content. Understanding the power, potential, and pitfalls of new mediums is essential in order to understand whether they are better purveyors of fundamental messages about development, or whether they contribute to making it more difficult to highlight these. Either way, it is clearly critical to engage with them and not remain entrenched in old ways of seeing and doing things. To this end, we hope this volume will stimulate further research into popular representations of development in ways that go beyond simply mapping these out to actively seeking to harness them, in order to engage the enduring challenges of global development with twenty-first century mediums and sensibilities.

Certainly, the possibility that broadening the canvas could challenge narrow-minded or fixed perspectives is becoming increasingly recognized (Nossel, 2016).[11] For example, in an article in the Cinema Journal Negar Mottahedeh (2018: 150) describes how he had been shocked by the 'black-and-white overlay' applied to the world by the use of the polarizing 'axis of evil' rhetoric in Goerge W. Bush's post-9/11 State of the Union address. In response he organized a film festival—which he called Reel Evil—for his students at Duke University, featuring films from North Korea, Iran, Iraq, and other countries that had been singled out in the speech. In the same piece, however, he wonders, on the basis of an interview with Bush in the *New York Times* (21 March 2017),[12] whether the former president's new interest in painting might be enabling him to see the world differently.

There are also other promising signs of such moves to diversify our understandings of the world more broadly. There are active ongoing debates in many universities about taking steps to 'decolonize' the curriculum, and these have

[11] Suzanne Nossel (2016: 103) makes the argument that 'Art has the ability to change our minds – inspiring us to take on different perspectives and to reimagine our worlds'.

[12] Mimi Swartz, '"W." and the Art of Redemption', New York Times, 21 March 2017, available at https://www.nytimes.com/2017/03/21/opinion/w-and-the-art-of-redemption.html.

gained further momentum following the #BlackLivesMatter movement and the outcry that followed the murder of George Floyd by police in Minneapolis. In addition to raising important questions about the ideas and identities of scholars on course reading lists, the debate also engages with the narrowness of what is considered acceptable forms of representation of knowledge. A recent student-led study conducted in the London School of Economics (LSE)'s Department of Media and Communications, for example, documented a range of views among students and led to the drawing up of ten 'decolonising the curriculum principles' (see Salih and Banaji, 2019). The sixth of these directly addresses the issue of diversifying the types of reading and media on course reading lists, and included the point that 'diversification in the content of readings through the recognition of other media such as songs, poetry, fiction, comics and animations, and film will work to enrich how we think about things'.[13]

But at its best, an exchange between the arts and development does more than just call more compellingly for change—diversify the range of perspectives being considered, subvert 'single stories',[14] or present key ideas in innovative forms—vitally important as these all are. If the arts achieve all these things and more—if a truly 'better', more just, locally authentic outcome is actually attained—a prosaic reality of development is that, come Tuesday morning, a team of people still has to show up and make things work in this brave new world they've helped create. Succeeding in resistance or advocacy is one thing; making the greener trains run on time—reliably, affordably, safely, for everyone, every day—is another. The political cliché bears repeating that one campaigns in poetry but governs in prose.

The best artistic works, however, can powerfully remind us of this reality—i.e., they can also anticipate and inform the 'prose'. Doing so is one of the many compelling contributions of *Hamilton*, perhaps the most influential new musical of recent years (at least in the Global North), which creatively retells the story of American independence (e.g., by casting non-white actors to play the founding fathers) through the life of a senior bureaucrat, Alexander Hamilton (a poor immigrant who became the first US Secretary of the Treasury). Or more accurately, Hamilton's story is told by his nemesis, Aaron Burr (Thomas Jefferson's Vice-President), and equally importantly by his wife Eliza Hamilton, whose painstaking work on his behalf—in obscurity, for fifty years after her husband's death (killed by Burr in a duel)—is how Alexander, over time, became revered. The full scope of *Hamilton* encompasses not just a creative retelling of complex events, but an incisive and compelling reflection on how stories get told, by whom and to whom; the visceral power of actively contributing to and experiencing change (of 'being

[13] Also available at https://www.lse.ac.uk/Events/2019/03/20190306t1830vHKT/Decolonising-the-Curricula

[14] On this point, see Chimamanda Ngozi Adichie's famous TED talk, available at https://www.ted.com/talks/chimamanda_ngozi_adichie_the_danger_of_a_single_story.

in the room when it happened'); and ultimately on coming to terms with success, of being equally committed to doing the less glamourous follow-up work if one's initial goal is to be fully realized. As journalist Alissa Wilkinson astutely concludes:

> Art alone doesn't change the world; it just ploughs the soil. Hamilton is a show about revolution, and a show about the trouble with revolution: After you've turned the world upside-down, you have to figure out what comes next. You have to figure out your laws, your economy, your foreign policy. You also have to figure out who matters, who makes the rules, and – maybe most importantly – who tells the story. Every culture war is about who gets to define the terms and control the narrative, and that's no different now than it was in 2016 or 1812 or 1776.[15]

So understood, *Hamilton* is an illuminating development production, doing all this sophisticated rendering of complex change processes—political and personal conflict, history remembered and forgotten, failure and success, ambition, entitlement, comeuppance—in a three-hour show that has been seen live or on television by millions of people. Doubtless many equally insightful productions on corresponding dynamics in other countries have also been prepared. As a powerful complement to—not substitute for—scholarly research, we hope that such work can inspire a rising generation to expand the range of ideas explored by the development community, increase the diversity of contributors and responders that comprise this community, and enrich the mediums in and through which these ideas are shared, debated ... and ultimately enacted.

Acknowledgements

The views expressed in this chapter are those of the authors alone and should not be attributed to the organizations with which they are affiliated.

References

Andrews, M., L. Pritchett, and M. Woolcock (2017) *Building State Capability: Evidence, Analysis, Action.* New York: Oxford University Press.

Bailey, S.C.M. (2021) *Approaching Recent World History through Film: Context, Analysis, and Research.* London: Routledge.

Balkin, J. (2018) *Symphony of Justice: Law as a Performing Art.* New York: Oxford University Press.

[15] See Alissa Wilkinson, 'We got comfortable with Hamilton. The new film reminds us how risky it is', Vox, 2 July 2020, available at https://www.vox.com/21308627/hamilton-movie-review-disney-2020.

Berg, G. and B. Zia (2017) 'Harnessing emotional connections to improve financial decisions: Evaluating the impact of financial education in mainstream media', *Journal of the European Economic Association* 15(5): 1025–55.

Berger, M. (1977) *Real and Imagined Worlds: The Novel and Social Science*. Cambridge, MA: Harvard University Press.

Booth, D. (2018) 'When are we going to stop giving solution-driven aid?' Valedictory lecture delivered at the Overseas Development Institute, London, 23 April.

Bui, T. (2017) *The Best We Could Do*. New York: Abrams.

Chwe, M. Suk-Young (2013) *Jane Austen, Game Theorist*. Princeton, NJ: Princeton University Press.

Cooke, P. and I. Soria-Donlan (2020) (Eds) *Participatory Arts in International Development*. London: Routledge.

Coser, L. (1972) *Sociology through Literature* (2nd edn). New York: Prentice Hall.

Gardner, K. and D. Lewis (2015) *Anthropology and Development: Challenges for the Twenty-First Century*. London: Pluto.

Geertz, C. (1980) *Negara: The Theatre State in Nineteenth-Century Bali*. Princeton, NJ: Princeton University Press.

Gharib, M. (2019) *I Was Their American Dream: A Graphic Memoir*. New York: Clarkson Potter.

Greenblatt, S. (2018) *Tyrant: Shakespeare on Politics*. New York: W. W. Norton.

Hirschman, A.O. (1991) *The Rhetoric of Reaction: Perversity, Futility, Jeopardy*. Cambridge, MA: Harvard University Press.

Jasonoff, M. (2017) *The Dawn Watch: Joseph Conrad in a Global World*. New York: Penguin.

Kabanda, P. (2018) *The Creative Wealth of Nations: Can the Arts Advance Development?* New York: Cambridge University Press.

Kristoff, N. and S. WuDunn (2010) *Half the Sky: Turning Oppression into Opportunity for Women Worldwide*. New York: Vintage Books.

Leigh, A. (2018) *Randomistas: How Radical Researchers Changed our World*. New Haven, CT: Yale University Press.

Lewis, D., D. Rodgers, and M. Woolcock (Eds) (2014) *Popular Representations of Development: Insights from Novels, Films, Television, and Social Media*. London: Routledge.

McCloskey, D. (1998) *The Rhetoric of Economics* (2nd edn). Madison, WI: University of Wisconsin Press.

Marsh, H. (2021) 'Our culture's not for sale!': Music and the Asamblea Popular de los Pueblos de Oaxaca in Mexico, *Bulletin of Latin American Research* 40: 416–31.

Morson, G.S. and M. Schapiro (2017) *Cents and Sensibility: What Economics Can Learn from the Humanities*. Princeton, NJ: Princeton University Press.

Mottahedeh, N. (2018) 'Reel evil', *Cinema Journal* 57(4): 146–50.

Nossel, S. (2016) 'Introduction: On "artivism," or art's utility in activism'. *Social Research: An International Quarterly* 83(1): 103–105.

Piketty, T. (2013) *Capital in the Twenty-First Century*. Cambridge, MA: Harvard University Press.

Posner, R.A. (2009) *Law and Literature* (3rd edn). Cambridge, MA: Harvard University Press.

Salih, L. and S. Banaji (2019) 'Decolonial Curriculum Project Report for Media and Communications', Unpublished report, Department of Media and Communications, London School of Economics and Political Science.

Snow, C.P. (1993) *The Two Cultures*. Cambridge: Cambridge University Press.
Spradley, J.P. and G. E. McDonough (1973) *Anthropology through Literature: Cross-Cultural Perspectives*. Boston, MA: Little, Brown.
Yoshino, K. (2012) *A Thousand Times More Fair: What Shakespeare's Plays Teach Us about Justice*. New York: HarperCollins.

PART I
TRANSLATION

1
The Sounds of Development
Musical Representations as (An)other Source of Development Knowledge

David Lewis, Dennis Rodgers, and Michael Woolcock

Introduction

To our knowledge there has been little research to date on the relationship between international development and popular music—for example, on the ways in which familiar development themes are rendered in popular music, or how music might constitute part of development interventions.[1] As with our earlier explorations of popular representations of development in the contexts of novels and films,[2] in this chapter we aim to make the case that music is a useful but largely unexplored repository of knowledge about development that also critically helps to shape ideas, perceptions, and practices. We are particularly interested in how music may offer distinctive insights into the way development issues—broadly defined as both aid and projects, as well as wider ideas about international poverty, inequality, and societal change[3]—take on public significance in social, cultural, and political terms, as well as the ways they are sustained in everyday life. Certainly, the centrality of music to social life should not be underestimated. As ethnomusicologist John Blacking (1973: 89) has put it: 'because music is humanly organised sound, it expresses aspects of the experiences of individuals in society'. It is a characteristic of virtually all societies and their constituent groups, and as such has long been a medium through which ideas are contested, collective memory is stored, and shared experience is conveyed.

[1] Some exceptions, usefully summarized by Korum (2017), include Clammer (2014), Stupples and Teaiwa (2016), and Howell (2018). More broadly, as John Clammer (2014) has pointed out, there has arguably been a relative lack of attention paid within development research and practice to the cultural and artistic dimensions of societal change. See also Long (2013).

[2] Lewis et al. (2008, 2013, 2014).

[3] For present purposes we take a broad and inclusive view of the concept of development. Lewis (2019) unpacks the dialectical relationship between development as unfolding change with winners and losers, and development as deliberate intervention, and argues that ideas about development are relevant not only to the Global South but also to the Global North.

David Lewis, Dennis Rodgers, and Michael Woolcock, *The Sounds of Development.* In: *New Mediums, Better Messages?.* Edited by David Lewis, Dennis Rodgers, and Michael Woolcock, Oxford University Press.
 DOI: 10.1093/oso/9780198858751.003.0002

Indeed, music is arguably one of the most immediate forms of art in the cultural repertoire, something that gives it a distinctive power. Smith and Jacobs (2011: 906), for example, suggest that

> music is arguably more pervasive than literature in the sense that one needs to choose to read a particular book in order to be influenced by its contents whereas one can encounter popular music in the supermarket, at sporting events or in one's motor vehicle regardless of whether one actually likes a particular song or chooses to listen to it.

In its pervasiveness, music can be understood both as experience and as message. This makes music a potentially rich source of information about how ideas about development are manifested and represented, as well as a potentially powerful tool for shaping public perceptions, either unconsciously (as in the reinforcement of lazy stereotypes) or consciously (as in the case of efforts to use music to empower, inform, or persuade). Or both, as with the now notorious charity singles issued in the UK and the US in 1984 as part of the response from western countries to the Ethiopian famine. Drawing on the work of Lilie Chouliaraki, Schwittay (2015: 32) identifies events such as the 1985 'Live Aid' concert as examples of 'the spectacle mode of affective engagement' where such events serve as entertainment that 'incite(s) Northern publics to care and share in order to alleviate the suffering of distant others'. Music—along with celebrity—is central to the increasing dependence of humanitarianism on the power of representation and spectacle (Richey, 2016).

Our primary (though not exclusive) focus is on the Global North as a site for the production and exchange of music as a cultural product that refers to representations of the 'Global South'. In line with our own areas of regional knowledge and experience, we also engage with examples of other music from developing contexts (though of course make no claims that we are somehow providing a comprehensive or representative 'survey' of the form and content of music about development, whether from the Global North or South). Nor do we wish to present an unnecessarily romantic view of the power of music, which Dillane et al. (2018: 1) and Dave (2019) remind us can also be used for 'malign' purposes of exclusion, incitement, and disinformation. Rather, we aim in this article to unpack a new issue for development research along five related lines of initial enquiry: the tradition of western 'protest' music; musical resistance in the Global South; music-based development interventions; commodification and appropriation; and, finally, music as a global development vernacular. This is far from an exhaustive list, but—extending our previous attempts to connect development studies and other forms of popular culture—we present them in the spirit of encouraging further contributions to both research and practice.

Traditions of 'Protest' Music in the Global North

Protest music in the western world has a long history. Its heyday is often seen as the 1960s, notably with the music of Joan Baez, Bob Dylan, Buffy Sainte-Marie, Malvina Reynolds, and Pete Seeger in North America; Ewan MacColl, John Lennon, Leon Rosselson in the UK; or Leo Ferré, Jean Ferrat, and Georges Brassens in France, for example.[4] Each of these had different origins. In the US, the African–American blues traditions that emerged at the end of the nineteenth and early twentieth century, connecting the historical experience of slavery with enduring forms of inequality and injustice in post-Emancipation USA, informed records such as Edwin Starr's 'War'.[5] Other key influences were the 'hobo' songs and ballads such as 'The Dishwasher' or 'The Bum on the Rods and the Bum on the Plush' described by Nels Anderson (1923: 200–2) in his classic study of homelessness in the US, and the folk music of Woody Guthrie about the Great Depression.[6] In the UK, protest songs also emerged from the labour movement and the Campaign for Nuclear Disarmament, while in France they were associated with the anarchist movement. Reflecting its multiple origins, the nature of protest music has ebbed and flowed in the decades since the 1960s, and what might today be looked back upon as the 'classical' protest tradition is in many ways but one moment within a series of evolving forms of musical resistance within wider cultural trends and histories of social change in the Global North.

For example, Rachel's (2016: xxi) oral history of the 1970s Rock Against Racism movement in the UK documents how 'through music, and through a general sense of disenfranchisement, both first generation black British and disaffected white youth ... began to recognise common grievances'. The politics of solidarity created connections between emerging traditions of punk rock from the Global North and reggae from the Global South, linking subcultures of resistance with forms of hybridity and fusion. Later during the 1980s, other political and cultural movements built further on these foundations. UK-based musician Jerry Dammers launched an initiative 'to make the British public aware of the plight of the banned ANC', which culminated in an Anti-Apartheid concert in London in 1988 that 'demonstrated how pop music could awaken the conscience of a generation' (Rachel, 2016: xxv). Emerging from the '2 Tone' movement of racially integrated political

[4] See Rice (2014) for a broader anthropological survey of 'the study of music in times and places of trouble', a topic on which he argues that formal research by ethnomusicologists only 'began relatively recently' (p. 193)—that is, since the mid-1990s. Works in this specific field that are relevant for development include Barz and Cohen (2011), Harrison (2013), and Berger (2014).

[5] Songs such as Billie Holiday's 'Strange Fruit', written in reaction to the lynching of Thomas Shipp and Abram Smith in Indiana in 1930, or Huddie 'Leadbelly' Ledbetter's 'Take This Hammer', which denounced the harsh prison conditions he endured in Louisiana, are classic examples, and were subsequently taken up as anthems by the Civil Rights movement in the 1950s and 1960s. See Margolick and Als (2000), and Blackman (2008).

[6] See https://www.woodyguthrie.org/.

pop music that developed first in the UK (drawing heavily on Jamaican influences), the Special AKA's 'Free Nelson Mandela' record was supported by the Anti-Apartheid Movement.

As Dillane et al. (2018) have argued, 'songs of social protest' are relational, involving exchanges between audiences and musicians. Protest music has long served as a means through which the politics of solidarity can be expressed, but it has also served as a channel through which a range of different ideas about global inequality and injustice have been communicated to mass western audiences. For example, long after his brief 1960s protest phase, Bob Dylan's 1983 song 'Union Sundown' was an observational critique of globalization centred around the fact that most consumer items bought in the United States were now being made elsewhere, mostly by relying on cheap labour and exploitative working conditions: 'You know capitalism is above the law, it say "it don't count unless it sells", when it costs too much to build it at home, you just build it cheaper someplace else.' Later that decade, Tracy Chapman's 'Talkin' 'Bout a Revolution' pondered the likelihood (and hope) that sustained economic dislocation would eventually lead to fundamental social change.[7] More recently, the 2016 song 'Poem' by the British psych pop group 'She Drew the Gun', explicitly tackles inequality and exclusion in neoliberal Britain. Moving from the economic to the more explicitly political, the Canadian activist and singer-songwriter Bruce Cockburn's song 'If I Had a Rocket Launcher' dealt with his outrage and anger at the injustice of US involvement in the wars in Nicaragua and El Salvador. The song's accompanying video brought some controversy to MTV but the track was also commended by solidarity campaigners as helping to make young audiences more aware of the political situation in Central America. Finally, Joni Mitchell's song 'Big Yellow Taxi' connected with the burgeoning western environmental movement and has subsequently been recorded by almost 500 other artists.

The role of protest music within social processes is of course contested—between those who see it as a force for change, and those who understand it as primarily reflective of change. For Thom York, singer of the rock band Radiohead, this structure/agency tension is essentially contingent. As he put it in an interview in *The Guardian* newspaper, there have been times and places where music has shaped events, but others—such as the present-day West—where it seems to have lost much of its power to do so:

> In the 60s, you could write songs that were like calls to arms, and it would work. If I was going to write a protest song about climate change in 2015, it would be

[7] This song was subsequently covered by musicians in the Middle East during the Arab Spring in the early 2010s, and in 2016 was used by Bernie Sanders as the unofficial theme song of his candidacy to be the Democratic nominee for President of the United States.

> shit ... It's not like one song or one piece of art or one book is going to change someone's mind.[8]

Protest music is normally associated with a political message, which distinguishes it from music aimed primarily at fund raising. For example, one of the best-known and earliest musical events linked to development issues in the western public imagination was the 1971 'Concert for Bangladesh' organized by former Beatle George Harrison and Indian musician Ravi Shankar to raise the profile and resources for the new country—one that faced natural disaster and the aftermath of a war that led to Bangladesh's secession from Pakistan following a popular liberation struggle and India's military intervention. Yet this event was primarily framed in charitable terms as a humanitarian response to famine and hunger rather than one that engaged with the underlying structural or political conditions that lay behind the crisis. This set the template for the similarly framed 'Live Aid' in the 1980s or today's 'Comic Relief' in the UK, although more recent initiatives, such as the Lilith Fair music festival, founded by the Canadian singer Sarah McLachlan in the late 1990s, which showcases solely female solo artists and female-led bands to counter the pervasive gender imbalance in the music industry, suggest that new approaches are also emerging.

The protest tradition has not simply communicated ideas but has also shaped global representations in particular ways. For example, the 2012 video release of a song by 'Radi-Aid', created by the Norwegian Students' and Academics' International Assistance Fund (SAIH) illustrates the use of musical parody as an instrument for protest. Taking its cue from the persistence of passive images of African societies first promoted by Live Aid, this faux campaign produced a 'We Are The World'-style video in which singers and rappers called upon people in African countries to donate radiators to Norway to help them deal with their extreme weather conditions. SAIH was an organization first established to support anti-apartheid movements and had continued to engage with global issues. The aim was to make people in the West think about global relationships, challenge representations, and influence public debate. The video surprised those who made it by garnering huge attention, receiving (as of this writing) almost 3.5 million viewings on YouTube.[9] According to its producers:

> SAIH has strived to promote a more nuanced image on countries in the global south than is usually portrayed in the media and by some charitable organisations and fundraising initiatives. While there are negative issues that need to be reported and a lot of organisations are doing very important work, we are frustrated at the constant repetition of the same negative images. Since the narrative

[8] See https://www.theguardian.com/music/2015/nov/25/thom-yorke-tony-blair-advisers-tried-to-force-me-to-meet-pm.

[9] For the video, see https://www.youtube.com/watch?v=oJLqyuxm96k.

> tends to be the same as it was when development assistance first started some 50 years ago, it might give the impression that none of these efforts have produced any results and thus lead to apathy.[10]

The protest song has continued to evolve in ways that ensure its relevance. For example, in the current turbulent political climate in both the US and UK, there are signs that the protest song is once again in the ascendant in the Global North. *Time* magazine reported on 24 January 2017: 'They say music flourishes in times of protest—and already, a slew of anti-Trump songs have sprung up in the lead-up to his election and inauguration.'[11] Similarly, a concert attended by one of us in Geneva, Switzerland, featured British hip-hop jazz artist Soweto Kinch premiering an anti-Brexit rap song. More generally, the Russian Pussy Riot feminist punk collective invaded the pitch during the 2018 World Cup final in protest against the Putin regime's human rights abuses. Questioning the idea that the 1960s was the golden age of protest, Jeneve Brooks (2009) found far more US protest music being written and circulated during the Iran and Afghanistan conflicts than during the Vietnam War; but also noted that changing modes of music production and consumption, including media fragmentation and radio consolidation, now limited its exposure and collective impact.

Musical Resistance in the Global South

Protest music obviously also has a long history in the Global South, to the extent that it can be associated with most of the major political struggles of the past half century. The Nicaraguan revolution of 1979–90, for example, was inextricably linked with the protest and then revolution-supporting songs of the Mejía Godoy brothers, Luis and Carlos, as well as the Katia and Salvador Cardenal sister and brother *Guardabarranco* duo. Similarly, in South Africa, the singer-songwriter and activist Johnny Clegg, with Sipho Mchunu, combined Zulu styles with Celtic folk to challenge apartheid in South Africa during the 1980s with their band Juluka, while the Miriam Makeba—aka 'Mama Africa'—song 'Soweto Blues', about the 1976 Soweto uprising and its brutal repression, became one of the anti-apartheid movement's most iconic anthems At the same time, however, the idea of protest music in the Global South can also be approached differently: not so much as intentional attempts to raise awareness or shift opinion, but as situated within the wider frame of music as reflective of social values and as a site of cultural resistance. In this sense, music becomes a site for both construction and contestation of postcolonial identities, something that is perhaps especially obvious in the music of

[10] See https://www.theguardian.com/world/2012/nov/26/radiaid-norway-charity-single.
[11] See https://time.com/4643778/trump-protest-songs/.

Argentine singer Mercedes Sosa or Senegalese artists such as Youssou N'Dour or Ismail Lo.[12]

Certainly, Randall (2017) argues that music and politics have long been interwoven in West African societies, with musicians playing a role alongside workers in the liberation struggle. For example, Ghana's 'high life' dance music shifted during the 1940s to reflect support for Kwame Nkrumah's movement for national self-determination. In post-colonial settings, music is a site of ongoing contestation over the direction of national development processes. As Senegal's Geji Hip Hop collective illustrates, it is also a site of resistance to gender violence and cultural stereotyping.[13] In Mali, Tuareg musicians, some of whom had fought against the Malian military regime in 1990–91, have fused African and Western rock (via links with western audiences built through the 'world music' networks),[14] and serve as rallying points for opposition to Islamist takeovers in parts of the country. In Pakistan, guitar-based heavy rock bands have long worked within and adapted western traditions, where the music serves as a signifier for a certain kind of liberal middle-class identity that pushes back against both secular and Islamist political interest groups. For example, Sufi-rock band Junoon were censored by the government and banned from state TV for songs such as 'Ehtesaab', which attacked political corruption.[15]

Contests between musical traditions and national state identities reflect wider structural political themes in contemporary Bangladesh. What role does religion play in a society that fought to separate from Pakistan, a state that was supposed to have been defined by a shared Muslim identity? Bangladesh contains different religions (Islam, Hinduism, Buddhism, Christianity) as well as different traditions within each one. After 1971 these differences were initially subordinated to the single idea of a new 'Bengali' nation primarily defined by a shared language but given its polyvalent nature other aspects of identity have continued to assert themselves. A key recurring fault line is that between multicultural or secular traditions and more conservative religious ones. One established religious identity is a local syncretic 'Bengali' Islamic tradition, shaped by a wide range of influences, including Hinduism and Sufism. Another is an orthodox Islamic tradition more in tune with the earlier history of the country as part of Pakistan, and more recently linked to international trends in the *sunni* Muslim world, heightened by people's increased

[12] At the same time, Dave (2019) undermines the assumption that music necessarily forms part of freedom struggles, resistance, or contestation, showing instead how music served to support authoritarianism and was used to sidestep dissent in Guinea.

[13] See https://www.theguardian.com/world/2019/dec/31/rap-does-not-shut-up-hip-hop-women-of-senegal.

[14] Although western rock music of course itself drew on African traditions imported to the US through the slave trade that later evolved into jazz, blues, and rock.

[15] See https://timesofindia.indiatimes.com/india/In-Pakistan-protest-music-is-a-tradition/articleshow/10562389.cms.

exposure to more conservative Islamic ideas from Saudi Arabia and the Gulf, to which many Bangladeshi migrant workers have travelled since the 1990s.

These questions of rights and identity play out at the national level through formal politics but are also recreated in the cultural sphere. For example, a popular Sufi gypsy folk music is seen by some people as forming an important part of syncretic culture, because it speaks explicitly to a distinctive local fusion of Hindu practices and Islamic beliefs. One of the central figures within this *Baul* tradition was the poet Lalon Shah (*c.*1774–1890), whose work embodied the values of a tolerant form of spiritualism and a rejection of organized religion (Ohlmacher and Pervez, 2014). Lalon's music is kept alive as part of post-1971 multicultural or 'secular' nationalist tradition, and adapted and commodified by generations of young and old listeners who view it as an important and increasingly relevant element of Bengali/Bangladeshi identity.

This music has become a highly visible arena in which these identity tensions are contested. For example, in 2008 the government commissioned a piece of public art in the form of a sculpture that commemorated practitioners of *Baul* music who were represented as statues. During construction the sculpture was attacked and damaged by religious extremists, prompting counter-protests organized on social media, and later a human chain street rally:

> When an Islamist group pulled down Mrinal Haq's in-progress sculpture of Baul musicians near the airport, there was an intense mobilization of cultural activists to defend Baul cultural icons. Just as 'Islam in danger' is a frequent rallying cry for Islamists, 'Bangla culture under attack' mobilized and temporarily brought together many disparate cultural organizations.
>
> (Mohaiemen, 2014: 127)

Music traditions can also become elements of contestation in other ways, however. *Narcocorrido*, a type of Mexican folk ballad that extols drug traffickers and glorifies drug trafficking is a good instance of a counter-example. A hugely popular musical genre, it has significant crossover appeal to broader youth and Mexican musical culture more generally, as well as internationally. At the same time, as Mark Edberg (2004: 25) has highlighted, *narcocorrido* music is associable with 'the creation of a particular cultural archetype or persona' that ties the violence, power, and money; and drugs narcotraffickers are known for to broader 'political, social, and regional themes'. In particular, *narcocorrido* ballads tend to represent the figure of the drug dealer as a community hero or a 'Robin Hood' figure who defies the threats posed by a corrupt Mexican state and who exploits the USA's demand for drugs to benefit Mexico's poor. Yet while undoubtedly 'at the margins of society, drug traffickers are far from being an exploited, suppressed, powerless subaltern group for whom musical expression functions as symbolic empowerment in its struggle for social betterment' (Simonett, 2001: 316)[16], and *narcocorridos* are perhaps better seen as a symptom of a broader struggle for what Christina Baker (2017: 179) has called 'the sounds of the modern [Mexican] nation'.

Seen from the perspective of both the *Baul* and the *narcocorridos* traditions, if we are to understand processes of development and change within post-colonial societies then there clearly is value in broadening the frame of reference: it enables music and its associated tropes and identities to be included alongside the more familiar elements of economy, politics, and civil society. We might, for example, pay more attention to the way that community level music making and music sharing can be understood as part of people's efforts to process their traumatic history and as a contribution to nation building and reconstruction, as in the case of Timor Leste, for example (Howell, 2018). But we must perhaps do so in ways that go beyond simply taking music as a point of reference, instead including it into our analyses and modes of presentation and representation. Indeed, this is something that some academics have begun to experiment with very successfully, including for example the French political sociologist Jean-François Bayart, who in May 2018 combined with the Senegalese dancer Alioune Diagne to give a powerful multimodal presentation on 'Violence and religion in Africa' that involved academic lecture, dance, music, and poetry-reading.[17]

Music-Based Development Interventions

Moving from the ways in which music shapes and reflects wider society and its development values and directions, we turn now to consider how policymakers and aid professionals have experimented with using music as a practical development tool. To what extent has music been part of formal development interventions? As a starting point, it is interesting to note that while numerous musicians have established foundations to encourage and fund development initiatives—such as the Colombian singer Shakira's 'Barefoot/Pies Descalzos' foundation, or the British singer Elton John's AIDS foundation, for example—few, if any, are actually based on the promotion of musical activities. An exception is Venezuela's El Sistema youth orchestra, acclaimed as an inclusive social programme that empowers vulnerable children, but also criticized for its authoritarian culture and middle-class origins.[18] Another is the Aga Khan Music Initiative, which supports musicians

[16] See Malcomson's (2019) analysis of agency in the writing of narco-rap for a stark reminder of the way that drug dealers can ruthlessly deal with singer–songwriters who disappoint them.

[17] See https://www.youtube.com/watch?v=HuxuqEwmfxA. See also the rendering of the 20th-century Asian American experience (migration, internment camps, the Vietnam War) by cultural historian Julian Saporiti, innovatively integrating 'art and scholarship' for broad audiences; available at https://www.nonoboyproject.com/.

[18] See https://www.theguardian.com/music/2014/nov/11/geoff-baker-el-sistema-model-of-tyranny.

and music educators around the world working to preserve, transmit, and further develop their musical heritage in contemporary forms[19]

A relatively small but growing project literature is documenting efforts to use music as a component within NGO work in fields as diverse as health, community development, and peace building. One of the fields that has received particular attention here is that of post-conflict settings. Howell (2018) has developed a useful four-level typology of the different intentions that lie behind such interventions: (i) music education (building new knowledge, skills, and learning as part of wider education); (ii) cultural regeneration (in the context of efforts to restore or rebuild cultural resources); (iii) social development (effecting social change, rebuilding trust, and challenging disadvantage); (iv) healing and health promotion (individual and group-based therapeutic use of music and promotion of public health and well-being). While optimistic, Howell resists the temptation to be naive about such work, noting that intentions may not lead neatly to clear outcomes and are often subject to overreach. Yet these risky 'beginnings', informed by 'optimistic and sometimes idealistic aims and goals', can create opportunities on which other plans and activities might build (Howell, 2018: 63).

In community health, Frishkopf (2017: 50) describes a pilot project which experimented with the idea of using music to support changes in sanitation behaviour in post-conflict Liberia. Based on participatory action research (PAR), this aimed to build a form of 'collaborative ethnomusicology' that in turn sought to create 'music infused relationships' to challenge cultural and linguistic differences. Such work centres on the idea of 'giving voice' as a form of collaboration with real-world effects. This consisted of video production and media dissemination in which local musicians and producers were encouraged 'to take the lead' in developing and promoting health messages. Although it is not unusual for international NGOs to contract local musicians to disseminate such messages, the PAR approach seeks to move beyond what Frishkopf (2017: 50) characterizes as 'simply an exchange of money for art' without meaningful participation:

> By contrast, musical creativity was integrated into the project through serious commitment by local artists, musicians, and producers whose roles extended far beyond the musical domain, drawing on their general knowledge of Liberian society, culture, and health practices as well.

Approaches like this draw on the power of music to shape beliefs, values, and norms. In another documented case, Bolger (2012) examines the use of music therapy as a psychosocial support tool within a women and children's refuge in rural Bangladesh, as part of a collaborative international project. A weekly women's music group was established at village level and created a forum where stories were

[19] See https://www.akdn.org/akmi.

shared and people sang and danced. As well as helping to facilitate forms of peer support and solidarity, the project aimed to develop the leadership and coping skills that women would need to rebuild their lives.

Music can also play a less positive, more instrumental role beyond the community level. For example, anthropologist Mark Schuller (2012) describes musical performances encouraged by NGOs in Haiti in their efforts to build their relationships with local beneficiaries—involving singing development and solidarity songs together in camps—that primarily served for donor consumption rather than the actual building of local community relationships.[20] In his account, the main aim was to produce a lively set of representations of NGOs' organizational engagement with local communities—in the form of photographs and video—that met NGOs' need to make their work visible to a select international audience.

There also exists a (more limited) number of development initiatives promoted at a more macro-scale by international organizations and national government agencies, including two instructive cases promoted respectively by the World Bank and the UK Department for International Development (DFID). The first relates to the World Bank's work with multiple donors in Aceh, Indonesia, following the horrendous devastation wrought by the tsunami in December 2004.[21] If there was a 'silver lining' to this tragedy, it was the impetus it gave to the forging of a peace agreement between secessionist factions and the government that, heretofore, had been engaged in a violent civil war lasting many years. The peace agreement was of pragmatic necessity negotiated and signed in Finland, leaving Indonesian and Acehnese officials with the daunting task of not merely conveying the news of the peace deal, but relaying to a sceptical population still deeply traumatized by the tsunami the details of the agreement while credibly conveying its legitimacy in the eyes of all key stakeholders. A two-part communications strategy was implemented. In addition to printing enough copies of the agreement for every household in Aceh—so that it could literally be pinned to the walls of every residence—a popular Acehnese musician was hired by the World Bank to produce a rap song consolidating and celebrating the end of the civil war. Crucially, the song's words were not drawn from the peace agreement itself, but from Acehnese school children, who were asked to submit a single sentence summarizing what the peace agreement meant to them; the musician arranged the best of these sentences into a catchy song which was then recorded and played across local radio stations, becoming a huge hit. The medium and the message aligned: in desperate, fraught

[20] In this sense, they can be seen as 'performances', as social acts intended for symbolic consumption by a particular audience (like the performance of charity—see Lewis, 2019).

[21] The material that follows is drawn from personal communications with Patrick Barron of the World Bank in 2007. Barron played a major role in conceiving and implementing the World Bank's response to the 2004 tsunami and the ensuing opportunity for forging a peace agreement to end the decades-long civil war in Aceh. For a broad overview of this process, see Barron and Burke (2008).

circumstances, domestic and international development actors used locally credible people (musician and children), content (words penned by the children), and communication tools (an original, memorable Acehnese song) to disseminate and legitimize a peace agreement that endures to this day.[22]

A more recent—and contested—case is the Girl Hub (later Girl Effect) project established in 2010 with a reported £15.6 million of DFID funds in partnership with the Nike Foundation and a number of other philanthropic and business organizations. The main aim of this venture was to contribute to the well-being and development of adolescent girls in Ethiopia, Nigeria, and Rwanda by challenging and changing how girls are socially valued and perceived. Its approach was less conventional than many development projects and included working through a variety of media including radio drama, music, talk shows, and clubs. The project became controversial because of both its achievements and its limitations. In 2012 the Independent Commission for Aid Impact (ICAI) reviewed the project and identified some potentially positive impacts, along with some doubts about how these could be measured, and some concerns about objectives, learning, and delivery. This made it similar to many such projects, but it was popular media coverage that was to play a more significant role in the project's subsequent trajectory.

In 2017, elements of the anti-foreign aid British media picked up the Girl Hub project as a prime example of its argument as to why foreign aid itself was a waste of money. The *Daily Mail* newspaper in particular built a series of stories around one part of the project taking place in Ethiopia. It focused on Yegna, a five-piece Ethiopian women's popular music band, described as a 'multi-platform culture brand, rooted in Ethiopian culture, which inspires positive culture change for girls'. Through Yegna's music and videos, the project was aiming to improve access to schools and health facilities across the country, and to address issues such as forced marriage, gender violence, and genital cutting—in part through the messaging effects of Yegna's music and videos. For Farah Ramzan Golant, speaking at the time as CEO of Girl Effect, Yegna is justified as a pioneering example of 'innovative, unconventional and efficient solutions to combating poverty at scale'. A key part of the *Daily Mail*'s strategy, however, was to trivialize these efforts: Yegna was pejoratively characterized as 'the Ethiopian Spice Girls' and therefore undeserving of UK taxpayer support. Development was understood narrowly as economic support or technology transfer but not as the promotion of rights through intervention and exchange in the cultural sphere. This led to the withdrawal of government funding before the expected end of the project due in 2018.[23]

According to the BBC, Girl Effect was reported as stating that its aims had been 'wilfully misrepresented' by the media, but the case highlights both the ways in

[22] See also Kartomi (2010) for a historical–anthropological account of the role of music in shaping Aceh's experience of civil conflict and the 2004 tsunami. No-one, of course, claims that these interventions singularly 'caused' the peace process to be forged or to endure.

[23] See https://www.bbc.com/news/uk-38538631.

which experiments with using music to promote social change have recently become more mainstream. While music may be seen as an arena in which more exploratory and innovative development interventions are being conceived, there are reasons to be cautious about how this might be playing out within the current climate of development agencies and intervention. There are deep challenges associated with verifying the positive 'impact' of development ventures involving music/popular culture in an age of austerity that not only shrinks aid budgets but increasingly generates wrenching resource trade-offs—music or medicines?—and intensifies demands for taking a narrow 'evidence-based' approach to aid and project-level results. As the Ethiopia case above suggests, innovative forms of development interventions grounded in popular culture are inherently going to struggle for legitimacy in such an environment. At the same time, considering the neoliberal environment within which development increasingly operates, combined with so-called 'donor fatigue', turning to music-related development initiatives might also be a means through which to generate income and self-fund development.[24]

Music, Commodification, and the Global South

Paradoxes clearly arise from contradictions contained within the collision of popular music, politics, and commerce, as Way (2017) has highlighted in his analysis of the role that music played in the 2013 Gezi Park protests in Turkey. Focusing on music by the Turkish indie rock duo Dev, and more specifically their song 'Dans Et', he shows how it helped communicate about the protests, which began as a demonstration by a few protesters seeking to protect a green public space, but quickly spread and eventually led to thousands of arrests and six deaths after a violent police crackdown. At the same time, however, Way (2017: 114) shows how the song, 'through a number of strategies identified in lyrics, images and musical sounds', also legitimized Dev as an authentically anti-establishment band, something they—somewhat ironically—benefited from enormously in commercial terms after the protests, leading to criticisms of their countercultural credentials.

The issue of 'authenticity' is something that has long been at the heart of the consumption of music from the Global South in the Global North. Gilroy (1993: 99) famously noted how 'authenticity enhances the appeal of selected cultural commodities and has become an important element in the mechanism of the mode of racialisation necessary to making non-European and non-American musics acceptable items in an expanding pop market'. In a similar vein, Hutnyk (2000: 20–2)

[24] See Kabanda (2018) on the broader, sizeable, rising but often ignored contribution of 'the arts' (including music) to the economies of low-income countries.

argues that the famous World of Music, Arts and Dance (Womad) festival, founded in 1980 by English rock musician Peter Gabriel, relies on a combination of the exoticization of 'traditionalism' and an 'evacuation of politics' in order to 'offer ... the commercialisation of everything'. At the same time, he also recognizes that 'Womad brings acts to Britain that [which] would otherwise not be widely seen, and in this sense it serves a progressive and explorative, innovative role unlike any other organisation in the UK' (Hutnyk, 2000: 23), something that can be said to correspond to the initial, more modest objective that drove the origins of Womad's founding by Peter Gabriel, namely 'bringing the world to the world'.[25]

The example of Womad begs the question of how—and how far—music from the Global South becomes commodified within the production and marketing systems of the Global North. Cultural industries are concerned with the reproduction of aesthetic categories through the linking of technologies, content producers, and consumers. Music has always travelled along trade networks, and colonialism led to the imposition of western cultural forms as well as the incorporation of other traditions of music through the festivals and exhibitions that were held in the cities of colonizing countries (Connell and Gibson, 2004). At the same time, cultural fusions and artistic hybridity can be regarded as positive strategies of both resistance and accommodation across the nineteenth and twentieth centuries.[26]

Processes of commodification have also been facilitated by wider historical shifts in the technologies available for mediating communication between human beings. The advent of recorded music created a form of 'technological mediation allowing for remote exposure to other forms of music' (Connell and Gibson, 2004: 391) that in turn made possible its circulation as a commodity within a commercial economy at the global level. This also led to the distinct *separation* of sounds from the societies and communities that produced them, which led both to forms of disjuncture as well as to new conjunctions or mixtures arising from within these wider forms of circulation (Arom and Martin, 2011). In this regard, the invention of 'world music' as a selective category designed to sell records illustrates key issues within the commodified representation of development. The idea can be pinpointed to a meeting in a London pub on 29 June 1987. Recognizing its dynamism and originality—and increasing popularity due to festivals such as Womad—veteran broadcaster Charlie Gillett aimed to bring together non-western music for sale to consumers in the UK. In response, eleven small record labels raised a total of £3,500 to introduce a new section in record shops where African, Asian, and Latin American music could be highlighted as distinct from rock, classical, reggae, and folk.[27]

[25] See https://www.youtube.com/watch?v=ztPXTOpYzb0.
[26] See, respectively, Bayly (2004: 366–92) and Bayly (2018: 215–30).
[27] See https://www.theguardian.com/music/2011/jun/16/world-music-term-invented.

World music has been identified by geographers as a prime example of the way that places are constructed, commodified, and contested within the shifting context of market power, cultural products, and migratory flows of people. As Connell and Gibson (2004: 344) put it:

> World music acts as both a metaphor for, and agent of, global cultural-economic change. 'World music' defines both a subject category and branding exercise, intended to increase the appeal of certain commodities: consequently, through world music, discourses of the 'global' and 'local' are produced and disseminated. World music relies on its being perceived as both global and 'distant', with connections to specific places.

The marketing and consumption of world music extends what these authors term an 'aesthetic of exoticism' that had been long been part of the western gaze, since it presents the music as a cultural product distanced from commercial business, and imbued with an authenticity and purity of expression no longer found in western forms.[28]

The construction of the category was a successful record company marketing ploy by western record companies. Did it contribute to forms of international solidarity and multiculturalism, as its progenitors might have hoped, or simply reduce complex cultural traditions to single essentialized signifiers? In many cases the 'world music' that met with commercial success was that in which the artist had been forced into 'artistic compromise' (Connell and Gibson, 2004: 353). By the 1990s artists such as British Indian musician Nitin Sawhney were reported as resisting the implicit marginalization embodied in the category and describing it as 'a form of apartheid' (Connell and Gibson, 2004: 357). In an article published in *The Guardian* on 24 July 2019, Ammar Kalia pronounced the term world music not just as 'flawed and problematic' but 'dead'.[29] In 2017, Oslo's long-running World Music Festival changed its name simply to Oslo World partly in recognition of the outmoded nature of the term.[30]

Music as a Global Development Vernacular

Certain forms of music seem to travel well. Reggae, for example, driven by the twin forces of migration and by the powerful marketing of Bob Marley's music, has spread throughout the world (Dagnini, 2010). Similarly, a striking feature of

[28] In this sense, it extended the earlier examples of western artists attempting to renew their work through what might be seen as either opening up to, or the appropriation of, outside influences—the Beatles with Ravi Shankar, Paul Simon with Ladysmith Black Mambazo.

[29] See https://www.theguardian.com/music/2019/jul/24/guardian-world-music-outdated-global.

[30] See http://www.osloworld.no/en/news-2017/oslo-world-music-festival-endrer-navn/.

gang dynamics around the world is the way that—in some shape or form—for many gangs in extremely varied contexts US gangsta rap becomes a major element of their cultural baggage. According to Hagedorn (2008: 94), gangsta rap has its origins in US hip-hop, which in turn emerged from the street music and dance of African-American and Latino youth in the South Bronx in the early 1970s, 'an expression of the dispossessed's misery and defiance of racism and poverty'. The fact that such situations of socio-economic exclusion and political discrimination often led to the emergence of gangs is associable with the development of a particular form of hip-hop, namely gangsta rap, which 'expresses the rage of the gang member in the ghetto and his defiance of the white man's system, particularly the police'. In other words, gangsta rap is 'a creative expression of street-level reality', reflecting the 'harrowing experience of a life lived close to death' (Hagedorn, 2008: 97, 99–100).

Gangsta rap has become extremely commercialized—and even corporatized—since its origins, to the extent that much of it has become highly stereotyped, with lyrics becoming 'more mythical than factual' (Kubrin, 2005: 375). Indeed, as Hagedorn (2008: 100) puts it,

> gangsta rap's booming popularity, constant play, and erotic, money-worshiping music videos reinforce racist stereotypes among whites. On the other hand, these stereotypes also have had an influence on gang members themselves ...: life imitating art imitating life in a manner that would make Jean Baudrillard proud.

The latter is especially germane to the issue of making a case for including music sources within the corpus of development knowledge insofar as the global appeal of major figures of gangsta rap such as Tupac Shakur, the Notorious B.I.G., or N.W.A., among others, are arguably indicative of cross-cultural connection and commonalities. For example, Utas (2014: 173) describes how the post-conflict West Side Boys (WSB) group of ex-combatants that he studied in Sierra Leone 'adopted the global rebel and gang icon Tupac Shakur as a primary reference point for their social being', with their name taken from the introduction to Tupac's 1996 track 'Hit 'em up', for example. Utas (2014: 177–179) goes on to note that

> [t]he influence of Tupac Shakur is by no means surprising; he has been an inspiration for other youth militias around the world. Around the time the Sierra Leone WSB emerged, there was a Tupac Outlaws/West Side Outlaws militia group in Guadalcanal ..., while in both eastern DRC and Côte d'Ivoire, rebel groups were, a few years later, reportedly using Tupac T-shirts as their uniforms ... Even within Sierra Leone, the Tupac imagery was not restricted to the WSB but was also a major reference for youthful members of the RUF as well. As Jeremy Prestholdt (2009: 198) discusses in relation to the latter, they 'sought broader meaning for their experiences, justification for their actions, and psychological solace from the

> chaos they were unleashing' in the lyrics of Tupac. Borrowing from Appadurai, he points out how 'Tupac appeals to diverse self-images in ways that constitute and reflect a disjointed community of sentiment across differing, even political landscapes.' Certainly the lyrics of his songs can be said to be 'steeped in the rhetoric of resilience, of overcoming unjust conditions ... Tupac's perceived invincibility offered psychological solace for young people who experienced violence as part of their everyday life' (Prestholdt, 2009: 201). ... At the same time, however, Prestholdt (2009: 206) also suggests that the invocation of Tupac indicated a broader youth discontent—with clientelism and corruption, exclusion, poverty, and inequality.

In a broader academic context marked by an 'ontological turn' suggesting the incommensurability of cross-cultural communication, at least at the verbal level, examples such as the WSB's and RUF's appropriation of Tupac's gangsta rap perhaps suggest that music holds a particular power to communicate meaningfully across contexts about key development issues that other forms of human expression might not have. Certainly, in a more general way, the frequent crossover of music from one context to another—e.g. the popularity of salsa or tango beyond Latin America, or the ever-increasing influence of Bollywood music beyond the Indian subcontinent, including within mainstream, conventional European and North American musical culture (as evidenced by the western success of musicals such as 'Basmati Blues' or 'Bride and Prejudice')—suggest that music may well have some form of universality that other forms of communication do not.[31] Seen from this perspective, a case can perhaps be made, as Henry Wadsworth Longfellow famously put it long ago, that 'music is the universal language of mankind.'[32]

Conclusion

The case for taking music seriously as a realm within which potentially important claims about development are made and contested rests not on providing 'rigorous evidence' that popular culture constitutes an effective 'tool' for promoting more equitable and effective development. Perhaps it can verifiably do this, under

[31] An interesting reverse example is the film 'Blinded by the Light' (2019), which conveys the moving 'true story' of how two Pakistani immigrants to England in the 1980s—living in Luton as factories are closing (rendering parents unemployed) and finding themselves (and their families) the frequent targets of racial taunts and vandalism—are inspired by the music of Bruce Springsteen, with its common theme of hope amid frustration, isolation, and constraints in depressed communities, to envision and enact alternative futures. In lesser hands such a narrative could be trite or condescending, but as conveyed in this instance it is a thoughtful depiction of how forms of elective affinity can be forged, via music, across lines of age, race, class, and nation.

[32] Although such a sentiment is not without controversy—see Kang (2016).

particular conditions—on which we would welcome evidence—but that is for others to discern.[33] In our (now long-standing) view, the broader and vastly stronger arguments are threefold. These arguments apply to the link between popular culture and development in general, but here we have sought to show the distinctive ways in which they apply to music and development in particular.

First, novels, films, and music are part of the communicative media through which many citizens in the Global North 'encounter' stereotypical images and perceptions of life in the Global South, and are thereby key mechanisms by which development debates are framed for and experienced by the general public.[34] These mechanisms, in turn, shape the nature and extent of development's broader political support, whether as a stand-alone venture or within the ambit of foreign policy—with corresponding consequences for the resources and legitimacy afforded it. As we have shown here, for example, the mainstream media can itself portray popular culture as a trivial or even profligate use of public resources for realizing development objectives, doing so as part of explicit campaigns to undermine support for it. At the same time, in previous decades, most notably the 1980s, music was mobilized—albeit often in deeply problematic ways—as part of global campaigns to focus attention on those suffering the ravages of war and famine. In today's increasingly globalized world, in which the barriers to producing and sharing music (and related visual material) have been greatly lowered, it is thus to be expected that music will increasingly be used as a medium in and through which the public experiences a wide array of emotive claims pertaining to the strategic importance, moral virtue, or political/economic folly of development. We have argued that music derives its distinctive power and influence not through appeals to reason, rationality, or 'evidence' but by harnessing and authentically generating shared memory, experience, and primal emotions—perhaps especially those emotions uniquely encountered and amplified collectively (e.g. in concerts, in national or religious anthems, military marches, etc.). Therein lies music's potential for political deployment, whether aiding, abetting, or challenging prevailing development practice.

Second, popular culture offers communicative mediums vastly more attuned to and resonant with the lived realities of marginalized groups, and the 'terms of recognition' (Appadurai, 2004) by which their views are conveyed, received, and interpreted. This implies that making development truly more 'inclusive' will entail not only expanding participation in meetings in narrow terms (where such participation can be readily counted and accounted), but enabling marginalized

[33] Indeed, we applaud recent efforts by researchers to engage in such studies. See, for example, the World Bank's Entertainment Education program, which attempts to assess the effectiveness of various social media campaigns on behavioural change (see https://www.worldbank.org/en/research/dime/brief/edu-tainment).

[34] And vice versa, of course: in our interconnected age, it is also how South increasingly encounters North.

groups to make and defend claims about themselves, their rivals, their concerns, interests, aspirations, and priorities in ways they find most resonant and compelling. These modalities of communication are unlikely to be those of educated elites in the policy, donor, and research communities, whose medium of choice overwhelmingly consists of lengthy written texts (often in English), numerical assessments (preferably 'hard evidence' derived from 'rigorous methods'), and analytical claims grounded in formal notions of 'expertise'. This is patently *not* how the vast majority of development's ostensible 'clients' communicate with one another, and the rest of the world. Taking inclusion seriously means taking seriously the predominant (and often preferred) modes of communication that the poor, illiterate, and marginalized themselves deploy. Music is—unlike novels and films, the focus of our previous analyses of popular culture and development—perhaps the one communicative medium shared by all of humanity, even if 'learning to hear' inherently requires considerable work by all parties. Insights from such material, as we have also previously stressed, should be regarded as a complement to, not substitute for, conventional social scientific evidence; even so, to the extent a distinctive power of music is its capacity to broadly convey human experience and speak directly to our complex emotions, all participants in the development space surely have much to be gained from exploring it more intentionally and carefully, on its own terms. For better and for worse, music is perhaps, while not immune to the reproduction of class and difference, a 'language' that humanity truly shares—or has the capacity to share. As such, it matters for deep intrinsic reasons, beyond whatever narrow empirical 'case' can be made for or against its instrumental significance.

Third, there are 'truths' about development that are best conveyed in popular mediums. These include the importance of power and representation, and the unequal relationships and 'disjunctures' between key development categories including developers and developed, rich and poor, and West and non-West. This is true of novels and films, as we have previously showed, but it also holds for music. Indeed, across all five of the analytical categories discussed above—western 'protest' music; musical resistance in the Global South; music-based development interventions; commodification and appropriation; music as a globalized development vernacular—one can readily discern themes and issues which are optimally expressed, and perhaps uniquely express-able, in musical form.[35] Biting political critique, satire, and advocacy can be conveyed musically in ways that might otherwise be regarded as seditious or treasonous, even as music can be used to construct and perpetuate patronizing stereotypes. Music can give voice to

[35] It is not lost on us that we are making these arguments using English academic discourse, but alas conveying them in musical form is, at least for present purposes, beyond our collective talents and far from our comparative advantage (although it should be noted that one of us—Lewis—is individually both an academic and a semi-professional musician—see https://store.cdbaby.com/Artist/DavidLewis1).

marginalized groups' experience of development in their own way, on their own terms, even as that same music can also be commodified, in ways that can reduce complex singing styles, lyrics, and instrument playing to packaged products sold on global markets, with few of the profits going to the music makers themselves. Today's technology enables music to be a culturally distinctive source of income, and be used to directly convey (or indirectly support) important pro-development initiatives in locally meaningful ways, even as it also risks public ridicule and unwarranted attacks on the entire development community. And yet, despite the vast array of economic, political, and cultural differences between groups worldwide, perhaps one of the few forms of common 'language' we share is our ability to make, celebrate, and share the human experience in musical form.[36]

At any given time and place, which of the possible development outcomes music can yield will inevitably be a function of innumerable contingencies. But music's status as a unique entry point into the experience of development processes, as a means to championing and resisting development practice, and as an active contributor to mainstream development outcomes, only means that specifying those contingencies more precisely can be a distinctive, interesting, and insightful field of research. We invite development scholars and practitioners, especially those in the 'rising generation', to take up this challenge.

Acknowledgements

The views expressed in this paper are those of the authors alone and should not be attributed to the organizations with which they are affiliated. For helpful comments and suggestions, we wish to thank Deval Desai, Oliver Haas, Eve Hopkins, Gillian Howell, Oliver Jütersonke, Solveig Korum, Laura Partridge, Gerry Rodgers, and Dennis Whittle.

References

Appadurai, A. (2004) 'The capacity to aspire: Culture and the terms of recognition', in V. Rao and M. Walton (eds) *Culture and Public Action*. Palo Alto, CA: Stanford University Press, pp. 59–84.

Arom, S. and Denis-Constant Martin (2011) 'Combining sounds to reinvent the world: World music, sociology, and musical analysis', in M. Tenzer and J. Roeder (eds) *Analytical and Cross-Cultural Studies in World Music*. Oxford: Oxford University Press, pp. 388–414.

Anderson, N. (1923). *The Hobo: The sociology of the homeless man*. Chicago: University of Chicago Press.

[36] Indeed, this may even be the case at an even deeper, genus-level (see Hattori and Tomonaga, 2019).

Baker, C. (2017) 'Sounds of a modern nation: From *Narcocorridos* to Hugo Salcedo's *Música de Balas*', *Symposium: A Quarterly Journal in Modern Literatures* 71(4): 179–94.

Barron, P. and A. Burke (2008) *Supporting Peace in Aceh: Development Agencies and International Involvement*, East West Center Policy Studies No. 47. Washington, DC: East West Center.

Barz, G. and J. M. Cohen (Eds) (2011) *The Culture of Aids in Africa: Hope and Healing in Music and the Arts*. New York: Oxford University Press.

Bayly, C. A. (2004) *The Birth of the Modern World 1780–1914: Global Connections and Comparisons*. Oxford: Blackwell.

Bayly, C. A. (2018) *Remaking the Modern World 1900–2015: Global Connections and Comparisons*. Oxford: Wiley Blackwell.

Berger, H. M. (2014) 'New directions in ethnomusicological research into the politics of music and culture: Issues, projects, and programs', *Ethnomusicology* 58(2): 315–20.

Blacking, J. (1973) *How Musical Is Man?* Seattle, WA: University of Washington Press.

Blackman, D. A. (2008) *Slavery by Any Other Name: The Re-Enslavement of Black Americans from the Civil War to World War II*. New York: Doubleday.

Bolger, L. (2012) 'Music therapy and international development in action and reflection: A case study of a women's music group in rural Bangladesh', *Australian Journal of Music Therapy* 23: 22–41.

Brooks, J. R. (2009) 'The Silent Soundtrack: Anti-War Music from Vietnam to Iraq', unpublished PhD dissertation, Department of Sociology and Anthropology. New York: Fordham University.

Clammer, J. (2014) *Arts, Culture and International Development: Humanizing Social Transformation*. London: Routledge.

Connell, J. and C. Gibson (2004) 'World music: Deterritorializing place and identity', *Progress in Human Geography* 28(3): 342–61.

Dagnini, J. K. (2010) 'The importance of reggae music in the worldwide cultural universe', *Etudes Caribéennes* 16, available at https://journals.openedition.org/etudescaribeennes/4740.

Dave, N. (2019) *The Revolution's Echoes: Music, Politics and Pleasure in Guinea*. Chicago, IL: University of Chicago Press.

Dillane, A., M. J. Power, A. Haynes, and E. Devereux (2018) 'Introduction: Stand up, sing out – The contemporary relevance of protest song', in A. Dillane, M. J. Power, A. Haynes, and E. Devereux (eds) *Songs of Social Protest: International Perspectives*. London: Rowman & Littlefield, pp. 1–10.

Edberg, M. C. (2004) *El Narcotraficante: Narcocorridos and the Construction of a Cultural Persona on the U.S.-Mexico Border*. Austin, TX: University of Texas Press.

Frishkopf, M. (2017) 'Popular music as public health technology: Music for global human development and "Giving Voice to Health" in Liberia', *Journal of Folklore Research* 54(1–2): 41–86.

Gilroy, P. (1993) *The Black Atlantic: Modernity and Double Consciousness*. London: Routledge.

Hagedorn, J. M. (2008) *A World of Gangs: Armed Young Men and Gangsta Culture*. Minneapolis, MN: University of Minnesota Press.

Harrison, K. (Ed.) (2013) 'Music and poverty', special half-issue of the *Yearbook for Traditional Music* 45.

Hattori, Y. and M. Tomonaga (2019) 'Rhythmic swaying induced by sound in chimpanzees (Pan troglodytes)', *Proceedings of the National Academy of Sciences* 117(2): 936–42.

Howell, G. (2018) 'Community music interventions in post-conflict contexts', in B.-L. Bartleet and L. Higgins (eds) *The Oxford Handbook of Community Music*. Oxford: Oxford University Press, pp. 43–70.

Hutnyk, J. (2000) *Critique of Exotica: Music, Politics and the Culture Industry*. London: Pluto Press.

Kabanda, P. (2018) *The Creative Wealth of Nations: Can the Arts Advance Development?* Cambridge: Cambridge University Press.

Kang, S. (2016) 'The history of multicultural music education and its prospects: The controversy of music universalism and its application', *Update* 34(2): 21–8.

Kartomi, M. (2010) 'Toward a methodology of war and peace studies in ethnomusicology: The case of Aceh, 1976-2009', *Ethnomusicology* 54(3): 452–83.

Korum, S. (2017) '"He who pays the piper, calls the tune": A study of values and practices in two multi-agency musical development projects in Palestine and Sri Lanka', unpublished paper presented at the 'Music 2020' workshop, University of Agder, Norway, 14 June.

Kubrin, C. E. (2005) 'Gangstas, thugs, and hustlas: Identity and the code of the street in rap music', *Social Problems* 52(3): 360–78.

Lewis, D. (2019) '"Big D" and "little d": Two types of twenty-first century development?', *Third World Quarterly* 40(11): 1957–75.

Lewis, D., D. Rodgers, and M. Woolcock (2008) 'The fiction of development: Literary representation as an authoritative source of knowledge', *Journal of Development Studies* 44(2): 198–216.

Lewis, D., D. Rodgers, and M. Woolcock (2013) 'The projection of development: Cinematic representation as (an)other source of development knowledge', *Journal of Development Studies* 49(3): 383–97.

Lewis, D., D. Rodgers, and M. Woolcock (Eds) (2014) *Popular Representations of Development: Insights from Novels, Films, Television and Social Media*. London: Routledge.

Long, N. (2013) 'The power of music: Issues of agency and social practice', *Social Analysis* 57(2): 21–40.

Malcomson, H. (2019) 'Negotiating violence and creative agency in commissioned Mexican narco rap', *Bulletin of Latin American Research* 38(3): 347–62.

Margolick, D. and H. Als (2000) *Strange Fruit: The Biography of a Song*. Philadelphia, PA: Running Press.

Mohaiemen, N. (2014) 'Fragile fourth estate: A history of censorship in Bangladesh (1972-2012)', in B. Shoesmith, J. W. Genilo, and M. Asiuzzaman (eds) *Bangladesh's Changing Mediascape: From State Control to Market Forces*. Bristol: Intellect, pp. 113–32.

Ohlmacher, J. and A. Pervez (2014) 'Negotiating identity: Islam in the films of Tareque and Catherine Masud', in B. Shoesmith, J. W. Genilo, and M. Asiuzzaman (eds) *Bangladesh's Changing Mediascape: From State Control to Market Forces*. Bristol: Intellect, pp.153–74.

Prestholdt, J. (2009) 'The afterlives of 2Pac: Imagery and alienation in Sierra Leone', *Journal of African Cultural Studies* 21(2): 197–218.

Rachel, D. (2016) *Walls Come Tumbling Down: The Music and Politics of Rock against Racism, 2 Tone and Red Wedge, 1976–1992*. London: Picador.

Randall, D. (2017) *Sound System: The Political Power of Music*. London: Pluto.
Rice, T. (2014) 'Ethnomusicology in times of trouble', *Yearbook for Traditional Music* 46: 191–209.
Richey, L. A. (2016) 'Introduction', in L. A. Richey (ed.) *Celebrity Humanitarianism and North-South Relations: Politics, Place and Power*. London: Routledge, pp. 1–24.
Schuller, M. (2012) *Killing with Kindness: Haiti, International Aid, and NGOs*. New Brunswick, NJ: Rutgers University Press.
Schwittay, A. (2015) *New Media and International Development: Representation and Affect in Microfinance*. London: Routledge.
Simonett, H. (2001) '*Narcocorridos*: An emerging micromusic of Nuevo L.A.', *Ethnomusicology* 45(2): 315–37.
Smith, D. and K. Jacobs (2011) "'Breaking up the sky": The characterisation of accounting and accountants in popular music', *Accounting, Auditing and Accountability Journal* 24(7): 904–31.
Stupples, P. and K. Teaiwa (Eds) (2016) *Contemporary Perspectives on Art and International Development*. London: Taylor and Francis.
Tenzer, M. and J. Roeder (Eds) (2011) *Analytical and Cross-Cultural Studies in World Music*. Oxford: Oxford University Press.
Utas, M. (2014) "'Playing the game": Gang–militia logics in war-torn Sierra Leone', in J. M. Hazen and D. Rodgers (eds) *Global Gangs: Street Violence across the World*. Minneapolis, MN: University of Minnesota Press, pp. 171–91.
Way, L. C. S. (2017) 'Authenticity and subversion: Articulations in protest music videos' struggle with countercultural politics and authenticity', in L. C. S. Way and S. McKerell (eds) *Music as Multimodal Discourse: Semiotics, Power and Protest*. London: Bloomsbury, pp.95–118.

2

The Pedagogy of Trash

Photography, Environmental Activism, and African Dumpsites

Danny Hoffman

Introduction

Trash, it seems, is everywhere. As a narrative thread in the larger stories of climate change, economic inequality, and chronic underdevelopment, trash is a powerful trope. How waste is managed, where it goes, who profits from, and who suffers from its presence are critical development questions with political, economic, and social implications. And like any development story, trash has its narrative conventions and its representational norms.

In sub-Saharan Africa the story of trash is generally told through hyperbole. A web documentary funded by the Bill and Melinda Gates Foundation calls Ghana an 'E-Waste Republic'.[1] A 2010 BBC documentary, *Welcome to Lagos*, implies that residents of that city's Olusosun dump are perhaps the only people on the planet truly prepared to face 'the extreme urban future'.[2] A 2014 Fox News story on West African dumps leads with the pithy headline 'Welcome to Hell'.[3] Visual staples of the African trash narrative are no less dramatic. Photographs and video footage show vast landscapes of garbage populated by grey men, women, and children picking through debris. The few trees are festooned with a thick canopy of plastic bags. In both art and documentary reportage, no single site, and no single image, seems to better capture the precarity of African environments and African political economy than the image of endless trash.

But not all photographs of the continent's notorious rubbish are the same. Using photography to teach the politics of trash on the continent is therefore not as straightforward as it might appear. In this chapter I contrast the work of two photographers who take up, in very different ways, the subject of African dumping grounds. Dakar-based photographer Fabrice Monteiro and South Africa's Pieter Hugo have each produced well-known and critically acclaimed bodies of work

[1] Available at http://interactive.aljazeera.com/aje/2015/ewaste/index.html.
[2] Available at http://www.bbc.co.uk/programmes/b00s3bmx.
[3] Available at http://www.foxnews.com/tech/2014/03/06/welcome-to-hell-photographer-documents-africas-e-waste-nightmare.html.

Danny Hoffman, *The Pedagogy of Trash*. In: *New Mediums, Better Messages?*.
Edited by David Lewis, Dennis Rodgers, and Michael Woolcock, Oxford University Press.
 DOI: 10.1093/oso/9780198858751.003.0003

Photo 2.1 Pieter Hugo, *David Akore, Agbogbloshie Market, Accra, Ghana*, 2010

on the subject of accumulating African waste. In doing so, they build on a longer tradition of trash as trope in African image production, a tradition that uses the visual iconography of garbage to educate publics and to make political claims. Both artists employ an activist camera, seeking to use their work to catalyse action around environmental issues on the continent. But the different approaches to visualizing trash in Monteiro's *The Prophecy* and Hugo's *Permanent Error* reflect a broader divide over how photography communicates urgent issues in global development and what photography has to offer in the particular discourses of African environmental and economic futures. The two projects point towards different interpretations of the environmental and social politics of waste, and each calls for a different response from the audiences of their work.

As an anthropologist offering undergraduate courses on African political economy, visual theory, and media studies, the politics of representation and development on the African continent are perennial themes in my teaching. And as a former photojournalist working in Africa, I have grappled with the limitations and possibilities afforded by different visual languages in the representation of

African issues.[4] In pairing these two projects in lectures and class assignments, I have drawn lessons from each of these spheres as I challenge students to think about both the potential and the limits of photography as a medium for engaging critical issues in Africa today. What students take from these projects is, of course, highly variable. But it is also at least somewhat prescribed by the photographic traditions in which these two artists work. These photographic genres speak differently to the common theme of trash, and leave their viewers with different tools for engaging Africa's environmental future.

Trash Matters

As a development issue, trash matters. A 2012 World Bank report on the global management of solid waste maps a familiar argument. The world's population is increasingly urban, with especially rapid growth across sub-Saharan Africa. Urban populations generate more solid waste, making waste management the single largest issue with which cities must deal. 'Solid waste management', as the report puts it:

> is almost always the responsibility of local governments and is often their single largest budget item, particularly in developing countries. Solid waste management and street sweeping is also often the city's single largest source of employment. Additionally, solid waste is one of the most pernicious local pollutants—uncollected solid waste is usually the leading contributor to local flooding and air and water pollution. And if that task were not large enough, local waste management officials also need to deal with the integrated and international aspects of solid waste, and increasingly with demographic change in the work force, employment generation, and management of staff—both formal and informal.
> (Hoornweg and Bhada-Tata, 2012: 1)

In other words, few aspects of the life in an urban space have quite the reach of trash. Over the past several years it has been not only domestic waste but the dumping of international refuse (notably e-waste) that has grabbed headlines. Materials that are too dangerous, expensive, or simply too inconvenient to be safely recycled or disposed of in Europe or the US are increasingly finding their way to massive dumps outside Accra, Lagos, Abidjan, and other African cities. According to a United Nations survey, much of the nearly 42 million metric tonnes of e-waste estimated to have been generated in 2014 was dumped illegally or informally, with West Africa being the principle recipient (Rucevska et al., 2015: 8).

[4] In my own visual scholarship, I have tried two very different visual approaches to representing social and environmental issues in Hoffman (2007) and (2014).

This despite the fact that, as a European Commission study argues, African cities are particularly ill-equipped to deal with their own or anyone else's trash (Scarlat et al., 2015: 1275).

As a result of this lack of pressing infrastructure, most solid waste in sub- Saharan Africa ends up in landfills and rubbish dumps (Munawar and Fellner, 2012). The dumpsite is, however, rarely the terminus of the complicated formal and informal networks of labour that collect, sort, and transport waste. Even at tightly regulated sites like Durban's Bisasar Road Landfill (perhaps the largest official dump on the continent) both licensed and unlicensed pickers, many of them living as well as working on the landfill, pick through the accumulated garbage in search of recyclable and saleable materials (see Bond and Sharife, 2012, as well as Myers, 2010; Fredericks, 2013, 2014). Yet in contrast to the dystopian, nightmare images of starving gleaners chaotically scrounging through mountains of garbage, much of this labour is well organized and at least modestly profitable—even as it is highly dangerous to the unprotected workforce (Spaull, 2015).

Complex as is the story of African trash, it continues to be depicted in simplified images. The cover of the World Bank's 2012 report 'What a Waste', a summary of the global state of solid waste management, perfectly illustrates the visual lay of the land: on the left of the cover is a Barcelona street scene with its neat line of colour coded bins for recyclable and non-recycling waste. On the right, two black youths stand atop a mountain of garbage. They stare vacantly out of the frame, digging sticks in hand, partly obscured by the smoke rising all around them. The juxtaposition is powerful: order and disorder, sanitary and deadly, responsible and grossly negligent.

These are naturalized, obvious images for most of my students. On the one hand, the smooth functionalism of the Global North; on the other, a Hobbesian world of destitution in the Global South. The pedagogical challenge is therefore to make these images more complex by exploring with students the ways that both are caricatures of reality, not separate histories but conjoined, mutually reinforcing ones. And, most significantly for my purposes here, the challenge is to push students to think about the representational politics of trash. If trash matters as a development issue, so too do the strategies by which photographers represent it, and the ways in which they visually link trash to the lives of those who produce it and those who must live with and among it.

The Image of Trash

The presence of trash in photography is a political presence. The earliest uses of photography as a tool of social activism often deployed uncollected trash as a signifier of social inequality and injustice. In Jacob Riis's *How the Other Half Lives* (1970 [1890]), an indictment of crowded tenement housing in New York, some of the more affecting images are those of boys sleeping (or pretending to sleep) on trash strewn sidewalks. Dorothea Lange's pioneering reportage deployed uncollected waste as evidence of the deplorable conditions facing labour migrants in the Depression era United States (see Spirn, 2008). For both photographers, as for countless others, accumulating garbage, and the image of a city's residents trying to create a life within it, signifies the failure of those in power to meet the most basic needs of a populace.

This has been a prominent theme in African image production. As Kenneth Harrow (2013) has argued, trash played a significant role in African cinema from the earliest days of the genre, where it marks the failures of both colonial and then post-colonial governments. In Ousmene Sembene's first narrative film, *Borom Sarret*, the great Senegalese film-maker contrasts the crowded African *quartiers* with the pristine but sterile European neighbourhoods in part through the medium of trash. The Cameroonian documentary film-maker Jean-Marie Teno shows mounting piles of garbage in Yaoundé across multiple films, each time serving as evidence that the country's ruling elite has betrayed the promise of equality that came with independence. And Salem Mekuria, the Ethiopian film-maker and video artist, uses the Addis Ababa city dump as a site for her Venice Biennale triptych *Ruptures*, a work intended 'to expresses the collective despair I felt about the state of the nation' (Mekuria, 2012: 16).

As the technologies of image making have expanded across the continent, so too have images of trash. For example, a dramatic drop in oil prices meant that in 2015 the Angolan government could no longer afford to collect trash in many neighbourhoods in the capital city, Luanda. As a result, a whole new genre of mobile phone photography emerged. The *selfie lixo*, or 'garbage selfie' images are posted online to shame city and state leaders for their corruption and ineptitude (see Gastrow, 2016).

Harrow (2013: 2) makes an important observation about the seeming ubiquity of trash, however. The visual signifier of garbage doesn't simply serve as a 'lament' over the failures of governments, past and present. 'There is more here than loss', he writes, 'more than decay and a descent. In fact, the descent is here only because of the belief that the depiction of it will serve to enable a change, an ascent, to become possible'. Drawing in part on Achille Mbembe's (1992) writing on the 'vulgar' aesthetics of post-colonial African politics, Harrow (2013: 4) argues that trash in African film-making has primarily been deployed to undermine autocratic regimes by mocking their excess and incompetency.

As solid waste management becomes an increasingly prominent issue in Africa's expanding cities—and an increasingly pressing *global* issue for environmental, health, and labour activists—images of accumulating African trash seem to function less as critical visual metaphors for generic failures of government and more as direct accusations of the unsustainability of the prevailing consumerist order. The activist camera poses a challenge to the attitude that waste can be dumped without cost at any level, from the individual consumer's plastic bag to the industrial materials shipped from points around the planet. Like all social activist photography, it rests on the basic premise that the photograph works by making visible that which would otherwise remain invisible or ignored. The photograph is an intervention by its very existence, and the photograph of trash serves as undeniable evidence of a broken system.

This is a logic that, for the most part, makes sense to the majority of my students. To a population that is primarily young and cosmopolitan, a call for action on environmental issues is generally uncontentious. A relatively media savvy (or at least media saturated) demographic, they are prepared to think of photography as a medium that both conveys information and constructs an argument. That photographers known mostly for their fine art imagery can speak to urgent issues in development studies does not seem counter-intuitive or illogical to most of them. Many are familiar with the genre-blurring reportage of photographers like Sebastiao Salgado or James Nachtwey, and accept the philosophical foundations of the camera-as-witness school of activism.

And yet I have been surprised at how many of my students do not approach these images with the same critical eye that they might bring to the written work of environmental activists, academic researchers, or policymakers. Many don't recognize the real and meaningful genre distinctions that structure how images communicate, or situate the images they see within specific aesthetic traditions. The 'myth of photographic truth' (Sturken and Carthwright, 2009), in which the photograph's peculiar magic lies in masking the conditions of its own production and is therefore assumed to have a neutral, indexical relationship to the world beyond the frame is a powerful one—even for a generation of students deeply immersed in many different kinds of image production. For me, then, the challenge in teaching trash as a development issue is also a challenge of locating the image of trash vis-à-vis the representational strategies that produce it. Nothing I have found works better towards that end than pairing two very different styles of work by two well-known African photographers.

Pieter Hugo, *Permanent Error*

The Agbogbloshie dump on the outskirts of Accra, Ghana, may be the most photographed of sub-Saharan Africa's landfills.[5] According to one international photographer visiting Agbogbloshie in 2015, the recyclers there had been so inundated with photographers that they began using mobile phones to photograph the photographers who visited the site, creating an archive of artists, journalists,

[5] The images in the *Permanent Error* series are available in Hugo (2011) and on the artist's website, at https://pieterhugo.com/PERMANENT-ERROR.

and activists who 'arrive as if going on safari, hoping to capture images of squalor' (Spaull, 2015).

South African Pieter Hugo may be the best known of the image makers to have taken up Agbogbloshie as a subject. Working with a large format field camera, shooting in colour, Hugo's Agbogbloshie images are primarily portraits, see Photo 2.1. Of the forty-four images collected in *Permanent Error*, sixteen are single individuals facing the camera. In another ten the principle subject is a group of people or individual recyclers turned away from the lens. There are five additional portraits, though in these the sitters are cows and goats, photographed in the same manner as the human portraits in the series.

Aesthetically, *Permanent Error* is consistent with Hugo's earlier work. In books like *Messina/Musina* (2007), *The Hyena & Other Men* (2008), and *Nollywood* (2009), Hugo uses large format environmental portraits to explore the connection between his African subjects and their context. The individuals in these images may dominate the frame, but what surrounds them is equally important to conveying meaning. In *The Hyena & Other Men*, a project documenting a troupe of Nigerian street performers and the hyenas, monkeys, and snakes they keep with them, Hugo writes that it is 'the hybridization of the urban and the wild' that interested him in the images. That line is blurred in the portraits in more ways than one; the signifiers of 'the urban' in these images (the rotting carcasses of cars, construction debris, and ubiquitous piles of trash) appear chaotic and untamed, and the animal subjects exhibit poses, looks, and demeanours that mirror the 'civilization' of their human handlers.

But if the aesthetic is consistent across Hugo's project, its effect in *Permanent Error* is different. In the Agbogbloshie images there is hybridity between the portrait subjects and their environmental context, but it is not an ambivalent or ambiguous hybridity. Here the human subjects read as part of the landscape of detritus. In only a handful of the images do the recyclers actually *do* anything, and even in these images their actions are mostly indecipherable and take place in the background. For the most part the gleaners in *Permanent Error* simply exist in the context of the dump, sometimes sleeping but mostly staring straight into the camera, posed with their unused sorting sticks. Interspersed with the animal portraits and with still lives of discarded floppy disks, keyboards, VHS tapes, and broken televisions, the images blur the line between human and waste by arguing that at Agbogbloshie, human and e-waste are equally abject.

As a result, *Permanent Error*'s activism falls squarely within the modernist tradition of socially engaged photography. Implicit in the project, just as it was in Jacob Riis's images of New York's urban poor, Lewis Hines's child factory workers and the combat images of American press photographers in Vietnam, is the idea of the camera as unimpeachable witness. The modernist photograph, shot according to the aesthetic principles of documentary realism, serves as evidence of an injustice. Done well, it is a call to arms. The documentary photographic tradition relies on a simple but compelling formula: confronted with the grim reality reflected in the photograph, a viewer has no choice but to feel interpellated in a moment of violence and violation, no choice but to feel the call to act. 'It's impossible not to feel guilty', wrote one reviewer about the *Permanent Error* images on display in a gallery in Cape Town. 'Impossible not to feel implicated in their situation. That culpability makes Hugo's work valid. You stay glued to the screen—like the subjects depicted—relieved not to be them—the ones photographed—relieved not to be contemporary paragons of misery' (Steiner, 2010).

That basic philosophical position on the power of documentary realism, an argument that making something visible is automatically a summons to intervene, is not, of course, uncontested. Susan Sontag's (1977, 2004) famous critique of photographs of violence and suffering disputed just this foundational logic. Not only did images of 'the pain of others' *not* lead to meaningful interventions. Frequently these images offered nothing more to a viewer than a perverse form of pleasure. Realist photographs of abjection, according to Sontag, become spectacles that offer no useful tools for political action, and in fact serve to foreclose real political engagement. It is a charge frequently levelled against Hugo by critics who have accused him of producing 'poverty porn', images of suffering as spectacle that become consumable commodities on the international art market.[6] Tom Leininger, reviewing *Permanent Error* in the *photo-eye* catalogue of photography books, nicely (though presumably inadvertently) captures the argument that images of social injustice might shock their viewers, but only invite them to further consume images: 'This [*Permanent Error*] is one of those books where I say it needs to be purchased since these pictures are important ... There are times when the first world needs a punch to the throat'.[7] What this 'punch in the throat' does, other than sell books, is not clear.

The undergraduate students with whom I have discussed Hugo's *Permanent Error* have generally resisted Sontag's more extreme critique. While ambivalent about the art market value of photographs of poverty and violence, they nevertheless remain largely committed to the principle of witnessing and of photographic realism as a form of activism. These are pictures, as one student put it after a 2016 lecture, 'that make me want to do something'.

Therein lies the more interesting, and more subtle, challenge in using *Permanent Error* to speak to the development problem of sub-Saharan African trash. Hugo's title does of course raise the question of whether any intervention into the scenes on the page is possible. Yet most students, as indeed most viewers, do find in the modernist tradition of documentary realism a meaningful summons. *Permanent Error*, like most projects of its kind, engenders outrage. 'Maybe someone should do something about this?', as Leininger put it in his review. The subjects

[6] Available at https://www.news24.com/citypress/voices/white-saviours-noble-savages-20160715
[7] Available at http://www.photoeye.com/bookstore/citation.cfm?Catalog=px145.

within the frame however, are rendered helpless, incapable of responding meaningfully to their own environment. Hugo's portraits can arguably be said to convey a kind of dignity on their subjects. Many seem defiant, almost noble, surrounded by garbage. But nothing in the images suggests that they have the resources or the wherewithal to interpret their own surroundings, let alone change their circumstances. Nothing in this situation can be altered from within. So, the questions raised here are all aimed directly at the viewer of the image, the presumed Global North consumer of both e-waste and art photography. If human beings have been reduced to the status of trash by the mass import of toxic waste, the response that these images seem to call for is an external intervention to eliminate these landscapes of garbage. We as viewers know all we need to know about what is happening at Agbogbloshie; all that is left is to figure out what we will do about it.

But Sontag's argument that the image itself contains little information on *how* to intervene is well taken. And indeed, the questions that Hugo's work provokes tend to be large and abstract, questions many steps removed from the realities of how waste in West Africa fits into the global political economy. 'Is technology good? Is the rush to update to the latest and greatest computer the problem? ... Can this phone last me a little longer? Maybe I do not need a new laptop', are the questions Leininger is left with in the face of Hugo's work. These are not, of course, meaningless questions and they are not unconnected from West African realities. But they seem inadequate in the face of the extreme dystopia of *Permanent Error*. Certainly, I have found that for students moved and motivated by Hugo's work, incremental changes in the way they consume technology do not feel sufficient to the task at hand. What they ask for are more immediate and more dramatic steps they can take to alleviate the suffering they read within the frame. And since the image itself contains no mystery, no invitation to further reflection on the scenes it depicts, what students (as any viewer) are left with is a standard rescue narrative, a well-meaning but poorly informed desire to save Africa and Africans.

As Edgar Pieterse (2011: 9) has argued in response to urban poverty more generally, in the absence of additional information about how people live and how cities function, the desire to 'fix' a city's problems alone generally reproduce simplistic, normative responses that have already been proven ineffective at best, counterproductive at worst. *Permanent Error* is not poverty porn, but it does not invite its viewers to ask how its subjects actually inhabit the world of trash. By offering moral certainty and outrage that what one sees in the images is *wrong*, that it requires an immediate and dramatic intervention from outside the frame, *Permanent Error* asks for action rather than further inquiry.

In short, what my students have tended to see in *Permanent Error* is a future that demands their intervention. Most see this as the unproblematic consequence of what Hugo's camera has done—rendered visible otherwise hard to access truths about the way the world dumps its refuse on helpless African subjects. They see truth in Hugo's work, not a set of modernist aesthetic conventions. Not, at least, until confronted with a very different representational style.

Fabrice Monteiro, *The Prophecy*

If Pieter Hugo's *Permanent Error* is heir to a high modernist tradition of activist photography, Fabrice Monteiro's *The Prophecy* is decidedly postmodern.[8] The origins of the project are instructive. Monteiro, a Dakar-based artist, conceived of the images as a series of fairy tales. Having asked Senegal's Minster of Ecology for a list of the top environmental threats to the West African nation, Monteiro selected nine scenarios around which to construct his images. Working with the fashion designer Doulsy, Monteiro outfitted models in fantastic costumes constructed of tar, plastic bags, cables, fishing nets, Saran wrap, and wood. Each untitled image features one of these mythical creatures rising out of some dystopian environmental context: a burning forest, a beach covered with animal parts, smog-belching vehicles, oil slicked waves, a trash-strewn landfill. Monteiro has described these figures as 'spirits' or 'genies' (*djinn*), sent by the Earth itself to 'to talk to the humans and tell them that they have to be aware of what is going on'.[9]

The lead image in the series, and the most widely circulated, was shot in Dakar's Mbeubeuss landfill, the largest in Senegal. A female figure with a towering skirt of plastic bags appears to be mid-stride, making her way through a smoking landscape of trash that is itself creeping outwards to replace the green mangrove swamps in the far background. Though her form is unmistakably human, with her face masked and her jewellery and clothing blending into the trash strewn foreground, Monteiro's model appears post-human, a kind of trash cyborg somehow birthed by the landfill itself.

While it is fair to argue that the de facto audience of Monteiro's work is, like Hugo's, an elite audience of transnational art consumers, Monteiro himself argues that his work is addressed to African viewers. In Marcia Juzga's documentary film about *The Prophecy*, Monteiro argues that 'as a photographer confronted by [a] lack of environmental public spiritedness, I wanted to create images that question us about our ways of consuming. The idea is to motivate an ecological consciousness in the upcoming generation by mixing art, culture, and tradition'. According to Monteiro, the fantastic forms into which he and Doulsy have transformed their models stemmed from a desire to reach Senegalese school children, young Africans who might still be open to his environmental message: '[F]rom living in Africa', he

[8] The images in *The Prophecy* series can be viewed on the artist's website, available at https://fabricemonteiro.viewbook.com/.

[9] Available at https://theglobalobservatory.org/2015/10/environmental-problems-africa-fabrice-monteiro/.

told one interviewer, 'I know that the solution is not going to come from the governments. It's going to come from the people. So I decided to write fairy tales for kids'.[10]

Unmistakably activist, Monteiro's approach nevertheless eschews the realist aesthetic that underpins Hugo's *Permanent Error*—and along with it much of the documentary photographic tradition. It isn't obvious how one should read the photographs in *The Prophecy* series. Where *Permanent Error* is jarring because it conflates familiar elements in an unfamiliar way (the bodies of its living subjects with the inanimate bodies of trash), *The Prophecy* is unsettling because its living subjects are so strikingly unfamiliar. As a result, *The Prophecy* isn't a call to action in the same way. It doesn't invite its viewers to intervene according to normative formulas, to fix an easily identifiable problem. What it demands of its viewers is that they look differently at the scene before them.

The figure emerging from the Mbeubeuss landfill may be an indictment of trash dumping, but it also conveys creation and genesis. Monteiro's camera captures a moment of creative adaptation. Whether one reads the emerging figures here as occult spirits or as science-fiction cyborgs, they are not simply victims of their debased environments. They are the products of it. They have found a way to inhabit their dystopic world. They are not abject, not reduced (in Giorgio Agamben's [1998] memorable phrase) to 'bare life'. Instead they invent new bodies and new relationships on the earth, apparently having succeeded in learning to live with the postmodern present's 'imperative to grow new organs, to expand our sensorium and our body to some new, yet unimaginable, perhaps ultimately impossible, dimensions' (Jameson, 1991: 39).

If Pieter Hugo's images ask how an external viewer will intervene to change the situation she or he sees in the image, Fabrice Monteiro's challenge is more complicated. Despite his claim to be making pictures primarily for Senegalese schoolchildren, *The Prophecy*'s primary audience has been the art, culture, and environmental activist markets of the Global North. (In addition to exhibitions and gallery shows on the blue-chip art circuit, Monteiro is a widely recognized fashion model and was named by *Foreign Policy* magazine as one of its 100 most influential global thinkers of 2015 for his environmental advocacy.) For that viewership, the challenge is to interpret what the subjects in the frame are themselves doing in response to their conditions of existence. Its invitation is to comprehension, or at least to further research, rather than action. Their imperative is to recognize what those who dwell within or on the landfill, literally or metaphorically, are doing themselves. These are deconstructive images, challenging their spectators to ask what they *don't* know or can't recognize in the scenes that unfold before them.

[10] Available at https://theglobalobservatory.org/2015/10/environmental-problems-africa-fabrice-monteiro/..

It is a deliberate strategy on Monteiro's part, as he has made clear in interviews about the project:

> I grew up in Benin. When I got back to Senegal four years ago, I couldn't believe how dirty it was. I realized that Africa had a serious, serious issue with environmental problems. So I thought I could do something, being a photographer, and I came up with the idea of mixing art and culture. Because to me, the mistake of a lot of NGOs that try to make Africans aware, they don't consider the culture. They come with ideas that are already all made, and the people there don't get it, because it doesn't talk to them.[11]

Indeed, confronted by Monteiro's very different rendering of the landscapes of trash and waste in West Africa, my students very often do respond positively to the provocation to ask what is going on in the image. They recognize the argument that they may not, in fact, know exactly what is going on in the story of trash in Africa. That there may be ways of inhabiting an urban landscape that are adaptive and emergent, that draw on histories they do not know, or that employ aesthetics with which they are unfamiliar.

Powerful and positive as that reading of Monteiro's work can be, however, it too comes with certain normative assumptions. In fact, Monteiro's own words can sometimes pose a challenge to using *The Prophecy* as a teaching tool for audiences uncritical of simplistic images of Africa and Africans. In describing his mythical figures as emissaries from the Earth itself, Monteiro repeatedly deploys a rather simplistic and totalizing vision of West African spiritualism:

> But using animism, the whole of West Africa believes in the spirits, and the idea was to use those spirits to deliver a message, instead of just saying, 'Oh, you shouldn't do this' or 'You shouldn't do that'. So my idea was to write beside the pictures—write a little tale for kids. The original idea was to have a little book published and distributed in schools in Senegal, because I believe the young generation is the one that we need to make aware of what is going on. They could bring it back home and say, 'Oh Daddy, you shouldn't throw the plastics there. We have to be careful about that, because the spirit of the plastic said now we have to be careful about that'. That was the whole idea of the concept.[12]

The risk here, of course, is that students already surrounded by images of West Africa as a space of primitivism, outside the modern world, cannot see past the idea of 'animism'. They risk understanding waste, its accumulation and its disposal

[11] Available at http://www.mantlethought.org/arts-and-culture/photographic-confrontations-fabrice-monteiro-interview.

[12] Available at http://www.mantlethought.org/arts-and-culture/photographic-confrontations-fabrice-monteiro-interview.

not as a complex question of global political economy, but as a problem of the spiritual fall from grace for Africa's noble savages. There are therefore two challenges in using Monteiro's *The Prophecy* as a starting point for engaging students. First, where employing Hugo's *Permanent Error* in the classroom requires deconstructing what students think they already understand, the challenge in using Monteiro's images to teach African environmentalism lies in reconciling *The Prophecy* with Monteiro's own interpretation of what his images mean. As Barrett (2000: 50–1) points out in his primer on photographic criticism, the intention of the photographer is not determinative of an image's meaning. I have therefore encouraged students to see in the series not djinn figures or animist spirits, *contra* Monteiro himself. Rather I have pushed students to see these figures as non-representative forces, creative but ambiguous. They are not subjects as much as they are visual, anthropomorphic signifiers of the potential to invent new possibilities. They express the latent possibility in any ruin space that the world might be imagined differently, that ameliorating a world of waste means not simply condemning it but employing it as part of the process of crafting new, locally meaningful visions of the future.

This is, of course, a less literal approach to the image than the modernist genre of documentary realism. And therein lies the second challenge for many of my students. Unlike the modernist tradition with its direct appeal to the viewer, many of my students see no point of entry for themselves through Monteiro's work. Some, in fact, read Monteiro's images as a foreclosure, a warning that they have no role to play vis-à-vis the scene before them. But once challenged to do so, most are willing to explore further the possibility that *The Prophecy* might simultaneously be a productive critique of both the politics of waste and the 'rescue' narratives that have so long plagued global development policy towards Africa.

Conclusion: Outside the Frame

Photographers who use the camera as a tool of activism make a range of choices in style, in dissemination, in equipment, and in message. Each of these decisions opens some communicative possibilities and forecloses others. There are messages the camera can convey and those it cannot, meanings that some types of photography make legible and others that they obscure. The same goes for those who use photography as a teaching tool. This is no less true of issues in development than it would be in any other sphere. The camera and the images it produces open certain avenues for exploration, and they risk shutting down others.

Teaching Fabrice Monteiro's *The Prophecy* and Pieter Hugo's *Permanent Error* together has allowed me to work with students to see the very different engagements that can be fostered with a modernist and postmodern approach to the communicative potential in photography. Both artists set out to intervene in the growing problem of solid waste in Africa, working to raise awareness of the human and environmental costs of indiscriminate dumping and the accumulation of trash. The two bodies of work speak effectively to one another, each addressing the elements weakest in the other. Hugo's work represents the urgent call to arms that has long been the hallmark of modernist photographic activism. But while it challenges a viewer to act, it does not necessarily challenge that viewer to act or think differently about what she or he sees. Monteiro's images, by contrast, force the viewer to confront what might be emergent from the environmental crisis. No less urgent than Hugo's work, it nevertheless suggests that any solutions to the continent's environmental challenges will require understanding what possibilities and potential there is to be found *in situ*. Existing narratives won't be enough. But that is a taller order than Hugo's, and one that risks becoming paralysingly obscure or complex. Inviting students to think these two works together makes it clear that development issues are representational issues, that understanding how to engage the politics and practices of development also requires the ability to effectively read an image.

It also requires an engagement with what is left entirely out of the frame. There are, for example, some parts of the story of African trash that simply cannot be told with the still camera in any style or genre. Recognizing these absences has been as important a part of the pedagogy of trash as challenging students to understand what they see within the frame.

Most obvious here is the incredible scale and diversity of activities that fall under the broad category of managing solid waste. As Nas and Jaffe (2004) argued over a decade ago, millions of people around the world exist on activities that are recognizable as forms of scavenging trash, and yet time, location, social, and economic context all give these activities very different local valences. Not surprisingly, still photography has gravitated towards the extreme end of what is, in fact, an enormously varied relationship between humans and their refuse.

Also largely absent from these frames is the deep history of trash as a site of contestation. It may be true that the environmental consequences of large-scale trash dumping are a rather recent development, but the politics of trash itself is not. Scholars working in various African cities have traced the ways in which the vocabularies of urban cleansing campaigns have blended the physical clean-up of city infrastructure with efforts to 'clean-up' city and state government (see, for just two examples, Diouf [1996] on Dakar, and Oppala [1994] on Freetown).

Finally, when told visually, the story of trash and its circulation tends to prioritize the dramatic landscape of the dumpsite and landfill. This obscures not just the transnational and national networks that carry waste to that point, but also the often-gendered labour that makes up these flows. As Rosalind Fredericks (2008: 2) points out, in Dakar as in many other places the collection of household trash is labelled as women's work, which in the neoliberal present has meant an expansion of such 'private' labour into more and more sectors of the city. The photographic focus on the predominantly male activity of gleaning a city's landfills risks obscuring these more complexly gendered 'geographies of trash labour'.

These are absences that, as an instructor, I labour to fill. They are the necessary second steps, though as someone invested in the complexities and nuances of contemporary African political economy, I find these details to be of the utmost importance. If they cannot be conveyed simply from looking at Fabrice Monteiro's *The Prophecy* or Pieter Hugo's *Permanent Error*, this is the fault of neither photographer. Photography as a medium simply does not operate at that order of meaning. But inevitably I find myself starting with the image of waste as a teaching tool. Because what both of these bodies of work do, and do far more effectively than any other medium, is to convey the sense that as a development issue, trash matters.

References

Agamben, G. (1998) *Homo Sacer: Sovereign Power and Bare Life*. Stanford, CA: Stanford University Press.

Barrett, T. (2000) *Criticizing Photographs: An Introduction to Understanding Images*. New York: McGraw Hill.

Bond, P. and K. Sharife (2012) 'Africa's biggest landfill site: The case of Bisasar Road', *Le Monde diplomatique*, 27 April, available at http://mondediplo.com/blogs/africa-s-biggest-landfill-site-the-case-of.

Diouf, M. (1996) 'Urban youth and Senegalese politics: Dakar 1988-1994', *Public Culture* 8(2): 225–49.

Fredericks, R. (2008) *Gender and the Politics of Trash in Dakar: Participation, Labor and the 'Undisciplined' Woman*, 'Thinking Gender' Papers, UCLA Center for the Study of Women. Los Angeles, CA: UCLA.

Fredericks, R. (2013) 'Disorderly Dakar: The cultural politics of household waste in Senegal's capital city', *Journal of Modern African Studies* 51(3): 435–58.

Fredericks, R. (2014) 'Vital infrastructures of trash in Dakar', *Comparative Studies of South Asia, Africa and the Middle East* 34(3): 532–48.

Gastrow, C. (2016) 'Toxic politics', paper presented at the 'Toxicity' conference, University of Durban, South Africa, 7–8 July.

Harrow, K. (2013) *Trash: African Cinema from Below*. Bloomington, IN: Indiana University Press.

Hoffman, D. (2007) 'The disappeared: Images of the environment at Freetown's urban margins', *Visual Studies* 22(2): 104–19.

Hoffman, D. (2014) 'Corpus: Mining the border', *Cultural Anthropology Photo Essays*, 31 January, available at https://culanth.org/photo_essays/1-corpus-mining-the-border.

Hoornweg, D. and P. Bhada-Tata (2012) *What a Waste: A Global Review of Solid Waste Management*, Urban Development Series Knowledge Papers no. 15. Washington, DC: The World Bank.

Hugo, P. (2007) *Messina/Musina*. New York: Prestel.

Hugo, P. (2008) *The Hyena & Other Men*. New York: Prestel.
Hugo, P. (2009) *Nollywood*. New York: Prestel.
Hugo, P. (2011) *Permanent Error*. New York: Prestel.
Jameson, F. (1991) *Postmodernism, or, the Cultural Logic of Late Capitalism*. Durham, NC: Duke University Press.
Mbembe, A. (1992) 'The banality of power and the aesthetics of vulgarity in the Postcolony', *Public Culture* 4(2): 1–30.
Mekuria, S. (2012) 'Representation and Self Representation: My Take', *Feminist Africa* 16: 8–17.
Munawar, E. and J. Fellner (2012) *Guidelines for Design and Operation of Municipal Solid Waste Landfills in Tropical Climates*. Rotterdam: International Solid Waste Association.
Myers, G. (2010) *Disposable Cities: Garbage, Governance and Sustainable Development in Urban Africa*. New York: Routledge.
Nas, P.J.M. and R. Jaffe (2004) 'Informal waste management: Shifting the focus from problem to potential', *Environment, Development, and Sustainability* 6(3): 337–53.
Oppala, J. (1994) "'Ecstatic Renovation!": Street art celebrating Sierra Leone's 1992 Revolution', *African Affairs* 93(371): 195–218.
Pieterse, E. (2011) 'Grasping the unknowable: Coming to grips with African urbanisms', *Social Dynamics* 37(1): 5–23.
Riis, J. (1970 [1890]) *How the Other Half Lives*. New York: Garrett Press.
Rucevska I., C. Nellemann, N. Isarin, W. Yang, N. Liu, K. Yu, S. Sandnæs, K. Olley, H. McCann, L. Devia, L. Bisschop, D. Soesilo, T. Schoolmeester, R. Henriksen, and R. Nilsen (2015) *Waste Crime – Waste Risks: Gaps in Meeting the Global Waste Challenge - A UNEP Rapid Response Assessment*. Nairobi and Arendal: United Nations Environment Programme and GRID-Arendal.
Scarlat, N., V. Motola, J. F. Dallemand, F. Monforti-Ferrario, and Linus Mofor (2015) 'Evaluation of energy potential of municipal solid waste from African urban areas', *Renewable and Sustainable Energy Reviews* 50: 1269–86.
Sontag, S. (1977) *On Photography*. New York: Farrar, Straus, and Giroux.
Sontag, S. (2004) *Regarding the Pain of Others*. New York: Picador.
Spaull, J. (2015) 'World's biggest e-dump, or vital supplies for Ghana?', *SciDevNet*, 5 October, available at https://www.scidev.net/global/digital-divide/multimedia/electronic-waste-dump-supplies-ghana.html.
Spirn, A.W. (2008) *Daring to Look: Dorothea Lange's Photographs and Reports from the Field*. Chicago: University of Chicago.
Steiner, L. (2010) 'Paragons of Misery', *Mahala*, 9 August, available at http://www.mahala.co.za/art/paragons-of-misery/.
Sturken, M. and L. Cartwright. (2009) *Practices of Looking: An Introduction to Visual Culture*. New York: Oxford University Press.

3

Writing a Development Play

'The soft bulldozer', or the Subtle Smashing of Self-Empowerment

Mark Ralph-Bowman

Introduction

It is 2011. I find myself copy-editing the contributions to a book. Initially, this book has no title but it becomes *Aid, NGOs and the Realities of Women's Lives: A Perfect Storm* (Wallace et al. 2013). The papers in it explore the complex and troubled intersection of two significant sets of stories. One set concerns the reality for those women in the Global South experiencing 'aid' for 'development' as its recipients and/or distributors. The other drills down into that reality as perceived by and explained to the North. One might expect those two sets to carry broadly the same payload. The bothersome fact is, they are radically at odds.

Besides the uncomfortable disconnect between the two sets, the book has another extremely disturbing dimension. I had lived and worked in Uganda and Nigeria for much of the 1970s. Reading the chapters, I am dismayed that the relationship between the North and South that I had witnessed over thirty years ago seems to have experienced little substantive change in the interim; it could even be argued that the relationship has become worse and more destructive.

Broadly, in the Global North, there are two well-rehearsed narratives about 'Aid'. One tells of the wasteful process of throwing good money after bad. The other tells of good folk in the North chuntering down to the South with buckets of goodwill and healthy bank balances to help those poor benighted citizens into the twenty-first century; this latter story is often given video validation in NGO promotional materials and fund-raising telethons. Unsurprisingly, neither narrative comes even close to reality. But they are much easier to tell than the real story of a complex, messy, often contradictory meeting of race, class, power, financial clout, and, fundamentally, gender, neatly summarized by David Lewis and David Mosse (2006: 5): 'Out of the messiness of practice, actor-networks constantly establish domains for the rule *of* expertise and universal principle that stand apart from the local, the arbitrary and continent world'.

Mark Ralph-Bowman, *Writing a Development Play*. In: *New Mediums, Better Messages?*.
Edited by David Lewis, Dennis Rodgers, and Michael Woolcock, Oxford University Press.
 DOI: 10.1093/oso/9780198858751.003.0004

The Decision to Write a Play

I have been involved in teaching, creating, and writing for theatre for much of my life including the years in Uganda and Nigeria. This theatre work in Africa was driven by both broadly 'artistic' motivations and an interest in theatre as an individual and societal development tool.

The papers in *Aid, NGOs* ... inspire me to write a play. This decision to explore the issues raised in the book proves to be the easy part. When the writing begins, I am confronted by the several common but complex and individual threads running through all the narratives in the book. The danger is that the complexity will be diluted by focusing on the commonality; the danger of falling into the trap of the single story persuasively argued by Chimamanda Ngozi Adichie's (2009) TED talk.[1] But there has to be some unifying image about which to construct the plot of the play.

As I begin the play that became *With You Always*, the issues raised in *Aid, NGOs* ... jostle with my own far-off experiences that seem still to be very much alive. People sometimes enquire as to what the play is about; I struggle to generate a coherent answer. When quizzed by a female director I reply, 'Oh, it's about women and overseas aid'. 'Good luck with that!' she observes, not unsympathetically.

The rule of unintended consequences applies to both playwright and development funder. And where one person might find an inspiring development project, another might see a piece of oppressive and costly neocolonialism. Since I am attempting an exploration of a dilemma it is important to avoid setting up simplistic polarizations between 'goodies' and 'baddies'; dilemmas, almost by definition, afford no easy moral solution. Thus it was that the tag line for *With You Always* became 'Doing no harm with "overseas aid" must be the easiest thing in the world, right?'.

Beginnings

An Old Testament image is provided by Meenu Vadera's (2013: 143–53) contribution to the book, *Aid, NGOs* ....—it's entitled 'Women on Wheels'. She describes her struggles in setting up an NGO to train women as taxi drivers in Delhi, a profession dominated by men. Hers is a compelling exploration of the David and Goliath narrative and contains many of the main themes in the book. The obstacle for me writing a play, however, is that I have never been to India and my sense of the place would be second, third, and fourth hand. In terms of the plot of the play I am writing, besides the David and Goliath image, there is a further debt to 'Women on

[1] Available at https://www.ted.com/talks/chimamanda_adichie_the_danger_of_a_single_story?language=en.

Wheels'. The current ending of my play is the beginning of Vadera's story; having been battered by the complex demands of meeting agendas set by the North, a woman sets out to build something independent.

Because I have lived and worked in two African countries and have some knowledge of the context, I decided to retain the David and Goliath image but set the play in contemporary Africa with an African woman as the central character.

I am cautious, however, partly because Peter Brook's 1970s London Roundhouse production of *The Ik* still sticks in my throat like cold, half-cooked porridge. Brook, as I do, drew on a book, *The Mountain People*, by the anthropologist Colin Turnbull (1972), which records his inability to understand the community he was studying in Uganda. Despite this inability, Turnbull seemed to assume an almost omniscient presentation of the people under investigation without benefit of knowledge of either their language or culture. As part of my thinking for this chapter, I decide to revisit *The Ik* in an attempt to understand my reaction to it, a visit that helps explain my visceral antipathy to the production at the time.

In the years since Brook's production, serious questions about Turnbull's representation of the Ik have been raised. In 1985, following his work with the Ik, Bernd Heine (1985: 1) wrote, 'Turnbull's account of Ik culture turned out to be at variance with most observations we made—to the extent that at times I was under the impression that I was dealing with an entirely different people'. Curtis Abraham concludes his 2002 assessment of *The Mountain People* by saying that 'ultimately the Ik saga says more about the internal hopes, dreams and aspirations of individuals like Turnbull rather than the external realities of the people they study'.

Certainly, what Turnbull writes in the Introduction to the published script of *The Ik* is astonishing (Higgins and Cannan, 1984: 9):

> Whether or not this [the story told in the play] was an Ik truth, we could not say. But it was truth for *us*, even though more than likely each of us in the company saw it differently; and it was a truth for the audience in terms of *their* individual experience. After all, it is for ourselves, including the audience, that we play, not for the Ik. The Ik we can only thank for having driven us to discover such a moment of beauty in our own lives and, no matter how discouraging the world around us may seem to be, perhaps to discover the hope, the faith, or whatever the truth is that for them also makes life worth living.

It is also revealing to set this conclusion in the larger context of Brook's 1972 African theatrical pilgrimage recorded in Heilpern's (1977) *The Conference of the Birds*. Having conquered the theatrical world in the Metropolitan North, Brook went to Paris, in Heilpern's (1977: 26) words, 'to discover the miraculous: a universal theatre'. There Brook created an acting troupe (including Helen Mirren) to travel through Africa to find that 'universal theatre' and its language. Heilpern's book follows that troupe through the highs and lows, the successes and failures in villages and towns in Algeria, Niger, and Nigeria. Pondering one disastrous performance Brook realizes that 'the audience couldn't understand what was happening because it couldn't share the convention' (Heilpern, 1977: 203).

In the context of *The Ik*, the point is that when it comes to 'understanding' them and creating a piece of theatre about their experience, unless you are Ik and are able to 'read' their history and social conventions, the likelihood is that you will impose interpretations and responses that are more about you than about them. In other words, you risk using the Ik as exemplars of some personal fixation. This danger is further intensified when, as later researchers such as Abraham have discovered, many of Turnbull's informants were not actually Ik but members of other, rival, ethnic groups who had their own agendas *vis-à-vis* the Ik. Turnbull's Introduction to the 1984 script quoted above demonstrates that he, at least, is aware of this dimension, though he presents it as an artistic merit.

In this respect, there is a wonderful, illustrative anecdote recorded by the anthropologist Laura Bohannan in relation to her work on Nigeria. In her 1966 article 'Shakespeare in the Bush', she describes how in the evenings during her fieldwork her hosts entertained her with stories. One evening they tell her that the next night it will be her turn to recount a story. She decides to recount the story of Shakespeare's *Hamlet*, which she thinks is universally understandable. She hardly starts with her narrative when her hosts interrupt, incredulous. They find the behaviour of the characters totally unbelievable and tell her she must have got it wrong and begin to reconstruct the story for her. Thus she learnt a simple but basic lesson: the sense and impact of a play is dependent on existing theatrical and social conventions.

So the challenge is to find a context in which the seemingly invincible Goliath of 'the North' might meet his (I use the pronoun deliberately) match in the seemingly powerless David, 'the South'. Also, I want to create real characters who are morally and psychologically complex, neither one-dimensional mouthpieces in an academic debate nor vehicles for polemical speechifying. With all these many and various caveats in mind, I begin to write my play. Since it is directed at a British audience, I feel it necessary to give them a way in via British sensibilities. So, the first draft of the (untitled) play begins thus:

NGO Play—2013

ACT ONE African drumming in the blackout. Women ululate. A slide projects an image of daylight in an African village onto a huge screen at the rear of the stage. A sequence of shots shows the building of a simple construction ending with shots of people dancing and singing in front of the finished building.

CLAIRE [voice heard over the drumming fading. The lights flash on as if fluorescent tubes being switched on. The final slide fades. As she speaks, CLAIRE appears addressing the audience.] And there it was. Complete. Months of work and uncertainty. The rains that washed so much of it away. The outbreak of measles. After so long and such difficult conditions, Kasangila, finally, had its new Lower Secondary School building—thanks to all of us and the money we raised here at 'Bringing Joy'. Never was a name more apt than ours. Truly we in 'Bringing Joy' can risk the sin of pride.

CLAIRE applauds the audience which breaks into 'For she's a jolly good fellow' the singing of which continues as CLAIRE is joined by OLAVE burdened with two wheelie suitcases and hand luggage which she shares with CLAIRE. The singing ends to be replaced by the tinnitus of airport muzak. They look about them flustered and anxious.

CLAIRE Do stop that, Olave.

OLAVE What?

CLAIRE Looking at your watch. This is Africa, dear. A completely different approach. No such thing as 'late' in African time. You'll find it most refreshing, liberating. If you can't be late, you see, there's no need to hurry. You'll just have to adapt.

OLAVE But we have been waiting rather a -

CLAIRE Thirty-seven minutes.

CHRISTOPHER approaches them.

CHRISTOPHER Excuse me, madame. You need taxi?

CLAIRE No, thank you. We are being met. A driver will meet us. I have it here.

She pulls a sheet of paper from her handbag and holds it towards him.

You see. An email. Confirmation.

CHRISTOPHER bends to read the proffered email.

CHRISTOPHER Ah! Tuko Pamoja.

CLAIRE Correct. Tuko Pamoja.

CHRISTOPHER [He reads] 'A driver will meet you in Arrivals.' This is Arrivals.

CLAIRE Indeed it is.

CHRISTOPHER No driver. I think, Madame, you are needing a taxi. My own is outside. Ready to go. Very safe. Comfortable.

CLAIRE Excuse me, young man. I do not need your taxi. I do not need any taxi. I am waiting for my driver. Good day to you.

CHRISTOPHER And a very good day to you, madame.

At this early stage of its development, the plot eases the audience into the unnamed African country through the journey of the redoubtable Claire and her friend Olave. Olave, however, does not make it through the first major re-write, though it took the observation of a fellow playwright to show that Claire's voice is enough to represent the good-hearted, charitable motivation of the liberal North's desire to 'help'.

One of the key issues the play needs to address is the confrontation between the altruism represented by Claire and the appropriation of that altruism by commercial interests, sometimes described as 'market forces'. So, I decide that, by chance, Claire's trip should coincide with that of accountants doing an audit of the local NGO she is visiting. [The NGO ends up being called *Tare Muke,* Hausa words which translate broadly as 'We are together.']

Caught in the spotlight of these two visitations is Dambisa, the young woman who runs the NGO. She is the central character in the play but in early versions she does not appear until Scene 5—like having Hamlet turn up in Act Two. It takes some time to find the courage to avoid pandering to the British sensibilities but the full theatre production of *With You Always* in 2016 at The Old Fire Station in Oxford puts her up front.

CAR HORNS BLARE. PLANES AND LORRIES ROAR. A SWIRLING CACOPHONY OF APPLE AND MICROSOFT START UP MUSIC AND ALL KINDS OF IT SFX.
MORPHS INTO ...

SCENE 1 OFFICE OF *TARE MUKE*

SOUNDS OF CICADAS AND BIRD SONG
DAMBISA HEARD OFF THEN ENTERING SPEAKING ON HER MOBILE

DAMBISA OK. OK. So, where are you? Sorry—you're breaking up. What? An hour ago? An hour? No, no, no. That's fine. Fine. No problem. Everything's set. Thanks. Bye. Bye.

SHE STANDS STILL. OUT OF NOWHERE SHE RELEASES A HUGE EXPLOSION OF FRUSTRATION.
AS CLAIRE AND CHRISTOPHER ARRIVE.

DAMBISA Oh my god! Er, welcome. Welcome to ***Tare Muke***. Christopher? Oh. You must be ... Mrs Boyden?

CLAIRE Please. Call me Claire.

DAMBISA How ... how was the journey?

CLAIRE Marvellous. I didn't expect such a bustling, modern city.

DAMBISA -

CLAIRE It's lovely to be here.

DAMBISA I am sorry for not sending the car. It slipped from my mind—some very important people are coming from the UK today. Not ... I mean, you are important also—I did not ... so ... ah ... yes, you see the car is with them. Claire Boyden—***Bringing Joy***, from Belper, isn't it? Our wonderful Derbyshire Support Group. Dambisa Jakande.

They shake hands

CLAIRE Christopher whizzed me here through the back streets. I say, these VIPs of yours, anyone famous?

DAMBISA Accountants. From your ***Hilarious Help*** organization.

CLAIRE Really? I'm rather fond of that young fellow. Does lots during those ***Hilarious Help*** telethon fandangos. You know him? Motorbike trips on the telly? Something on train spotting/one of our gang tells -

SAM ***[off]*** It's a Flame Tree, Alex.

CLAIRE Ewan McGregor!

SAM ***[off]*** Take a picture of every single flower in the city, why not.

SAM AND ALEX ENTER

Hi, hi. ***[SAM holds out her hand to CHRISTOPHER]*** I'm Sam. That's Alex.

ALEX TAKES A PHOTO OF SAM AND CHRISTOPHER SHAKING HANDS

His paparazzi act. So—good to visit Tear Mouk.

CHRISTOPHER You are welcome, Madame.

SAM Hi. Good to meet you.

CLAIRE My pleasure, er, Sam?

SAM Cool. Right, cool.

CLAIRE I'm Claire. Lukewarm. May I introduce Dambisa Jakande, the Director of ***[deliberate—correct pronunciation—Ta-(as in cat)ray Mookay] Tare Muke.***

SAM Oh. Right. Yeah. Um. Good. Alex? This is Dambisa? You know? Director of ***Tare Muke***?

SAM TAKES DAMBISA'S HAND. ALEX CAPTURES THE MOMENT

Great location. Loving the Flame Tree. Alignment—spot on, yeah? Feng Shui? No? Oh-kaaay. So—you're a volunteer?

CLAIRE No. I'm ***Bringing Joy***—from Belper. Supporting the New Kasalynga School.

SAM Ah, right—Belper—Awesome. Books, uniforms and stuff, cool. Sooo. Can we get right to it—er, Dambisa?

DAMBISA Will you take some coffee? Tea?

SAM Water for me. Alex? Water? Alex? Life support machine?

ALEX Oh, yeah, yeah. Whatever. Nice place, Dambisa. Cool.

DAMBISA Mrs Boyden, sorry, Claire. Excuse me for some moments. Sam is from DfID you see—your Department for International Development?

CLAIRE Department for International/Development—well I never!

SAM So—we're not DfID. INKE? Private sector?

CLAIRE As in South American savages? Bestial sacrifice of young girls/to satisfy some deity of the—

SAM Eye. En. Kay. Ee—pronounced inca. Yeah, like we need another acronym. Initials of the guys who founded it. Right, Alex?

ALEX Something like that.

SAM No vestal virgins slaughtered for this company, Claire.

CLAIRE !

DAMBISA I've made my office available as your base.

SAM Let's get on it.

THEY GO

Locating the play in Africa and making an African female the protagonist, however, creates a further challenge pointed out by Dr Eric Northey, one-time Professor of Mass Communications at Bayero University, Kano and later Senior Lecturer in Media at Manchester Metropolitan University. He observes that most people in the North are functionally ignorant about Africa past and present. For them it's represented by game parks, safaris, the 'Big Five', bloody conflict as represented in films like *Blood Diamond* and *Hotel Rwanda*, corruption ['The Interpreter'], the cynical clichés of Richard Bean's *The God Botherers* or the flyblown, malnourished children paraded by INGOs seeking funding. Even the geography seems to defeat them. When Ebola struck West Africa, tourism to countries thousands of miles away took a big hit. Northey predicts that the audience of a play set in Africa will go away disappointed if there is not a plentiful supply of 'native costumes', bare chests—preferably both male and female—and lots of drumming and dancing. Some responses to the production seem to indicate his prediction to be correct—but more of that later.

The Past Invades the Present

When editing *Aid, NGOs and the Realities of Women's Lives: A Perfect Storm*, and before starting to write *With You Always*, I frequently found my mind going back to late 1970s Nigeria with a strong sense of *déjà vu* and the disturbing realization of little substantial change in over thirty years. I was reminded of *The Project*, a theatre production created through workshops with Nigerian students.

Back then, the World Bank put up 50 per cent of the funding for a number of enormous projects that would, it was claimed, increase productivity of huge swathes of Nigerian agricultural land. Three of these projects focused on transforming relatively arid, sub-Saharan savannah land in the Kano, Sokoto, and Chad River Basins from their traditional agricultural use into industrial-scale cotton production. Cotton is a thirsty beast so rivers were to be damned, irrigation lakes established, and miles and miles of irrigation canals built and the indigenous population to be relocated from thousands of hectares of their traditional land.

It was a World Bank condition that 40 per cent of the loan [i.e. 20 per cent of the total cost of the project] had to be spent in the Global North. So 20 per cent of the multi-million dollar loan was used to import the gargantuan machinery required, pay the salaries and emoluments of the senior staff (recruited primarily from the North), to say nothing of the regular flights from Italy bringing fresh produce to the air-conditioned supermarket servicing those expatriate staff and their families. Ordinary Nigerians mainly profited from employment as unskilled and semi-skilled labour force.

But they also lost their land. Thousands were relocated, 'benefitting' in the process from visits of advisors ['Agricultural Extension Workers'] from various government ministries who would tell them how to make the best of the fantastic opportunities being made available to them thanks to their sagacious government and the World Bank. At the time, the Nigerian exchequer was relatively flush with oil money so projects such as these were not only a highly attractive investment for the World Bank but were also being replicated in five other states in Nigeria. And the loans for these projects had to be repaid in at an interest rate of 7–8 per cent. And here's the killer: repayment is in foreign exchange.

In a paper written in 1979, Tina Wallace (1979: 6) noted that 'it is essentially a technocratic approach to the causes of rural stagnation, which sees the solution in bringing new knowledge, inputs, technology efficiently to the recipient, the small farmer. Reliance is placed on "the expert" carrying change to the poor; the key actors in rural transformation include road engineers, dam builders, extension workers, seed multipliers, Project management'. She also noted that the World Bank project had no sense of the whole: 'they do not tackle such issues as rural health, nomadic groups, non-farming activities, rural industries, the role of women' (Wallace, 1979: 5).

Scroll forward to 2011. In *Aid, NGOs and the Realities of Womens' Lives*, I read Stan Thekaekara's essay 'Development from the ground: A worm's eye view', where he writes that since 1974, 'we have seen governments, civil society, philanthropists, and even corporations investing huge amounts of money. But has anything changed for the people living in poverty?' (Thekaekara 2013: 33).

The Project

Back in 1979, I was already engaged in creating theatre with students at Bayero University, Kano. I wanted to both explore with them the issues around the World Bank involvement in Africa and create a piece of theatre that would be accessible to a wider audience than the educated elite; motivation very similar to that behind the writing of *With You Always.*

Using the research being conducted by Tina Wallace at Ahmadu Bello University, Zaria, I began a series of theatre workshops exploring this subject of vast sums being spent with little discernible benefit for the poor. Week by week we would take a starting point suggested by the research and literally play with it. The outcomes of each workshop were recorded in written notes. Eventually, after several months of development, a story, or more accurately several narratives, began to emerge. And out of these a theatre production was formed. By the time it came to public performance the show had developed a fixed and loosely scripted format.

The only thing it did not have was a title. We spent an inordinate amount of time tossing ideas around until one of our number, Emman Usman Shehu, calmly announced 'It must be called *The Project*.' As we thought about it, we realized it was wholly apposite. Our work was indeed a Russian doll of projects. There was the context of the general North/South project, the specific World Bank project, the research project, our theatrical development project of workshops, and then the performance project of placing the results in front of audiences.

The Project was initially performed at Bayero and Ahmadu Bello Universities before being funded, without irony, by the Ministry of Agriculture to be shown in Kaduna, Jos, and Maiduguri. In many respects the latter show was the most inspiring. It took place in broad daylight on the racecourse before an audience seated in the stands by the finishing post. But the great thing was that much of the audience comprised 'ordinary' people from local communities, many of them speaking little English. *The Project* used a combination of RP, Pidgin, and occasional smatterings of indigenous languages. It was immensely rewarding for the participants in the show that the narratives portrayed spoke directly to this Maiduguri audience which responded enthusiastically.

A scene in the *The Project* that always received a spirited audience response was the visit of the 'Agricultural Extension Workers' to the farmers following their relocation from their ancestral lands. These characters arrive dressed in the height of late 1970s fashion—perilously high platform shoes, swirling flared trousers, extravagantly patterned tailored shirts with collars big enough to take flight on, and the ubiquitous shades. They proceed to lecture the farmers on how to do their jobs. The farmers are sceptical. At one point in the conversation, the Extension Workers explain:

BASIL The problem is fertilisers. I have studied fertilisers in Britain.
OGUNLEYE So in Britain they go teach you?
BASIL Yes. I studied fertilisers, soil conservation and soil analysis. I studied phosphates. I studied nitrates. I studied all the things in a laboratory in Birmingham.
OGUNLEYE Tell me. This soil wettin you go study. Which kind soil be that?
BASIL Why?
OGUNLEYE So you go study English soil?
BASIL Well, yes. I was in England you see.
OGUNLEYE This soil, now. The one we dey sit on. Which soil be that?
DELE How long you go study the soil for there?
BASIL Six months—six whole months.[2]

[2] From my working notes on *The Project*. The 'script' recorded here was the outline script, and actors improvised around it.

In the final scene of *The Project,* a small group of rich young Nigerians brag to each other of their experiences in the yuppie high spots of Europe and the USA. As these young swells talk, the audience becomes aware of murmurings that slowly coalesce into the chants of street beggars. Ragged mendicants, some with ugly deformities, inexorably appear quite literally from among the audience and forcefully importune the audience for alms. Initially, the audience tends to laugh but as the chants continue, the demands strengthen to be made directly to individuals in the audience; they begin to feel uncomfortable. After what feels like an age, the chanting abruptly cuts—an awkward silence falls.

One of the challenges currently facing the world is the tens of thousands of people from many African countries risking untold hardship in search of a better life in the Global North. As I read the reports of refugees drowning in the Mediterranean and hear Office of the High Commissioner for Human Rights (OHCHR) condemnation of the horrors of Libyan detention camps, in my ears I hear those chants and recall the deprivation and depredations ongoing since the 1970s and before.

Aid, NGOs … and With You Always

Looking back on *The Project,* I realize that its point of view was unremittingly male. One reason for this is the fact I, a man, was initiating, facilitating, and probably—though not deliberately—manipulating it; there's something of Peter Brook in all theatre directors. Another reason is that the majority of student participants were male. Bayero University students were primarily, though by no means exclusively, Muslim. For most female Muslim students, appearing in mixed theatrical performances was problematic.

On this issue of the dominance of the male perspective, *Aid, NGOs and the Realities of Women's Lives* unsurprisingly has many telling comments that give me pause. Kate Grosser and Nikki van der Gaag (2013: 80) write, for example, that in the South, 'most girls have little power to change their situation, and it is not because they are stupid or uneducated or lack skills'. Somehow this comment encapsulates the related and intensely complex issues of gender and power that I also want to explore in *With You Always.*

Ashish Shah's (2013: 206) essay in *Aid, NGOs...* reminds us that many of the issues around gender, power, and class are universal:

> I realize the difference between attending a gender training and actually understanding and trying to empathize with the different world that women live in. As men, as people with different positions of power (whether we are men or women), as people from biased professions, as outsiders, even when we make significant

> efforts to try to understand a problem or context, we are always getting only a partial picture. While we will never fully grasp the realities experienced by women, as men, and as people who want to do good development work, we owe it to ourselves to break out of our comfort zones and try to experience reality from the perspectives of those we say we work for.

The universal nature of the challenge is neatly put by Chris Mowles (2013: 58) in his contribution: 'Citizens in the developing world are not distant abstractions, or objects of our "treatment", but are self-organizing, meaning-making animals, and our moral equals. They interact with each other and with us, enabling and constraining in relationships of power, as the future emerges in highly unpredictable ways and in response to our plans and actions as we differently construe them.'

And then there is the significant challenge that, in the thinking of funders of development, reality is a nice, neat, concrete entity. Wallace and Porter (2013: 9) disagree, arguing that 'reality is unpredictable, and often messy. Local knowledge is frequently strikingly at odds with well-crafted projects; what actually happens often falls far outside "the scope" of planning documents. And yet what happens in "real life" is what INGOs and their partners can build on to create better interventions, based on people's lives and priorities.'

This complex reality is one that I struggle to explore in *With You Always*. At the time of the 2016 production of the play, the final scene turns out to be one of its more problematic features and the most difficult to get right. In it, through a confrontation between two central characters, the issues of male assumptions around relationships with women are addressed head on. This confrontation draws on discomforting realities for both characters. Many audience members also find it challenging and uncomfortable, especially since it provides no reassuring solutions to the dilemmas raised. The reason for not providing them is that there are no solutions 'out there'. These are dilemmas, the solutions to which each and every one of us has to find for ourselves in and through our own relationships.

Whose Soil Is it?

Ashish Shah's (2013: 203) record of his encounter with a farmer in Kenya to whom he, a confident young development worker, had offered help, is particularly revealing. The farmer said to him:

> I don't think you have ever farmed before in your life. You don't know what it's like to grow sugarcane or any other crop. You are just a little boy from Nairobi who has studied in university and who is now working for an NGO driving a big car pretending he knows what he's talking about! I don't have time for people like you.

To his credit, in order to fill this knowledge gap, the young Shah then set to and farmed a small patch of land.

But then came another shock when he met a woman sugarcane farmer, who said to him 'Everything you talk about is from a man's viewpoint ... I don't think you understand what it means to be a woman sugarcane farmer' (Shah, 2013: 205). She challenged him to live and work alongside the women farmers. He did so and discovered that:

> I did not understand how difficult, if not impossible, it was for women sugarcane farmers to claim payments compared to their male counterparts, for a multitude of reasons. I did not understand the actual workload involved for women engaged in the multiple roles forced on them by society; coupled with the expectation to be a good sugarcane farmer. I did not understand the level of abuse and exploitation that women faced at all levels of the farming process, or the impact of cultural practices and women's vulnerability in areas of their life that they could not control—be it their bodies or their land. I did not understand the levels of violence against women and its psychological, social, economic and political impact on them. I did not know about the internal organising structures of women cane farmers, how different these were to the formal organising structures for most of the male farmers, or that women were trying to introduce complexity into mono-crop sugarcane farming systems to counter the growing hunger periods.
>
> (Shah, 2013: 206)

Our jokes in *The Project* about whose soil it is seem pretty mild in comparison to this dark and complex reality for farmers in general and women farmers in particular. In 1970s Nigeria, initiatives like the Kano River Project were asking some disturbing questions regarding ownership of the land and who had the right to work it. This was not the first time that the World Bank had been involved in the displacement of large numbers of people. In 1962, for example, it put up US$47million for the Volta River Project in Ghana that displaced over 80,000 people (Wallace, 1979).

By 2014, however, the plundering of land had become common in Africa and beyond. Across swathes of the South, international businesses, including though not exclusively agribusinesses, are hoovering up vast tracts of land with the complicity of national governments in both the North and the South. Much of this process is justified by appeals to efficiency and progress. David Lewis (2013: 115) expresses the underlying principle at work thus:

> [A]s Western development policy has recently become more and more concerned with the management of aid resources, relationships and impacts, so the lives of ordinary people in developing countries have, perhaps paradoxically, become even more remote from policymakers and development professionals.

In 2017 this process of effectively recolonizing land in Africa was set in stark relief when the UK government, without irony, decided to call its strategy for developing bilateral deals with African countries 'Empire 2.0'. The beauty of this moniker is that it declares precisely and exactly the way that the North regards its relationship with the South. While the British demonstrated an extraordinary lack of intelligence in naming their strategy thus, we need to be clear that their approach to their dealings with the South are not only common in the North but also in the emerging economies of Asia.

These are the kinds of issues that I am attempting to dramatize in *With You Always*. As I have suggested above, I am trying to use the point at which these issues intersect in the lives of half a dozen people as a sort of peephole through which an audience can sense that what they are seeing is but a small example of the whole.

Journey to Performance

This journey is exhaustive and exhausting. When I have finally produced something I am reasonably happy with, we give a public rehearsed reading using professional actors. This took place at the Ark T Centre in Oxford in April 2014. As so often with such readings, the rehearsal period is short. The actors and director, despite being talented and committed, are largely unfamiliar with many of the issues being explored in the play. Because they are embodied in character and situation rather than expressed through debating points, the actors have to drill down into the social and political context to find not only their character's motivations but also the issues being addressed.

These challenges for the actors are almost a microcosm of the whole. There is a complex reality that we are trying to capture in the play so as to avoid the simplistic caricatures exploited by fund raisers. But not only do we need to avoid an audience throwing up its hands saying 'I don't get this' and walking away but I also need to avoid alienating the actors with material way beyond their lived experience. So we spend a lot of time unpicking and clarifying character and issues.

Some seventy or so people came to the 2014 Rehearsed Reading. The key points from the feedback—besides a lot of encouragement—are that it is too long and too wordy. An interesting reaction, however, came from a manager in the UK's public sector: 'It's just like that where I work.'

In 2015, supported by an Arts Council Grant, a series of workshops culminated in the performance of a truncated version of the play at the Simpkins Lee Theatre in Lady Margaret Hall, Oxford in front of an audience again of about seventy (though a largely different seventy!). By this time the actors—most of whom were also involved in the Rehearsed Reading—are getting to grips with the challenge.

Jo Noble, who plays Claire, the Englishwoman visiting *Tare Muke*, talks of it as an ongoing process (Promotional video for *With You Always*, 25 August 2015):

> It made me think, I want to investigate (Aid) further and I want to investigate what strings are attached for the recipients. Who made the decisions? Are the decisions really in the best interests of the people they are supposedly trying to help?

In the same video, Amantha Edmead who plays the character of Edriam, an African woman running a small cooperative enterprise, says:

> Even though this play is full of lots of issues, it's still very character driven so it's about bringing individual characters—who are real people—to life. And the subject matter, cos you can't get away from the issues particularly now when you're seeing lots of refugees showing up and when you're looking at Africa whether it's the Chinese coming in or the fact of what we do with the world's resources, whose benefit that is for.

In the Q & A that follows the Showcase—unusually, most of the audience stay on—three comments broadly summarize the reactions:

> 'A strong piece of theatre. There's so much in it I feel I want to take it away and think about it.'
>
> 'What I enjoyed most about it was the differences on both sides as well as between the sides so there's a lot going on.'
>
> 'You were really good on the individual relationships and the characterisation.'

Which brings the story to the first full production at the Old Fire Station in Oxford on 4 and 5 November 2016. The showcase at Lady Margaret Hall had incorporated some elements of singing. A number of those who saw that Showcase are clearly expecting further development of the musical elements in the production at the Old Fire Station (one of the audience in the Simkins Lee who had not been to Africa said the singing and dancing made him feel he 'could manage going there'!). Some are surprised, therefore, and some are disappointed, that the production has moved into a more conventional, naturalistic performance style.

It is not entirely naturalistic, but predominantly so. The reason for this decision is worth noting. Emma Webb has taken over as director due to the previous director, John Sailsman, not being available. She is very much a physical theatre practitioner. But she feels that the central strength of *With You Always* lies in the characters, their relationships, and the issues; she wants to focus on those aspects. Since the play runs around two hours with a fifteen-minute interval, she is throwing down a huge gauntlet to the stamina of the actors and the powers of concentration of the audience.

Feedback on the show broadly divides into two. There are those who come to see the production primarily because they are attracted by the subject matter exemplified in the tag line 'Doing no harm with overseas aid must be the easiest thing in the world, right?' Their interests are in arts and theatre that engage with important issues. They are not there to see the latest innovations in theatricality, though probably would not be averse to them if used to explore challenging ideas. The second group are people of the theatre. For the most part they are less interested in the issues than in the ways in which theatricality is being employed. Unsurprisingly, therefore, the latter group, while recognizing the importance of the subject matter, tend to find the play 'worthy' but unexciting.

Earlier in this chapter I mentioned Eric Northey's comments that people would be expecting lots of drumming, naked torsos, and exotic costumes from a play set in Africa. I recall going to buy postcards in Kano in 1975 and expressing disappointment at the shortage of cards with animals or picturesque landscapes. The woman in the shop smiled. 'Ah,' she said. 'Europeans always want to keep us back in the past. They don't want pictures of the way we are now'—one of those chance comments that still resonates. I had not anticipated that it would be the theatrical people who would be making a demand of me similar to mine of that woman in that shop all those years ago.

Many of those principally committed to and interested in development issues tend to be both engaged and excited by the production. Not uncommon the following comments from development practitioners and academics made to the author at the Simpkins Lee Q & A in May 2015 and emails in November 2016:

> 'I thoroughly enjoyed it, and many people who I knew there have said how much they appreciated both the drama itself, and the introduction it gave them to the issues.'
>
> 'The play was insightful, moving and pertinent, strategically directed. The casting was excellent; the acting attuned to the text.'
>
> 'In my experience that happens a lot (manipulating the data). It's the only way to get things done. That too is an ethical challenge.'

But there were also development practitioners and academics who felt that the play fell short on some of issues. Such viewpoints are exemplified by the following comments also from the 2015 Q & A and emails in November 2016:

> 'I wanted more on the structural power relationship between people both on the ground and in the development sector.'
>
> '(More projects are mentioned but we) didn't get enough of a sense of the other work. Too limited a lens on the work of *Tare Muke*.'

> 'I want to know how to change that world – a plan offering the solution to that problem.'

Initially I was dismayed by such comments from development practitioners. Naively I had assumed that they at least would be fully appreciative of what I was attempting to achieve. But then I recalled the response of some colleagues in the Theatre Department in Ahmadu Bello to *The Project*, back in 1979. They complained that it was merely bourgeois *agit prop*; somewhat like complaining that an African elephant is merely a *Loxodonta Africana*. In many areas of human endeavour, the most critical responses sometimes come from those in the same discipline. Certainly, as Lewis and Mosse (2006: 11) have highlighted,

> the development encounter between developers and people is far more complex and nuanced than is allowed for either (at the level of practice) by the crude approaches of interventionist developmentalism that still exist in many parts of the development industry, or (at the level of theory) by the poststructuralist critiques of anthropologists in the 1990s. Meanings are contested and organizing space is negotiated at multiple levels, blurring the range of insider/outsider, indigenous/scientific or formal/informal dualisms that are common in both development theory and practice.

Conclusion

A review of the play appears in the January 2017 edition of *Dub* magazine in Oxford. Though the magazine is dedicated to 'Celebrating *Roots Reggae* music in the Thames Valley region' it is the only publication that reviewed the production. The review by Natty Mark (2017) began thus:

> What do you do with the good heart that is misguided? Especially when that misguidance might result in the appearance of the soft bulldozer; the subtle smashing of self-empowerment. The play I went to see tonight addressed this question.

I suspect there can few experiences more satisfying for a playwright than reading a review of your play that simply gets it.

References

Abraham, C. (2002) 'The Mountain People revisited', available at https://www.thefreelibrary.com/The+Mountain+People+revisited%3A+Curtis+Abraham+went+to+Ik-land+in...-a082802101.

Bohannan, L. (1966) 'Shakespeare in the bush', *Natural History Magazine* 75: 28–33, available at http://www.naturalhistorymag.com/editors_pick/1966_08-09_pick.html.

Grosser, K. and N. van der Gaag (2013) 'Can girls save the world?', in T. Wallace and F. Porter with M. Ralph-Bowman (eds) *Aid, NGOs and the Realities of Women's Lives: A Perfect Storm*. Rugby: Practical Action, pp. 73–87.

Heilpern, J. (1977) *Conference of the Birds: The Story of Peter Brook in Africa*. London: Faber & Faber.

Heine, B. (1985) 'The Mountain People: Some notes of the Ik of North-Eastern Uganda', *Journal of the International African Institute* 55(1): 3–16.

Higgins, C. and D. Cannan (1984) *The Ik*. Woodstock, IL: The Dramatic Publishing Company.

Lewis, D. (2013) 'Reconnecting development policy, people, and history', in T. Wallace and F. Porter with M. Ralph-Bowman (eds) *Aid, NGOs and the Realities of Women's Lives: A Perfect Storm*. Rugby: Practical Action, pp. 115–26.

Lewis, D. and D. Mosse (2006) 'Encountering order and disjuncture—contemporary anthropological perspectives on the organization of development', *Oxford Development Studies* 34(1): 1–13.

Mark, N. (2017) 'The soft bulldozer', *The Dub* 8: 30–1, available at https://issuu.com/thedub/docs/the_dub_issue_8__january_2017.

Mowles, C. (2013) 'Evaluation, complexity, uncertainty – theories of change and some alternatives', in T. Wallace and F. Porter with M. Ralph-Bowman (eds) *Aid, NGOs and the Realities of Women's Lives: A Perfect Storm*. Rugby: Practical Action, pp. 47–60.

Shah, A. (2013) 'I don't know ... and related thoughts', in T. Wallace and F. Porter with M. Ralph-Bowman (eds) *Aid, NGOs and the Realities of Women's Lives: A Perfect Storm*. Rugby: Practical Action, pp. 199–211.

Thekaekara, S. (2013) 'Development from the ground: a worm's eye view', in T. Wallace and F. Porter with M. Ralph-Bowman (eds), *Aid, NGOs and the Realities of Women's Lives: A Perfect Storm*. Rugby: Practical Action, pp. 33–46.

Turnbull, C. (1972) *The Mountain People*. London: Pimlico.

Vadera, M. (2013) 'Women on wheels', in T. Wallace and F. Porter with M. Ralph-Bowman (eds) *Aid, NGOs and the Realities of Women's Lives: A Perfect Storm*. Rugby: Practical Action, pp. 143–53.

Wallace, T. (1979) 'Some issues raised in Rural Development by World Bank projects in Nigeria', paper presented at a Seminar for Commissioners and Permanent Secretaries, Minna, Niger State, Nigeria, 6 November, mimeo.

Wallace, T. and F. Porter with M. Ralph-Bowman (eds) (2013) *Aid, NGOs and the Realities of Women's Lives*. Rugby: Practical Action.

4
Entering the Fictional World of Development
Writers, Readers, and Representations

Hilary Standing

Introduction

Over a decade ago, I decided to write a novel about 'development.' The decision came about partly because I have always been a secret scribbler of odd bits and pieces—short stories and narratives of events that have engaged me in ways for which social science doesn't quite work. But it was also because the story behind the novel presented itself to me unbidden in a country where I have worked and lived and that is very close to my heart. That country is Bangladesh and the story which came to haunt me is one of good development intentions gone disastrously wrong.

In the 1970s, following a very successful programme to construct deep tubewells for irrigation to increase agricultural production, international agencies turned their attention to using this technology to provide clean drinking water for the rural population. The tubewell pumps were adapted for domestic use and from the 1970s onwards, millions of wells were dug. Rural people soon adapted to this new technology and stopped drinking bacteriologically contaminated surface water from ponds and other shallow water sources. The availability of groundwater from tubewells was a major contributor to the rapid decline in morbidity and mortality due to diarrhoea and other waterborne diseases, especially among children. It looked like a textbook example of well spent international aid money.

But over the decades it became clear that there was something deadly in this water. The first reports had come from over the border in India in the 1980s, where tubewells were also common. That something turned out to be arsenic—naturally occurring in many deltaic regions and liberated from under the layers of sediment by the action of constructing a deep bore well. As infant mortality rates were tumbling, millions of people were being slowly poisoned by some of the highest arsenic levels ever recorded in drinking water. While various mitigation measures exist, the scale of the problem has so far defeated a comprehensive solution. Estimates

Hilary Standing, *Entering the Fictional World of Development.* In: *New Mediums, Better Messages?*.
Edited by David Lewis, Dennis Rodgers, and Michael Woolcock, Oxford University Press.
 DOI: 10.1093/oso/9780198858751.003.0005

are that 50–80 million people remain affected by what has been described as the world's worst mass chemical poisoning.

It is a terrible story which raises many questions about the project that we call 'development'. Where does accountability for this disaster lie? Could it have been foreseen? Which actors and agencies should take responsibility for resolving it? There are many sober, well-researched accounts of the arsenic situation in Bangladesh. I wanted to tell it differently, to explore these troubling questions through the prism of individual lives, to imagine how characters caught up in this situation in different ways might respond, and to reach audiences beyond academia.

It is these individual and interconnected stories that I tell in my novel *The Inheritance Powder* (2015, 2016). The novel is told from the alternating viewpoints of a visiting British consultant working for a European development agency that wants a grand plan for dealing with the arsenic situation, and a Bangladeshi woman leader of a grass-roots organization that is working to develop local solutions. Their subsequent emotional entanglement throws into painful relief the dilemmas and compromises inherent in their relationship as a consequence of their very different positions in the world of development.

In this chapter, I begin with a general discussion of the role and value of fiction in writing about the world of development and the ways in which its forms of representation both converge and diverge with other modes of development writing. I then move on to discuss some key questions about power, authority, representation, and the positionality of the author, which confronted me in writing my novel. In the final section, I draw on my experience with writing a novel about development to consider relationships between writers, the publishing world, and readers.

Fiction and Non-Fiction in the Writing of Development

In one of the first scholarly articles on the value of fiction as an important form of development knowledge Lewis et al. (2008, 2014) argue that fiction can sometimes give us a 'better' representation of development realities than academic accounts. They suggest that fiction accomplishes this in two main ways. The first is through exploring the private and informal worlds of people and institutions and giving voice to the experiences and emotions of those who often go unheard. Fiction, they argue, can reveal the complexities that are so often glossed over or selected out of academic accounts.

One example cited is Helen Fielding's debut novel *Cause Celeb*, a satirical comedy about a young Englishwoman who goes to Africa to work in a humanitarian organization involved in famine relief efforts.[1] In a study of non-governmental organizations (NGOs) in the Philippines, Hilhorst argues that Fielding's novel provides the kind of nuanced, behind-the-scenes account of how bureaucracies work and how their clients react to them, which is often missing from development writing about NGOs (cited and discussed in Lewis et al., 2014: 25–6).[2] Humour, idiosyncrasy, individual characters and their emotions and motivations are of course the very stuff of novels and the material that academic writing is generally obliged to leave out. There are sound research and ethical reasons for much of this. It is unclear, though, why humour—whether as rhetorical device or as subject—is so strikingly absent from works of social science, except perhaps from fear that other social scientists will not take the writer seriously.

The second way in which fiction may provide a more effective representation of development is through its quality of 'being there'. This grounds the reader in rich, multilayered contexts and realities. One might add that it also engages directly with the reader's emotions and empathy. In focusing on the tragedy of one man's rise and downfall against the context of enforced transformation of a society by colonial rule, the Nigerian novelist Chinua Achebe's depiction of Igbo society in *Things Fall Apart* (1958 [2006]) carries unique emotional and dramatic, as well as empirical truth.

But the boundary between fiction and non-fiction in writing about development is not a fixed one. As Lewis et al. note, this 'being there' quality has much in common with ethnographic modes of representation which offer 'thick description' of a society and its social relations (2008: 14). Within this methodology, there is room for detail and nuance and multiple stories. Indeed, the anthropologists James Clifford and George Marcus go further in arguing that '(ethnography) ... is always caught up in the invention, not the representation, of cultures ...' (1986: 2). This problematizes the boundary still further. Are all accounts of the social in some sense fictions—not in the 'made up' sense—but as constantly contested imaginaries? I will explore this problematic further below in the context of wider questions about power, authority and representation in all forms of 'development' writing.

Writing about development in ways that blur the boundaries between forms and styles of writing is not new. The epistemologies of feminism and participatory approaches, grounded as they are in debates about subjectivity and positionality, have encouraged some social scientists towards greater self-reflection and reflexivity in their writing practice—the 'who am I in this narrative and what is my relation to the subjects of my research?' (Harding, 1988; and for a literary account, see

[1] Fielding is best known as the author of the *Bridget Jones* novels.

[2] While Hilhorst may be right about the tendency to focus on the normative and the formal rules of organizations in a lot of this writing, this critique does ignore a substantial body of work outside development studies that has centred attention on the informal rules and worlds of organizations. See, for example, Cooperrider et al. (1995).

Lenz, 2004). Equally, they have encouraged the use of personal narratives and testimonies, the giving of voice particularly to the marginalized (e.g. Narayan and colleagues, 2000). More recently, Rosalind Eyben's reflective writing on the experience and dilemmas of being an 'aid professional' (Eyben, 2014) and on what it means to be a feminist in an aid organization (Eyben and Turquet, 2013) draws on some of the techniques of fiction. It uses conversation and personal reflection to open up fresh perspectives on insider–outsider positionality and complex power relationships in the world of development aid.

In their vividness, some ethnographic accounts have much in common with the narratives of fiction. One example is Thomas Belmonte's classic account of an impoverished Neapolitan neighbourhood, which plunges the reader right into its streets and homes (2005 [1979]). Within the increasingly porous borders of fiction, memoirs and 'life writing' genres can provide in-depth understanding of and insights into development processes. One of many great examples of African life writing is the historian Toyin Falola's memoir of his Nigerian childhood (2005).

There are thriving genres of non-fiction writing and reportage that draw on the immediacy of authors' experiences, such as Katherine Boo's account of a Mumbai slum (2012) and the 'literary reportage' of international issues of the acclaimed Polish investigative journalist, Ryszard Kapuściński (see, for example, *The Shadow of the Sun,* 2001, which reflects on development questions in several countries of sub-Saharan Africa). The ever thriving subgenres of 'travel writing' span a wide range of modalities and styles from the light-hearted holiday account to the 'epic' journey.[3] David Lewis has also drawn attention to the 'personalised style and form' of the 'development blockbuster' which relies on simultaneous appeal to the writer's scholarly authority and their individual on-the-spot experience (Lewis, 2014: 11).

So, as Lewis et al. (2014: 21) point out, 'the line between literature and the social sciences becomes a very fine one'. Similarly, when we consider social science research as the predominant form in which development writing appears, the (re)presentation of research is also accomplished through narratives—research is a form of storytelling in the sense that data do not speak for themselves but require selection, interpretation, and crafting into a plausible narrative. This applies particularly but by no means exclusively to qualitative research. These narratives may call on a range of rhetorical devices such as metaphor and the use of the particular to illustrate more general truths. Research also treats subjective experience as an important source of insight. These devices and insights are, of course, at the heart of fiction writing. We are dealing therefore less with a line than with a spectrum of overlapping approaches to style and representation.

[3] For a critical appraisal of western travel writing, see Pratt (1992).

It is important also to recognize the links between creative writing and research. Novels often 'contain' considerable research. This is true not only of novels adhering broadly to realist conventions of writing.[4] Narrative plausibility relies on an implicit pact with the reader that a novel located in a specific place, or time, or event does not violate empirical truth unless for particular creative purposes signalled in the style. There is a difference between importing factual error and engaging in creative licence. The latter is not infinitely elastic. The city of London is not in the south-west of England unless it is an otherwise signalled fictional entity. Errors simply annoy readers who spot them.

In *Mother London* (1988) the novelist Michael Moorcock gives us a London that is simultaneously empirically recognizable as itself and dazzlingly off-kilter. Seen and excavated through three characters who are mental health patients—part of London's floating, marginalized flaneurs—the city becomes mythical, existing more in its network of presumed or real tunnels below the ground and in the congealed history of war-time bombing than in its empirical geography. The 'truthfulness' of London lies in its narratives of dislocation. But a novel like Mother London could only be written by someone with an intimate knowledge of the city and its history and who is self-consciously muddying the common-sense boundaries between fact and fiction.

The novelist J. G Farrell is a writer of particular relevance to the fiction of development. His 'Empire Trilogy' consists of three novels completed in the 1970s. Each focuses on three diverse but critical moments in the decline of the British Empire.[5] The final one, *The Singapore Grip,* is set in the few months leading up to the fall of Singapore to the Japanese in 1942. On the surface, privileged life in the European enclave continues as usual, despite World War II in Europe and the Sino-Japanese war to the east. The early waves of the dispossessed arriving from China and the Malayan peninsula barely disturb the garden parties of the colony's ruling and business elites. The hierarchy of empire, exemplified in the spatial layout of the colony and in its racial and sexual orders, is intact. But underneath, the old order is being chipped away as global economic and political power shifts.

The novel draws heavily on real events. Farrell further blurs the line between fact and fiction: as well as quotations from contemporary sources such as newspapers, he includes several real historical figures and makes us privy to their (imagined) thoughts. With its long and detailed treatment of the colonial economy of commercial rubber production in Malaya, *The Singapore Grip* can also be read as a shout against political and economic exploitation. Farrell undertook very substantial research and added an afterword on his sources and a long bibliography. Farrell's

[4] See Head (2002: 2) for an extended discussion of realism in novels: 'the novel, through its ability to fictionalise and reimagine, affords a reinvigorating perspective on the real.'

[5] *Troubles* (1970), *The Siege of Krishnapur* (1973), *The Singapore Grip* (1978).

Singapore is, however, a gloriously fictional universe. He makes it a city of invented architecture, enabling him to deploy his gifts for the fantastical and the tragi-comic (it is extremely funny) while keeping historical faith with the events that preceded and followed its fall.

This critical distinction between error and invention accompanied me throughout the writing of *The Inheritance Powder*. I was able to draw upon my experience and knowledge of Bangladesh. I have both lived in the country and been involved in research, consultancy, and academic links over several decades. I also researched the arsenic situation extensively. I was clear from the start that I must maintain complete fidelity to the empirical truth of the issue.

This is because it felt to me too serious an issue to tamper with the facts and realities. So every statement that contained a specific fact was checked and rechecked for veracity. The novel is set in 2003, and I was as meticulous as I could be in ensuring that the situation as presented accorded with how it was at that time. This is harder than it first appears. The numbers and the known facts are different now. Other things have changed significantly, such as the means of communication. Then, it was largely faxes and emails. I am still haunted by the thought that there are unwitting anachronisms. I was, I suspect, over-meticulous (or simply being 'true' to my calling as an academic). But if, as a novelist, you decide to take on specialist and technical issues and to anchor your narrative to a specific time, you can expect some of your readers to know more than you do. It feels imperative to respect those readers as well as the reality you are trying to represent.

The novelist Ian MacEwan has perhaps best articulated this challenge for the fiction writer who ventures into specialist areas. In an interview for the New Yorker (Zelewski, 2009), he described how he needs to do field research whenever his characters work in complex areas (he has written novels on topics as diverse as brain surgery, climate change, and law). He further commented that, 'It's worth knowing about ten times as much as you ever use, so you can move freely', a sentiment that many social scientists would identify with. I can testify to this need from the paper and electronic mountains of material I amassed and studied on water engineering, the geology of the Bengal Delta, and the history of arsenic.

I also wanted to convey a real sense of place in my depiction of Bangladesh, to be as faithful as I could to its geographical and social landscapes. I was very conscious that I was writing for different audiences. One is mainly 'western' in that it is written in English and was first published by a UK publisher. This audience is also segmented in that there are readers (particularly in the development studies community) who know Bangladesh and readers who do not. The other audience is Bangladeshis having their country represented back to them by a non-Bangladeshi.

I return below to the larger issues contained in the concepts of representation and audiences, but from the perspective of the kind of story I was telling, this seemed to me to require fidelity to both place and social relations as well as to time and knowledge. Thus, the city of Dhaka appears as itself. It would not have advanced the narrative to make changes to its geographical and social contours. They would simply appear arbitrary. On the other hand, I did invent the district where part of the action takes place, giving it a name ('Shimulganj') which was carefully checked to ensure that it had no actual counterpart. I also located it with deliberate vagueness a few hour's drive from Dhaka city.

This invention was a narrative necessity. Shimulganj is the location of one of my two main characters, Zafirah Rahman, leader of the organization working on local development solutions to the arsenic problem. Her story is very particular and deeply entwined with the history of her activist grandmother who was a prominent figure in the district. I needed an invented space for her story to unfold, unencumbered by concerns that I might be trespassing into the realms of actual places and people. In that sense, the decision was one made specifically with Bangladeshi readers in mind.

The line between fact (in the sense of a generally agreed empirical truth) and invention was thus always at the forefront of the novel's development. I wanted readers to know where the line is drawn, so included a preface making this perhaps pedantically clear. Writers of realist development fiction must also be mindful of the possibility that too close a resemblance to actual people and organizations might incur legal challenge!

But these are choices all fiction writers make. There is nothing intrinsic here to the writing of 'development' fiction. My choice to adhere broadly to realist conventions reflects more my personal disposition and capacities as a writer as well as my reading preference for novels with real world 'stuff' in them, rather than my training as a social scientist. Development could as well be written as satire or magical realism. Indeed, these modalities—in pointing up absurdities, and using myth and magic to confront political and other forms of denial, would illuminate the project of development in important new ways.[6]

And realism in fiction does not mean a worthy adherence to empirical reality. My novel has a third main character, Arsenic, that stands in a certain way for the limits of human intervention. This imagining of a chemical element as a persona allowed me considerable dramatic licence. In one chapter, the women members of the NGO create a drama for their anniversary day in which they put Arsenic on trial in front of the village court. Their eventual judgement embodies a wisdom that challenges the taken-for-granted technical discourses of the experts.[7]

[6] In these senses, the novelist Gabriel Garcia Marquez can be seen as a major commentator on Latin American forms of 'development'.

[7] For social scientists, there are parallels here with Latour's sociological extension of the concept of 'actants' to things as a way of breaking down what he sees as the artificial distinction between human and technical ways of acting in/on the social universe. Agency can also be invested in objects (Latour, 2005).

I have drawn attention to the ways in which fiction and non-fiction modes of writing about development overlap, particularly in their narrative styles and often common reliance on research. I have also noted the epistemological fluidity of the boundary in terms of the kinds of truths that both forms of writing may be seen to represent. Nonetheless, I would argue that critical differences remain between fictional and non-fictional endeavours. In relation to the role of research, for example, novels are often 'researched' but they are not social science texts, or ethnographies, or attempting to be authoritative accounts of their subject matter. While I have noted the tacit rules and conventions in fiction writing regarding the difference between invention and error, research is always in service to the narrative, not the other way round.

When I was writing the novel, one of the hardest things was having to constantly jettison my own research knowledge, to remove the didacticism that would keep intruding into the narrative and the material that did not advance the story. This may serve as a general warning to social scientists who turn to fiction writing. A novel is not primarily about informing or improving the reader's specialist knowledge. It is about telling stories. I would nevertheless agree with the literary critic John Sutherland on the important role that novels can play in democratizing specialist knowledge and that: 'Fiction can make us better, or at least, better informed citizens' (2007: 257).

What is refreshing about writing a novel is that the novelist is under no obligation to be 'fair' or to render interpretative judgement based on a careful weighing of evidence. Fiction is not required to meet the canon of 'balanced reporting'. On the contrary, fiction allows and frequently foregrounds the outrageous and the controversial and gives voice to societies' rogues and outlaws and bigots. In their conclusion to the earlier volume in this series, Lewis et al. suggest that a critical role for popular representations of development is to articulate otherwise unacceptable views that may equally come from professional 'insiders' (2014: 244). One minor but important character in my novel—an old (and white, male) development hand—consistently punctures the pious tendencies of the main male protagonist with his robust commentary on the failings of the aid industry and the queasy compromises that working in it so often entail. For an applied social scientist in particular, there is relief in escaping from the straightjacket of the normative, to be able to create characters that are wilfully subversive and politically 'incorrect'.

Lewis et al. (2014: 27) refer to 'the freedom of fabrication' that fiction offers. This is not a freedom without limits. As I have argued, fiction also has its rules and conventions. But in letting the imagination off the leash, fiction opens up the everyday world in uniquely different ways. Fictional characters can be cynical, deluded, inadequate, foulmouthed, and have bad consciences or no consciences. These same characters can at the same time be sympathetic and heroic. The best characters are always the flawed ones, the ones whose lives veer off-course in unexpected ways. Fiction thrives on contrariness.

Unlike social science, fiction privileges the irrelevant, the individual, the playful, and the particular. Characters become known by their tics and idiosyncrasies. In a wonderful piece of sustained metaphorical writing in *The Singapore Grip,* Farrell gives much space to an ill-favoured, diseased stray spaniel which resists all attempts at humane 'disposal', cropping up in all kinds of unlikely places and finally getting itself onto the last ship to leave Singapore before the Japanese invasion. Someone nicknames the animal 'The Human Condition'.

Through its concern with emotional truths and truths of the imaginary, fiction amplifies interpretational possibilities. By unfettering us from the literal and empirical, it allows the imagination to roam through places that we may think we know until that familiarity is unsettled or upended by a different narrative. In its exploration of character and motivation, fiction invites us into our own interior worlds, into our dreams and desires, our secret fears and personal failures. We identify with characters even while finding them unlikeable.

I would argue therefore that the differences between fiction and non-fiction lie less in narrative forms and styles and more in what fiction 'does' and how this 'doing' arises from its relationship with audiences of readers. Freedom of fabrication is part of, and dependent on, unspoken pacts with readers. Novels are 'read' differently, not just through the willing suspension of disbelief that they require but also through the different sensibilities that they invoke. Nabokov's *Lolita* is not a manual on paedophilia.[8]

However, this freedom is not insulated from wider questions about power, authority, and positionality in representation. In an essay on exile, the writer Leon Edel argued powerfully that, 'One's citizenship in literary discourse is determined ... by the landscape of the imagination' (1982: 50). But neither citizenship nor landscapes are neutral zones. Edel's vision is a contested one at given historical and political moments. I turn now to how these issues played out for me in the writing of *The Inheritance Powder.*

Representing 'Development': Writing Ourselves and Others

When I first conceived of my novel, it had one central character from whose point of view the story was to be told. This was a British economist called Carl Simonovsky from a London-based research institute, who is visiting Bangladesh for the first time. He is first and most obviously an outsider and 'Bangladesh' is thus filtered through his vision and consciousness. As I wanted the novel to speak

[8] I am aware that there may well be readers who would make that claim or view it as such, but even if such a view is granted validity, it is arguably incidental.

also to issues of identity in a globalized world, I made his origins deliberately ambiguous. But as the novel progressed, I became increasingly dissatisfied with the restrictions that this format imposed. I felt it lacked any counterweight or challenge to the naive outsider's point of view. Furthermore, I was finding him hard to write and I was particularly troubled by a sense in which I felt the novel risked repeating hackneyed tropes about ignorant foreigners and 'bumbling Brits abroad'.

I realized that I wanted to write a counterpart point of view, and that the obvious contender was the woman with whom he falls in love—Zafirah Rahman, the NGO leader. This would open up a freedom to write from 'within' the context and to make their very different positionalities central to their conflicted relationship. The decision to write this other point of view was itself a conflicted one. Writing Bangladesh through the eyes of a foreigner had enough potential traps and pitfalls. Who was I to presume to write through the consciousness of a Bangladeshi woman? It was a reminder that in terms of the epistemologies of power and representation, the 'development novel' must be considered as part of the broader post-colonial landscape of fiction. It is in this context that I will now discuss both of these point of view challenges in more detail.

The term 'post-colonial' is simultaneously a contested one and one which it is difficult to dispense with, referring as it does both to a particular historical moment in the decolonization of Africa and Asia and to its associated political, economic, and cultural transformations. This corresponds broadly to the second half of the twentieth century. The concept of 'development' takes its current shape in this era, and this is reflected both in the locations that it focuses on and in the epistemologies of change which underlie its visions (see Eckert et al., 2010).

Definitions of post-colonial tend to be either spatial–temporal—focused on specific societies in a particular time period, or representational—based on the intersections of imperial power relations with language, text, or practice in colonial/post-colonial settings (Ashcroft et al., 1989; McLeod, 2000 [2010]). From a literary perspective, this latter understanding is more fruitful. It opens up to scrutiny the multiple forms within which power plays out textually in a whole range of cultural media. 'Othering' is one of the major tropes through which colonial/post-colonial discourses are enacted in fiction. In *Orientalism* (1979) Edward Said argues that the West has inscribed a homogeneous otherness onto its colonized spaces. They are not so much places as repositories of the fantasies and projections of the colonizer. A second, and related trope, is exoticization. Huggan describes this as 'an aestheticising process through which the cultural other is translated, relayed back through the familiar' (2001: ix–x).

A third way in which power relations are inscribed in literary text—and of particular relevance to my own writing practice—is resistance to and reappropriation of the terms of representation (see for example. Spurr, 1993; Cohn, 1996; Ashcroft et al., 1989). Edward Said, in asserting the right of the formerly colonized to represent themselves, notes: 'it is sometimes of paramount importance not so much what is said, but who speaks' (2001: 244). In this assertion, Said brings us up sharply against the reasons why Leon Edel's (1982) vision of an unbounded literary citizenship of the imagination is a contested one at certain historical and political moments. For 'representation' is not a neutral term.

Derek Attridge argues that the capacity to represent an 'other' in relation to oneself is intrinsic to the creative process and is 'something that is brought into being by an act of inventive writing' (2004: 29). But where the representation of self and otherness is tied to contexts of oppression it runs the risk of both exoticization and appropriation. It can misrepresent and disempower the other in claiming to 'speak for' their reality. This broader politics of representation was an ever-present accompaniment to the writing of my novel. It has important analogues with writing about international development and the sensitivity, for instance, around matters of authorship and co-authorship of academic papers—an issue that I was acutely aware of through long engagement in international research programmes with partners from the Global South.

An important exemplar of the politics of representation is the (white) British author Joyce Cary's novel *Mister Johnson* (1939 [2009]). This was written, unusually, from an 'African' point of view though the novel is also peopled by stock expatriate character types. Mr Johnson is a comic figure, a low-level clerk in the colonial apparatus. It is this novel that is said to have provoked Chinua Achebe to write his famous African trilogy, as a riposte to Cary's representation of Africans which he found offensively superficial (Slattery, 2010).

These are traps for the unwary writer, raising thorny questions about what is being represented and by whom. To make progress with my novel, I needed to explore these issues in more depth in order to feel creatively 'comfortable' with both of my point of view characters. I therefore wrote my creative writing Masters dissertation (2012) (*Only clowns, dupes or saviours? Writing 'ourselves' back into the postcolonial world*) around this central dilemma of representation.

In examining twentieth-century novels by white British authors that focused on encounters between expatriates and colonial/post-colonial settings, I found an interesting divide that appeared to open up as the century progressed. Up until the 1960s, it is not difficult to name internationalist writers who used such settings to explore wide-ranging ethical, moral, and political dilemmas. Writers such as E. M. Forster, Graham Greene, Paul Scott, Olivia Manning, and J. G. Farrell all wrote substantially and often critically on the relationships between Europeans and 'others'. While they have not always escaped critique from the standpoint of subsequent post-colonial reassessments,[9] this does not detract from their literary and thematic boldness.

In contrast, my review of those novels from white British authors that have ventured into 'post-colonial' settings since the 1970s found few that take on significant

[9] See e.g. Salman Rushdie's harsh verdict (1984) on Paul Scott's *Raj Quartet*.

social and political issues through the phenomenon of the transcultural encounter. Rather, 'Brits abroad' became increasingly the province of genre fiction. Novels took the form either of comedies or of thrillers. In representational terms, expatriates are either clownish or victims of sinister plots. Paradigmatic examples are William Boyd's (1981) *A Good Man in Africa* (comically unsavoury British diplomats make mischief in a comically unsavoury fictionalized African country), and John Le Carré's (2001) *The Constant Gardener* (self-sacrificing expatriates take on evil local and international forces of big business in Kenya). This, I realized, was at the source of some of my early discomfort with my white British male protagonist.

A third type, which can cut across these two, is the 'white saviour' novel, in which the expatriate becomes the fulcrum for improving the lot of the local population. Helen Fielding's comic heroine in *Cause Celeb* (1994 [2002]), undertaking voluntary work in an African refugee camp, calls in her rich and famous London friends to save the refugees from famine. In each of these genres or types, expatriates perform the roles of clowns, dupes, and/or saviours. As the writer Teju Cole (2012), among others, notes—the effect of these tropes is to reinforce a Europe-centred view of the world. There is, I concluded, something of a crisis of representation among 'white' fiction writers engaging with the post-colonial world.

There are many reasons for this. The end of empire brought the loss of a coherent narrative of power within which Europeans had held the authoritative place. For the (white) British writer in the decolonizing century representational options narrow once the British are no longer the orchestrators of action in the colonies. Critiques of the English novel in the post-war period have pointed to a sense of insularity and parochialism in its themes, a turning inwards to local concerns in the context of the post-war social contract (summarized in Head, 2002). Post-colonial voices have increasingly filled the literary space in terms of alternative narratives of empire and post-colonial power relations.

These diminished forms of representation can be seen to reflect a crisis of identity (how do we think about ourselves as Britons/Europeans in the post-colonial world?) which is linked to an awkwardness with colonial legacy. Comedies and thrillers, with their distancing devices of the comic expatriate abroad or the victim of sinister plots and forces, provide convenient modes for circumventing engagement with the complexities of this legacy and its implications for the politics and performance of identity.[10] But the anthropologist Benoit de l'Estoile points to the multiplicity of ways in which the colonial past is inscribed in the present, continuing to shape encounters and relationships across continents, while 'their meaning is actively reinterpreted and renegotiated' (2008: 277).

[10] They are essentially tropes of 'innocence' that bring to mind Graham Greene's (albeit now insensitive) warning in *The Quiet American*: 'Innocence is like a dumb leper who has lost his bell, wandering the world, meaning no harm' (2004: 29).

This fertile terrain for novelists has largely remained the province of (non-white) post-colonial writers. From the 1950s onwards, the empire itself was increasingly 'writing back'[11] as novelists of, or with a heritage in, those countries became the accepted literary voices for post-colonial settings. This has almost certainly led to some abdication of the territory by white writers, due particularly to nervousness about charges of neocolonialism through appropriation of the experience of the 'other.' In a *Guardian* interview, the novelist Philip Hensher described how his grant application to write about an Indian painter of miniatures was questioned by 'an academic who wrote an angry letter saying that this person should not write novels about India because he is not Indian' (Wroe, 2012).

Post-colonial critiques of representation have perhaps unwittingly placed the white metropolitan writer in an impossible bind. If writing which explores the experience of the 'other'[12] but is not written by that other risks being culturally embargoed, it severely limits the creative space. Any sense of the other becomes tainted by its authorship.

In the framing of both of my central characters, therefore, the representational dilemmas that I experienced were rooted in the challenges of writing in the historical moment loosely described as 'post-colonial.' The decision to move from a single, external point of view to a structure which interweaves a 'British' and a 'Bangladeshi' viewpoint needed much self-reflection. But so, equally, did writing a 'British' character in a post-colonial setting.

I found three recent developments and ways of thinking important in working through these dilemmas. First, I was influenced by reading post-colonial writers who have written British point of view characters into their novels in nuanced, reflective ways. Examples are Chimamanda Adichie in *Half of a Yellow Sun* (2009) (set in southern Nigeria), where the boyfriend of a key character is a young British historian; and Aminatta Forna in *The Memory of Love* (2011) (set in Sierra Leone), in which a British psychiatrist becomes involved in post-conflict mental-health care. This felt like a moving on, a shifting of the representational terrain: a 'permission', almost.

Second, and relatedly, was a sense that, in this (relatively) new century, writers have different realities to explore and negotiate. In a globalized world with ever increasing migrations, individual and collective lives are shaped by the intersections between new forms of connectedness, by the hybridization of identities, and the blurring of cultural boundaries.[13] As two contemporary scholars of transnational

[11] The phrase 'the empire writes back' was coined by Salman Rushdie (1982) to refer to a revisioning of colonial texts and a repositioning of voices in the telling of post-colonial experience (see Ashcroft et al. 1989: 32).

[12] To write from an expatriate viewpoint is necessarily to speak of the 'other' in relation to that viewpoint, even through silence.

[13] For a non-fiction exploration of expatriation against this changing context, see Fechkter and Walsh (2012).

English fiction argue: 'there is no longer anything *absolutely foreign*. Accordingly, there is no longer anything *exclusively one's own*, either' (Schulze-Engler and Helff, 2009: 7, emphasis in the original). I became increasingly concerned to explore my characters' commonalities, making them boundary crossers whose passports fully define neither their identities nor the space called 'home'.

Third, it helps to keep in mind two simultaneous and seemingly contradictory things—that the positionality and self-reflectiveness of the writer matter to interpretation and that the text has a life of its own and is subject constantly to rereading. In testing the limits and possibilities of literary citizenship, therefore, the context of representation will always matter but will never be all-determining. All readings and literary labels are inherently unstable and subject to multiple forms of appropriation and re-appropriation by different audiences at different times. None of my readers so far has raised an objection of the kind that most concerned me—that I have used a privileged outsider's position to appropriate another reality. But that leads into my final section on the interfaces between writers, publishers, and readers.

The Hard World of Publishing and Finding an Audience for 'Development' Fiction

The writing of any novel is a complex and often tortuous journey from having an idea and a compulsion to having a completed manuscript. Most ideas never get to final execution, and the vast majority of finished manuscripts does not get published. Of the few that do, sales in most cases are very small (Piersanti, 2020). This is particularly true for first-time authors with no reputation to trade on, and with manuscripts that do not fit any obvious category—or worse—are consigned to the barely read zone of 'literary fiction'.

This reflects the changes that have taken place in publishing over the last few decades. In *Merchants of Culture*, Thompson (2010) points to several factors which have produced a very different industry in the twenty-first century. These include mergers of smaller publishing houses into large conglomerates and a focus on the publishing and marketing of a narrow range of commercial bestsellers in order to make publishing 'pay' while book sales decline. This has come at the expense of diversity and books that have merit but are only ever going to achieve modest sales. At the same time, the digital revolution has opened up self-publishing and other forms of hybrid publishing as a viable route for authors either struggling to break into traditional publishing or actively choosing to take control of their own distribution and marketing. So, over the last decades, the number of books actually published has grown exponentially. According to a newspaper article, 'UK publishers released more than 20 new titles every hour over the course of 2014, meaning that the country published more books per inhabitant than anywhere else in the world' (Flood, 2014). The irony is that fewer and fewer of these books get noticed, purchased, and read, in either print or electronic form. Without the marketing power of the large conglomerates behind them, authors are lucky if they earn back their modest advances for the publisher.

What does this mean for trying to get a 'development' novel into print? First, there is no such concept or genre in mainstream publishing. A novel about development has to conform in some way to the categories that the market recognizes. One of the first questions an agent asks is 'What is it like?' In order for it to be pitched to a publisher, it has to have a recognizable market. This means finding books that it can be compared with. This gave me a lot of problems as I struggled to think of any. Pitches to agents and publishers also have to be crafted with this highly competitive market in mind. The ten-word pitch is normal, as is the one paragraph summary. For social scientists whose lives are dedicated to the complexity principle, these marketing devices can feel akin to a violation.

The Inheritance Powder did attract some interest from literary agents. One agent from quite a prestigious London agency expressed a strong interest. But it became clear he was looking for a thriller, a new version of *The Constant Gardener*. He also wanted me to remove the female point of view character as he was only interested in the 'outsider's' narrative. My description of the novel as an ambivalent post-colonial love story ticked no genre boxes for him. Another commended me on my writing style and said she would be delighted to read a different novel from me. However, she would not want to take on *The Inheritance Powder* as she was looking for books written from an 'authentic' point of view rather than that of an 'outsider'. Both of these ostensibly contrasting responses have strong echoes in my exploration of the challenges of writing such a novel in the long shadow of post-colonial literary criticism and the ways in which this has become refracted in publishing discourse.

'Development', it turned out, was not a saleable concept for commercial publishing. Another agent put it bluntly: 'Who is interested in novels about international development?' The only sensible advice to anyone contemplating writing a development novel is to write anyway but without expectation. Eventually it found a UK home with a small, new, independent publisher whose business model is realistic about the market for unknown authors of niche books. This left me with a further dilemma. Although it meant that the novel was available worldwide via Amazon and other global distribution platforms, this requires purchasers to have access to the means to pay, such as an international credit card. This ruled out many potential readers in Bangladesh. In 2016, following discussions between RedDoor—the UK publisher, and UPL, the main publisher of English language books in Dhaka, UPL negotiated the rights to publish and distribute it for the South and South-East Asia region. This edition was launched at the Dhaka Lit Fest in November 2016.

Conclusion

Who are the readers and how have they responded? For the most part, readers have come from the development community itself—at least judging from most of the reviews on my Amazon author's page and to an extent from Goodreads.[14] Of course, family and friends have kindly bought it and told their friends about it. But amid the deluge of fiction now available, book sales require a huge and continuous marketing effort by authors themselves, and it is surprisingly difficult to get feedback beyond the small circle of known readers. The marketing strategy with my publisher has focused particularly on development studies academics and students. What I had not factored into this is the fact that students no longer buy books and that, despite encouraging emails from course tutors and one request to talk to a development studies department, the teaching of fiction in development studies course programmes remains a minor enthusiasm. I suspect this reflects the sheer volume of topics and material that programme convenors feel they already need to cover.

Much feedback to authors is informal and personal ('just read your novel, loved it'). Those who do not love it probably keep quiet. The main source of formal reader feedback comes from big sites like Amazon and Goodreads author pages. Responses on those pages from 'expert' readers (i.e. those working in international development or familiar with Bangladesh) have been very favourable, to quote from a few:

> 'If you have lived in Bangladesh and worked in the development sector as I have, then reading (this) novel is like your life flashing in front of you.'
>
> 'This book should be required reading for anyone who aspires to work in development, join the Peace Corps, attempt to save the world.'
>
> 'Having worked for NGOs, government and the UN, I recognize many of the distortions, disillusionment, delays and dilemmas of development which the author portrays. As a development professional and trained anthropologist, she distils her experience well into the feel of "being there".'

For balance, I should add that my only two-star rating is from someone with a background in development and Bangladesh, who did not otherwise leave a comment. But in personal conversation they were most concerned with trying to work out 'who' my characters were 'really', and unconvinced by my categorical statement that no-one in the book is based on an actual person.

Reviewers also commented favourably on the portrayal of the country:

> 'It's easy to almost feel the sights and sounds of Bangladesh as you read.'
>
> 'I have not visited Bangladesh, but a sense of place shone through.'

[14] These are generally complimentary, with an overall rating of 4.5 stars from 26 reviews on Amazon and 4.1 from 12 reviews on Goodreads.

> 'Where an author is writing from their own experience the resulting book normally oozes with authenticity and that is certainly the case with *The Inheritance Powder*.'
>
> 'It's so rare to get a book set in Bangladesh and she depicted the country with such insight and humour.'

There have also been very favourable reviews from readers who do not have a development or Bangladesh background:

> 'Great to read a novel which brings another part of the world to my door and tells me about an issue which I had never heard of previously. I really enjoy learning about history and the world when reading fiction.'
>
> 'This is a very easy to read novel and for me it is a huge plus that it is also very informative.'
>
> 'I found this novel gave a fascinating insight into Bangladesh, a country I have never visited, and the labyrinthine world of international aid.'

Gauging the response of Bangladeshi readers is somewhat harder as not many reviews have appeared, and there is no equivalent to Amazon for readers to post comments. But my author's public Facebook page has over 600 'likes', which are overwhelmingly from Bangladeshi Facebook users, though I have no way of knowing how this translates into actual readers. I have also been contacted by journalists in Bangladesh and Hong Kong, concerned to engage with the subject matter. One interesting reaction from Bangladeshi readers known to me personally has been to express gratitude that the 'story' of arsenic has been told. No-one so far has raised any concerns about representation and appropriation. At the launch of the Bangladesh edition at the Dhaka Lit Fest in 2016, audience questions focused for the most part on the substantive issues that the book raised. I feel that this provides some empirical support to my process of reflection on Edel's (1982) 'citizenship of the imagination', that issues of power and representation are a constantly shifting political terrain. Finally, to my relief, no-one has yet contacted me to point out any embarrassing factual errors.

References

Achebe, C. (1958 [2006]) *Things Fall Apart*. London: Penguin Classics.

Adichie, C. Ngozi (2009) *Half of a Yellow Sun* (2nd edn). London: Fourth Estate.

Ashcroft, B., G. Griffiths, and H. Tiffin (1989) *The Empire Writes Back: Theory and Practice in Post-colonial Literatures*. London and New York: Routledge.

Attridge, D. (2004) *The Singularity of Literature*. London: Routledge.

Belmonte, T. (2005 [1979]) *The Broken Fountain* (25th anniversary edn). New York: Columbia University Press.

Boo, K. (2012) *Behind the Beautiful Forevers: Life, Death, and Hope in a Mumbai Undercity*. London: Portobello Books.
Boyd, W. (1981) *A Good Man in Africa*. London: Hamish Hamilton.
Cary, J. (1939 [2009]) *Mister Johnson*. London: Victor Gollancz.
Clifford, J. and G. E. Marcus (eds) (1986) *Writing Culture: The Politics and Poetics of Ethnography*. Berkeley, CA: University of California Press.
Cohn, B.S. (1996) *Colonialism and its Forms of Knowledge: The British in India*. Princeton, NJ: Princeton University Press.
Cole, T. (2012) 'The white savior industrial complex', *The Atlantic*, March 21, available at http://www.theatlantic.com/international/archive/2012/03/the-white-savior-industrial-complex/254843/?single_page=true.
Cooperrider, D.L., F. Barrett, and S. Srivastva (1995) 'Social construction and appreciative inquiry: A journey in organizational theory', in D. M. Hosking, H. P. Dachler, and K. J. Gergen (eds) *Management and Organization: Relational Alternatives to Individualism*. London: Ashgate Publishing, pp. 157–200.
de L'Estoile, B. (2008) 'The past as it lives now: An anthropology of colonial legacies', *Social Anthropology* 16(3): 267–79.
Eckert, A., S. Malinowski, and C. R. Unger (2010) 'Modernizing missions: Approaches to 'developing' the non-Western world after 1945', *Journal of Modern European History* 8(1): special issue.
Edel, L. (1982) 'The question of exile', in G. Amirthanayagam (ed.) *Asian and Western Writers in Dialogue*. London: Macmillan.
Eyben, R. (2014) *International Aid and the Making of a Better World: Reflexive Practice*. London: Routledge.
Eyben, R. and L. Turquet (2013) *Feminists in Development Organizations: Change From the Margins*. Rugby, UK: Practical Action Publishing.
Falola, T. (2005) *A Mouth Sweeter Than Salt: An African Memoir*. Ann Arbor, MI: University of Michigan Press.
Farrell, J.G. (1970) *Troubles*. London: Jonathan Cape.
Farrell, J.G. (1973) *The Siege of Krishnapur*. London: George Weidenfeld and Nicholson.
Farrell, J.G. (1978) *The Singapore Grip*. London: Weidenfeld and Nicholson.
Fechter, A. and K. Walsh (2012) *The New Expatriates: Postcolonial Approaches to Mobile Professionals*. London: Routledge.
Fielding, H. (1994 [2002]) *Cause Celeb*. London: Picador.
Flood, A. (2014) 'UK publishes more books per capita than any other country, report shows', available at https://www.theguardian.com/books/2014/oct/22/uk-publishes-more-books-per-capita-million-report.
Forna, A. (2010) *The Memory of Love*. London: Bloomsbury.
Greene, G. (2004) *The Quiet American*. London: Vintage.
Harding, S. (1988) *Feminism and Methodology: Social Science Issues*. Bloomington, IN: Indiana University Press.
Head, D. (2002) *Modern British Fiction, 1950–2000*. Cambridge: Cambridge University Press.
Huggan, G. (2001) *The Post-colonial Exotic. Marketing the Margins*. Abingdon: Routledge.
Kapuściński, R. (2001) *The Shadow of the Sun*. London: Penguin Books.
Latour, B. (2005) *Reassembling the Social: An Introduction to Actor-Network-Theory*. Oxford: Oxford University Press.
Le Carré, J. (2001) *The Constant Gardener*. London: Hodder and Stoughton.

Lenz, B. (2004) 'Postcolonial fiction and the outsider within: Toward a literary practice of feminist standpoint theory', *National Women's Studies Association (NWSA) Journal* 16(2): 98–102.
Lewis, D. (2014) 'Commodifying development experience: Deconstructing development as gift in the development blockbuster', *Anthropological Forum* 24(4): 440–453.
Lewis, D., D. Rodgers, and M. Woolcock (2008) 'The fiction of development: literary representation as a source of authoritative knowledge', *Journal of Development Studies* 44(2): 198–216.
Lewis, D., D. Rodgers, and M. Woolcock (2014) 'The fiction of development: literary representation as a source of authoritative knowledge', in *Popular Representations of Development: Insights from Novels, Films, Television and Social Media*. London: Routledge, pp. 19–37.
McLeod, J. (2000 [2010]) *Beginning Postcolonialism*. Manchester: Manchester University Press.
Moorcock, M. (1988) *Mother London*. London: Secker and Warburg.
Narayan, D. with R. Patel, K. Schafft, A. Rademacher and S. Koch-Schulte (2000) *Can Anyone Hear Us? Voices of the Poor*. New York: Oxford University Press, for the World Bank.
Piersanti, S. (2020) 'The 10 awful truths about book publishing', Berrett-Koehler Publishers, 26 September, available at https://ideas.bkconnection.com/10-awful-truths-about-publishing?redirected=true.
Pratt, M.L. (1992) *Imperial Eyes: Travel Writing and Transculturation*. London and New York: Routledge.
Rushdie, S. (1982) 'The Empire Writes Back With a Vengeance'. Times 3 July: 8
Rushdie, S. (1984) 'Outside the whale', Granta 11, 31st March, available at https://granta.com/outside-the-whale/.
Said, E.W. (1979) *Orientalism*. New York: Vintage Books.
Said, E.W. (2001) *Reflections on Exile and other Literary and Cultural Essays*. London: Granta Books.
Schulze-Engler, F. and S. Helff (eds) (2009) *Transcultural English Studies: Theories, Fictions, Realities, ASNEL Papers* 12. Amsterdam and New York: Rodopi.
Slattery, K. (2010) 'The Igbo people: Origins and history', MA dissertation in Modern Literary Studies, Belfast: Queens's University.
Spurr, D. (1993) *The Rhetoric of Empire. Colonial Discourse in Journalism, Travel Writing and Imperial Administration*. Durham, NC and London: Duke University Press.
Standing, H. (2012) 'Only clowns, dupes or saviours? Writing "ourselves" back into the postcolonial world', MA Dissertation in Creative Writing, London: Royal Holloway, University of London.
Standing, H. (2015) *The Inheritance Powder*. Haywards Heath, Sussex: RedDoor Publishing.
Standing, H. (2016) *The Inheritance Powder*. Dhaka: University Press Ltd.
Sutherland, J. (2007) *How to Read a Novel*. London: Profile Books.
Thompson, J.B. (2010) *Merchants of Culture. The Publishing Business in the Twenty-First Century*. Cambridge: Polity Press.
Wroe, N. (2012) 'Philip Hensher: A life in writing', *The Guardian*, 30 March, available at http://www.guardian.co.uk/culture/2012/mar/30/philip-hensher-life-in-writing?newsfeed=true.
Zalewski, D. (2009) 'The background hum: Ian McEwan's art of unease', *The New Yorker Life and Letters* 23 February. https://www.newyorker.com/magazine/2009/02/23/the-background-hum.

PART II
ADVOCACY

5

From Poverty to Power

A Blogger's Story

Duncan Green, with Maria Faciolince

Introduction

As Ryan Manning (2014) wrote in the precursor volume to this book, *Popular Representations of Development* (Lewis et al., 2014: 213),

> recent years have seen an explosion of Internet-based communication and publishing forums, ranging from Facebook and Twitter to more traditional websites. These have dramatically lowered the barriers to producing and distributing content, and people can now easily share information, experiences, perspectives, artwork, and almost anything else with their fellow Internet users around the world. Some decry this proliferation of online publishing as chaotic, overwhelming, rife with minutiae, and lacking in standards. Others claim it heralds the emergence of a more democratic, inclusive world of free speech, public debate, open exchange of knowledge, and global collaboration.

The *From Poverty to Power* (FP2P) weblog was part of this dynamic explosion of web-based communication. It went live in July 2008, as part of the promotion for my new book, *From Poverty to Power: How Active Citizens and Effective States Can Change the World* (Green, 2008). It rapidly took on a life of its own, becoming one of the most widely read blogs on international development. This chapter explores the evolution of FP2P, how blogging compares with other representations of development, and the challenges of blogging within a large bureaucratic institution. It draws potential lessons for both academic and NGO blogging.

The Weblog (Blog) FP2P

As an erstwhile journalist and wordsmith, I took to the blogging format immediately, and early posts show that the blog rapidly settled down into a format which more or less continues to this day: comments on events—this being 2008,

Duncan Green, with Maria Faciolince. *From Poverty to Power*. In: *New Mediums, Better Messages?*.
Edited by David Lewis, Dennis Rodgers, and Michael Woolcock, Oxford University Press.
 DOI: 10.1093/oso/9780198858751.003.0006

'How will the meltdown affect development?';[1] reviews of new publications ('Does Grassroots Activism Work? Two new collections of case studies');[2] curtain raisers for important events ('What Happened at the G20 Summit on Saturday?')[3] tips for NGO activists ('Killer Facts: a User's Guide'),[4] discussions of 'big ideas' ('Will we ever be able to talk about limits to growth?'),[5] and the introduction of a more personal touch ('I just read four novels in a row').[6]

Over the last 11 years, the blog has evolved into something akin to an international community with shared interests and values, engaging in conversations on a daily basis. Blogging enables a timely discussion of a new or breaking issue or event, with more depth than other social media like Twitter. The exchanges are often intense, and both intellectual and emotional—bumping into regular participants in the flesh at conferences or on field trips is like an encounter with an old friend (or occasionally the opposite). It is both more democratic than many more conventional NGO and academic fora, and yet not democratic enough—a point discussed later in this chapter—but it has become one of the most rewarding parts of my current role at Oxfam.[7]

Over time, FP2P has made greater use of guest posts, with my role often being as much that of editor/curator, as of sole author. The blog has also run some fifty reader polls. In 2012, it added an active Twitter account, which both promotes and feeds off the blog. At the time of writing @fp2p has about 40,000 followers, high by the standards of the aid industry. I have also experimented with vlogging[8] (short video blogs), audio (summaries and podcast interviews),[9] and debates between high profile protagonists on controversial issues such as the role of evidence,[10] or private education.[11]

Rising visibility ensured that what had initially been a short-term promotional exercise was recognized as a useful part of my day job (as Head of Research, and subsequently as Oxfam's Senior Strategic Adviser), accounting for approximately 10 paid hours per week (and doubtless a few unpaid ones too). Most recently, the blog has also attracted funding from two US foundations to enable it to run the

[1] Available at https://oxfamapps.org/fp2p/how-will-the-meltdown-affect-development/.
[2] Available at https://oxfamapps.org/fp2p/does-grassroots-activism-work-two-new-collections-of-case-studies/
[3] Available at https://oxfamapps.org/fp2p/what-happened-at-the-g20-summit-on-saturday/.
[4] Available at https://oxfamapps.org/fp2p/killer-facts-a-users-guide/.
[5] Available at https://oxfamapps.org/fp2p/will-we-ever-be-able-to-talk-about-limits-to-growth/.
[6] Available at https://oxfamapps.org/fp2p/i-just-read-four-novels-in-a-row/
[7] For more on the motives and experiences of development bloggers, see Denskus and Papan (2013).
[8] Available at https://www.youtube.com/watch?list=UUCftgsFVGiAihCJu-HhR4dQ&v=ZiI2Aq2HG7Y.
[9] Available at https://open.spotify.com/show/5db71I4MLaABZmQBInBhy3.
[10] Available at https://oxfamapps.org/fp2p/the-evidence-debate-continues-chris-whitty-and-stefan-dercon-respond/.
[11] Available at https://oxfamapps.org/fp2p/education-wonkwar-the-final-salvo-kevin-watkins-responds-to-justin-sandefur-on-public-v-private-and-the-reader-poll-is-still-open/.

#PowerShifts project to raise voices and issues from the Global South, discussed in more detail below.

According to Wordpress, the platform on which FP2P appears, at the time of writing (September 2019), FP2P had hosted over 2,700 posts, and 13,000 reader comments (an average of 5 per post). At a typical word length of 800–1000 words per post, that comes to well over 2 million words, the equivalent of several academic volumes.

Readership and Impact

Data on readership is available from Google Analytics, which measures the numbers of direct hits on the site (though not reposts, excerpts, etc). After a slow start of fewer than 14,000 'unique visitors' (UVs)[12] in its first six months, traffic increased steadily for the first four years, and since late 2012, has fluctuated around an average of 30,000 UVs per month. Google Analytics provides some information on the location of readers. The most recent summary on FP2P (of data for 2018, Table 5.1)[13] shows that just over 40 per cent of its 330,000 UVs were based in the UK and US, with no other country exceeding 6 per cent of readership. Only three developing countries appeared in the top ten. Those used to academic download numbers will probably see these figures as high, while anyone from traditional print media outlets such as newspapers and magazines will find them strikingly low. The truth (at least in the case of FP2P) is that the blog has provided a platform for a specialist conversation with a relatively narrow, but global, readership.

Perhaps surprisingly, the most-read post over the 11 years of FP2P is a country specific post about climate change in South Africa[14]—I presume it is on a large reading list somewhere, but have been unable to track it down. Other 'greatest hits' include a 'funny': 'What Brits Say v What They Mean'[15] circulated endlessly on social media. The other most-read FP2P posts give a good sense of the breadth and randomness of the internet. They include practical/self-help advice posts ('How to get a PhD in a year without giving up the day job',[16]) the controversial ('How

[12] The term 'unique visitors' refers to the number of distinct individuals (or more accurately, IP addresses—individuals using more than one device will register multiple times) visiting a website during a given period, regardless of how often they visit.

[13] Available at https://oxfamapps.org/fp2p/2018-fp2p-report-back-stats-most-read-posts-and-some-big-plans-for-2019/.

[14] Available at https://oxfamapps.org/fp2p/how-is-climate-change-affecting-south-africa/.

[15] Available at https://oxfamapps.org/fp2p/what-brits-say-v-what-they-mean-now-with-author-credit/.

[16] Available at https://oxfamapps.org/fp2p/how-to-get-a-phd-in-a-year-and-still-do-the-day-job/.

Table 5.1 FP2P 2018 readership data

	Country	Users	% Users
1.	United States	77,597	23.34%
2.	United Kingdom	61,787	18.59%
3.	South Africa	17,348	5.22%
4.	France	15,931	4.79%
5.	Australia	14,648	4.41%
6.	India	13,662	4.11%
7.	Canada	11,307	3.40%
8.	Germany	6,149	1.85%
9.	Netherlands	6,050	1.82%
10.	Philippines	6,008	1.81%

Source: Google Analytics

much should charity bosses be paid?'[17]), and the campaign polemic (comparing country GDPs to the turnovers of the largest global corporations[18]).

Readers arrive at the blog through a number of channels. Around 7,000 people receive daily email notifications of new posts, while some 3,000 have signed up via the popular Feedly RSS feed.[19] The most recent survey of FP2P readers comes from 2017.[20] Based on approximately 350 responses to an online survey, roughly 40 per cent of the readers worked for NGOs. A further 18 per cent were academics and students, and 13 per cent came from government or multilateral organizations, suggesting a fairly specialized development sector audience.

Readership is, of course, not the same as impact (on discourse, policy, or practice), and here the evidence is much patchier. It is hard to pick out any one post as having had more influence than others. Instead, the impact appears to be cumulative, based on multiple posts exploring a range of themes that have evolved with my own interests and in response to external events. Threads of posts in the early years concentrated on the developmental impact of the global financial crisis, subsequently moving on to inequality and, most recently, governance and theories of change. It is these extended conversations that appear to have most resonance.

[17] Available at https://oxfamapps.org/fp2p/ok-so-how-much-should-charity-bosses-be-paid-plus-your-chance-to-vote/.

[18] Available at https://oxfamapps.org/fp2p/the-worlds-top-100-economies-31-countries-69-corporations/.

[19] Available at https://feedly.com., RSS (rich site summary) is a format for delivering regularly changing web content. Many news-related sites, weblogs, and other online publishers syndicate their content as an RSS feed to whoever wants it.

[20] Available at https://oxfamapps.org/fp2p/survey-results-who-reads-fp2p-what-jobs-do-you-do-how-would-you-like-to-improve-it/.

As far as I know, the only independent evidence that goes beyond the anecdotal is from a 2012 report on attitudes among 'influentials' in US, UK, China, France, and Germany (Intermedia, 2012). This involved a survey of 3,984 'interested citizens' in the UK, France, Germany, China, and the US, along with in-depth interviews of 88 'Influentials' across China, France, Germany, the UK, and the US, and 40 government decision makers in the UK, France, Germany, and the US.

The study identified FP2P as among the five most influential blogs on international development among 'influentials' in the UK, France, and Germany (though not the US and China), and among government officials in the UK. Interestingly it also drew a distinction between 'institutional' bloggers linked to a recognized organization (such as FP2P/Oxfam) and unaffiliated individual bloggers, finding 'Blogs sponsored by recognized institutions are popular, including those run by recognized development NGOs (e.g. Oxfam) and multilateral funders/agencies (e.g. the World Bank). Among new generation influentials, institutional bloggers appear to have much stronger links to government decision-makers than independent bloggers' (pp. 8, 28). I return to this issue below.

Swimming Pool-Gate and Bringing Internal Aid Debates to Life

The 'Nairobi Swimming Pool' post[21] has become somewhat notorious in the aid sector, illustrating both the reach and risks of blogging. It became a case study in Rosalind Eyben's (2014) book *International Aid and the Making of a Better World*. Its popularity lay in exposing the kind of difficult decisions and dilemmas that are a regular occurrence in aid work, but are seldom discussed in public.

> Nairobi is a major NGO hub, currently the epicentre of the drought relief effort, and Oxfam's regional office realized some years ago that we could save a pile of money if we ran our own guesthouse, rather than park the numerous visitors in over-priced hotels. It's nothing fancy, definitely wouldn't get many stars, but it's much more relaxed than a hotel.
>
> But there's a problem. As a large converted house in a nice part of town, and like most such houses in Nairobi, it has a swimming pool. But the swimming pool is covered over and closed, even though it would be cheap to keep it open. Why? Reputational risk—back in the UK, where swimming pools are luxury items, Oxfam's big cheeses saw a tabloid scandal in the making and closed it. It didn't help when some bright spark decided to advertise for a swimming pool attendant on the Oxfam website ...

[21] Available at https://oxfamapps.org/fp2p/the-great-nairobi-guesthouse-swimming-pool-dilemma-cast-your-vote-now/.

On my recent stay at the guesthouse, I asked everyone I met there and whether African or expat, they all said it makes sense to open the pool. Exhausted aid workers arrive hot and dusty from remote areas of East Africa for some R&R, but there's no chance of a refreshing swim. I need my exercise so had to go running instead—the combination of altitude, hills and choking traffic fumes nearly killed me.

On the other hand, there's no denying that most of our supporters back in the UK, let alone the people we are working to help, are not likely to have access to a pool in their back yard, so why should aid workers get special treatment?

So what do you think? Should Oxfam open the pool and take any bad publicity on the chin, or should we stop whining? It would probably cost about $200-300 a month to keep the pool open—if we could find a way to do it without creating an accounting nightmare, we could probably raise that from contributions from guests, and even have money to spare to plough back into Oxfam programmes.

The post sparked record numbers of comments (89 to date) and votes. Of 800 people who took part in the poll, 75 per cent urged Oxfam to reopen the pool, while only 7 per cent argued for keeping it shut. However, the post itself became part of the problem, when it was picked up by anti-aid journalist Ian Birrell in an article in *The Spectator*,[22] which argued that 'Mr Green's blog highlighted the contortions of a thriving industry that would go out of business if it succeeded in its stated aims'. In the middle of a famine response in East Africa, overworked Oxfam press officers were forced to handle enquiries from journalists about the Great Swimming Pool Debate. I had to apologize to them, and the pool remained closed.

Tapping into the Zeitgeist: Sausagefest

FP2P had its #MeToo moment in early 2018. On 10 January, I summarized a lecture by Stefan Dercon, outgoing DFID chief economist, to my LSE Masters students, which included a striking section on 'Big Ideals, Big Thinkers, Big Egos'.[23] Based on a briefing he gave to the incoming DFID Minister Justine Greening, he neatly summarized and critiqued the big-name authors in development economics (Sen, Sachs, Easterly, and co) that a UK Secretary of State was likely to have quoted at her. I thought it provided a useful set of ideas about the 'big names', and in particular the flaws and limitations in their arguments. The list had a heavy male bias—out of ten big names featured in his opening slide, only one (Esther

[22] Available at https://www.spectator.co.uk/2012/02/big-charity/.

[23] Available at https://oxfamapps.org/fp2p/10-top-thinkers-on-development-summarized-in-700-words-by-stefan-dercon/.

Duflo) was a woman, and even she is a co-author with her partner, Abhijit Banerjee, and Dercon also mentioned Dambisa Moyo in his wider list. I duly noted in my post 'who's he missed out? Can there really be so few women or people from the South among the top tier?'

Upon posting, it immediately became clear that it was going to get a lot of hits. When I tweeted the link, Alice Evans, a lecturer at Kings College and occasional FP2P contributor, tweeted '#sausagefest. Ignores so many, e.g. Merilee Grindle. Judith Tendler. Emma Mawdsley. Nancy Birdsall. Andrea Cornwall'. I invited Alice to write a riposte to Stefan's 'male gaze', which she duly did,[24] astonishingly in time to go up the next day. The two posts provoked enormous interest, and generated the most visits of any month on the blog (by a distance), but at some personal cost. Various commenters accused me of sexism, and the whole exchange became acrimonious and deeply upsetting. My conclusion? Controversy may generate clicks, but neither Oxfam nor my personality are well suited to it.

Handing Over the Stick: #PowerShifts

In April 2019, FP2P embarked on its biggest change of direction in its 11 years of existence. With a small amount of funding from two US foundations, it began a project to partially convert the blog into a platform for writing, opinions, and ideas from the Global South.[25] The project, subsequently named #PowerShifts,[26] partly responds to the *zeitgeist*—international NGOs like Oxfam are increasingly (often justifiably) criticized for failing to cede power and decision making to grassroots organizations and individuals in the Global South. It also partly reflects my own desire to try something new and challenging—after 10 years, the blog was becoming a little stale and repetitive, at least for its author.

#PowerShifts coincides with this moment of change and is being run by Maria Faciolince, a Colombian-Antillean anthropologist.[27] The project began as an attempt to 'hand over the mic' to more southern contributors, aiming to open up a space (this time within the development bubble) for ideas and perspectives that reframe the way we think and talk about development issues in diverse regions, and that shift power towards critical voices and people-led initiatives from the Global South. Putting the perspectives of people and communities with lived experience of any issue at the centre of the discussion is crucial for understanding it;

[24] Available at https://oxfamapps.org/fp2p/the-perils-of-male-bias-alice-evans-replies-to-yesterdays-sausagefest/.
[25] Available at https://oxfamapps.org/fp2p/were-changing-up-fp2p-heres-the-plan-but-we-havent-got-a-name-yet-please-help/.
[26] Available at https://oxfamapps.org/fp2p/category/power-shifts/.
[27] CV available at https://www.linkedin.com/in/mariafaciolince/?originalSubdomain=es.

our proposal is that we should be doing more *listening* instead of talking among ourselves.

Development itself as a concept and practice is deeply embedded in power relationships, involving issues of representation and the ways in which we produce and validate knowledge. So it was no surprise that featuring more critical perspectives from the South led to some fascinating engagement around complex topics concerning representation, genuine participation, and what solidarity can mean in future iterations of the development and aid system. Important discussions around the 'geopolitics of voice' have emerged, exploring not only what is being said, but who is being heard and how we're talking, to fundamentally challenge dominant notions of 'authority' and 'expertise'. For example, a collaboration with the (Silent) Voices collective at the Governance in Conflict (GIC) network from the University of Ghent on a series of blogs called the 'Bukavu Series', dealt with research ethics and the violence of academic knowledge production.[28]

The standard approach to 'raising' or 'tapping into' unheard voices has been, by and large, dictated in a top-down way from the northern Anglosphere. Being aware of the nuances and complexity of this, #PowerShifts is an effort to rebalance some of the asymmetries that continue to characterize a large chunk of development communications, and start making these conversations more horizontal, democratic, and centred on justice. But it comes with more questions than answers. How do we engage in genuine participation and mutual learning, without tokenizing or limiting inclusion to a mere invitation to 'sit at the table'? How can we nurture a spirit of collaboration and horizontal co-creation? How can we ensure these conversations create ripples in spaces of action and strengthen efforts to tackle the blind spots in local and global development?

We have begun exploring some possible pathways of co-creation alongside collectives such as 'Convivial Thinking',[29] in the academic sector, networks of youth activists such as the 'Global Changemakers',[30] and movements working to redesign funding structures within the development sector like #ShiftThePower.[31] These include thinking of ways to facilitate genuine participation and access, which involve coming up with new formats to have conversations online and in person, steering away from the written word, and co-posting on several platforms. This has involved not only creating more content, but also compiling links, stories, videos, interviews, and databases as a series of #PowerShifts resources on various topics,

[28] Available at https://oxfamapps.org/fp2p/?s=bukavu.

[29] Available at https://www.convivialthinking.org.

[30] Available at https://www.global-changemakers.net.

[31] Available at https://www.alliancemagazine.org/feature/shiftthepower-rise-community-philanthropy/.

ranging from perspectives of climate justice from the Global South,[32] to exploring tools such as collective mapping,[33] to topics like reclaiming representation.[34]

The project is set to run for two years. Although at the time of writing, we are only six months into its work, it is getting a good response and already changing the nature of the blog. So far, out of the fifty-two new contributors, all come from the Global South, with half coming from Africa. Over two-thirds of them are female. The editorial make-up of the content has had feminism, inequality, and activism as the top three thematic areas, with over a third of the posts directly addressing critical issues to rethink development. We have also seen a huge increase in southern engagement compared with the previous 6-month period (September 2018–March 2019): readership from Africa has risen by 80 per cent, Asia by 15 per cent, and South America 16 per cent. In due course we will have to decide whether to spin it off as an independent site, continue it in some way, or incorporate it into the daily functioning of FP2P.

Encouraging Debate

Individually authored posts may receive comments from readers, but the power imbalance is decidedly asymmetric: the author gets more space, a privileged position (original posts are seen as weightier than comments) and (if the author is also the blog's curator) has the option of the last word. Debates *between* authors are much more horizontal, and often attract considerable interest. Debate formats enlighten big debates and policy issues and allow practitioners and academics alike to take a step back from day-to-day routine and reflect. This is useful in particular for those field/operational staff who often have little time to access information on them.

Two of the most successful debates on FP2P covered the role of evidence and results[35] and private vs public provision of education.[36] On evidence and results, two senior DFID figures, Chris Whitty (Director of Research and Evidence) and Stefan Dercon (Chief Economist) took on two prominent academic critics of the 'results agenda', Chris Roche (Latrobe University) and Rosalind Eyben (IDS). Both sides came out roughly equal in a subsequent reader poll. I summarized the debate and reader reactions with some difficulty, as my sympathies were with the critics, but I had to acknowledge that the supporters of the results agenda had had

[32] Available at https://oxfamapps.org/fp2p/powershifts-resources-lessons-from-the-global-south-for-surviving-the-climate-crisis/.

[33] Available at https://oxfamapps.org/fp2p/powershifts-resources-collective-mapping/.

[34] Available at https://oxfamapps.org/fp2p/powershifts-resources-reclaiming-representation/.

[35] Available at https://oxfamapps.org/fp2p/the-evidence-debate-continues-chris-whitty-and-stefan-dercon-respond/.

[36] Available at https://oxfamapps.org/fp2p/education-wonkwar-the-final-salvo-kevin-watkins-responds-to-justin-sandefur-on-public-v-private-and-the-reader-poll-is-still-open/.

the best of the argument.[37] Writing the summary also highlighted the additional contribution made by the numerous comments (seventy-five in all, many substantial), which among other things, emphasized the gulf between the debates and what those in charge of gathering results in aid agencies actually face—highly constrained resources, crazy time pressure, and the overwhelming need to feed the aid machine with 'results'. On public vs private education provision, Kevin Watkins of ODI took on Justin Sandefur of the Center for Global Development through two rounds of erudite and occasionally bruising exchanges—one participant commented ruefully 'I hadn't realized blogging was such a blood sport'—generating fifty-six comments from a range of practitioners and academics.

Multi-author debates are time consuming to organize and to participate in—they work best when contributors respond swiftly to each other, and to comments from readers, which requires freeing up a considerable amount of time. Experts are often reluctant to be pigeon-holed as 'for' or 'against' a particular position. There is a tendency for antagonists to caricature their opponents' arguments (straw men) and to use cheap debating shots to score points, in addition to more dispassionate argument. But done well, debates attract readers and can be excellent at highlighting and comparing the different arguments around an issue. Some of the most searching discussions however take place around book reviews, which are usually popular on FP2P (although I fear that is because they save people time reading the actual books). Back-to-back reviews of new books on developmental success in China[38] and Bangladesh[39] triggered a third post comparing the two,[40] and a debate involving both authors and readers on the nature of development in those countries and the lessons for others. This kind of exchange shows the value of blogging in turning reading books from a passive to an active process.

Blogging vs Other Representations of Development

Over the years, I have been involved in a range of different roles in aid and development—as an activist, journalist, think-tank writer, scholar, civil servant, NGO researcher, and advocate. Each has involved talking and writing about development in different ways to different audiences through different media. Of all these blogging stands out as a form of continuous engagement with a specialist audience, in which ideas and arguments can evolve and be sharpened over time.

[37] Available at https://oxfamapps.org/fp2p/so-what-do-i-take-away-from-the-great-evidence-debate-final-thoughts-for-now/.

[38] Available at https://oxfamapps.org/fp2p/book-review-how-china-escaped-the-poverty-trap-by-yuen-yuen-ang/.

[39] Available at https://oxfamapps.org/fp2p/book-review-the-aid-lab-understanding-bangladeshs-unexpected-success-by-naomi-hossain/.

[40] Available at https://oxfamapps.org/fp2p/two-top-authors-compared-hossain-on-bangladesh-and-ang-on-china/.

The conversation can be searching and bad ideas can be easily shot down, as I found when I road-tested a 2×2 matrix on fragility and conflict in the final stages of writing a book, *How Change Happens* (Green, 2016).[41] The 2×2 never made it into the final text. At the same time, writing *How Change Happens* also revealed some of the limitations of blogging. I initially thought that a book could emerge from the blog in an organic way, pulling together the archive on particular issues and polishing it into a chapter form. That approach rapidly crashed and burned as I went back to a more traditional research and writing approach, although I did publish the draft text on the blog,[42] and got some useful commentary (and advance publicity).

But the conversation is undeniably asymmetric—in this field, the blogger presents themselves as an 'expert', or else no-one will click through. It also reflects the broader distribution of power and influence in both society and academia: most international bloggers on development are, somewhat paradoxically, 'pale, male and stale' (old white men), although national-level blogging is much more diverse. Although readership surveys suggest FP2P's readership is evenly divided between men and women, comments and guest posts tend to come from men.[43] Despite such flaws, blogging is often less asymmetric than journalism, film, or book-writing that allows little or no space for the 'consumer' to comment, or even academic exchange with students that are cowed by the power hierarchies within universities. This is particularly true when comments on a post take on a life of their own, with different commenters actively discussing a topic among themselves. Then a blog can come to resemble something more like a community of practice. In the words of one commenter on the draft of this chapter 'I've received emails from think tanks, researchers, academics, and students after engaging with your blog. So it helps me share my research, and build networks, despite being junior'.

The Individual and Institutional Benefits and Challenges

Writing, uploading, and managing several 1,000 word posts a week is a considerable personal and institutional commitment, but has brought significant benefits. At a personal level, writing a blog post forces you to clarify and nail down your analysis and opinion of the books, papers, or conversations that fill the day, and then test that analysis with a group of peers. Over time, posts become a cumulative

[41] Available at https://oxfamapps.org/fp2p/fragility-v-conflict-can-you-help-me-populate-a-new-2x2-please/.

[42] Available at https://oxfamapps.org/fp2p/first-draft-of-how-change-happens-now-ready-anyone-want-to-read-it/.

[43] For discussions on gender and development blogging, see https://oxfamapps.org/fp2p/why-do-so-few-women-write-or-comment-on-blogs/, and http://aidnography.blogspot.com/2012/03/is-writing-reflective-blogs-on.html.

archive of your work and thought, invaluable for responding to enquiries or overcoming memory loss. Emotionally, blogging is an antidote to the isolation that can accompany research. Professionally, a blog profile has proved an effective way to build a network. It has also stocked my bookshelves with free review copies.

Blogging is not for everyone of course. Conversations with Oxfam colleagues have shown that many find the informal tone and short format hard to manage—my advice to would-be bloggers is to 'write like you talk', but that can be hard for those with a more academic background, or steeped in the rather formalized, 'broadcast' nature of NGO public communication (what development blogger Owen Barder caricatures as 'flogging not blogging').[44]

Institutionally, Oxfam initially struggled with FP2P. NGOs have a default preference for personal anonymity and institutional control. The authorship of papers, if acknowledged at all, is buried in the small print. Egotism is frowned upon. Blogs, however, often benefit from having a personality and expressing doubt and ambiguity, asking questions rather than always claiming to know the answer. This makes institutional sign-off sometimes a contentious issue, especially when blogs depart from agreed institutional messaging, whether in tone or content, as it can create reputational risks (see 'Nairobi Swimming Pool'). Initially every FP2P post had to be signed off in advance by an Oxfam press officer. But as an early entrant to a relatively new field, the blog may have benefited from the lack of established procedures. After a few months, we agreed to abandon the practice (without telling anyone) and move from 'asking permission' to occasionally 'asking forgiveness' when I overstep the mark. My rule of thumb is that I should need to apologize once or twice a year—do so too often, and the blog risks being closed down; never get into trouble, and the blog is probably getting boring. The increasing institutionalization of social media in large organizations since then has probably made it harder for new blogs to improvise and evolve in this way.

As the readership built up, and anecdotal evidence of impact accumulated (for example in Oxfam's interactions with aid donors and governments), attitudes to FP2P became more positive. With many readers among staff in major aid institutions such as DFID and the World Bank, the blog provides an additional form of influence, alongside more formal channels of consultation, campaigns, and lobbying. As in academia, FP2P and other Oxfam blogs also play a useful role in boosting readership and downloads for its policy and research papers. World Bank research on economics blogging, published on the excellent LSE Impact blog[45] showed just how big the 'blogging effect' can be:

[44] Available at http://www.owen.org/blog/3150/.
[45] Available at http://blogs.lse.ac.uk/impactofsocialsciences/2011/11/15/world-bank-dissemination/.

> Blogging about a paper causes a large increase in the number of abstract views and downloads in the same month: an average impact of an extra 70–95 abstract views in the case of Aid Watch[46] (now sadly defunct) and Chris Blattman,[47] 300 for Marginal Revolution,[48] and 450–470 for Freakonomics[49] and Krugman.[50] These increases are massive compared to the typical abstract views and downloads these papers get—one blog post in Freakonomics is equivalent to 3 years of abstract views! However, only a minority of readers click through—we estimate 1–2% of readers of the more popular blogs click on the links to view the abstracts, and 4% on a blog like Chris Blattman that likely has a more specialized (research-focused) readership.

Similar effects appear to be obtained from Twitter.[51]

But increased acceptance also brought new tensions to be managed, namely an urge to 'instrumentalize' the blog as a mouthpiece for the latest Oxfam policy paper or campaign. I cope with that by ensuring that Oxfam colleagues and papers regularly appear on the blog (after all, Oxfam pays my wages), but push (and support) authors not to write in the standard NGO finger-wagging style. Another tension surrounds 'snark' and conflict. Nothing attracts web hits like a good brawl, but neither I nor Oxfam are set up for this. My skin is too thin for the more brutal variety of exchanges on social media, and Oxfam needs to be careful not to alienate elements of its broad constituency. Even attempts at humour can be minefields: when over Christmas lunch, my team edited the ten commandments as if they had gone through Oxfam sign off,[52] I was forced to apologize to the then Oxfam CEO for the offence caused (sample: 'You shall not commit adultery' [footnote: 'I know this represents something of a U-turn, but all this "you shall not" stuff goes completely against our new emphasis on positive frames; we have to transmit provocative optimism and possibility']).

In this respect, the existence of different blog formats may be important. Oxfam, like many NGOs, hosts a number of different blogs catering to different audiences. Compared to other NGO blogs, FP2P is unusual in being identified with a single author/curator, ranging widely in subject matter within a broad 'aid and development' envelope. Alternative formats include subject specific blogs, such as Oxfam's *The Real Geek* blog on issues around monitoring and evaluation, which has proved

[46] Available at http://www.nyudri.org/aidwatcharchive.
[47] Available at https://chrisblattman.com/.
[48] Available at http://marginalrevolution.com/.
[49] Available at http://freakonomics.com/.
[50] Available at https://krugman.blogs.nytimes.com/.
[51] Available at http://blogs.lse.ac.uk/impactofsocialsciences/2012/05/18/who-gives-a-tweet-860-downloads/. For other LSE Impact pieces on academic blogging see http://blogs.lse.ac.uk/impactofsocialsciences/?s=blogging.
[52] Available at http://oxfamblogs.org/fp2p/christmas-special-what-happens-when-an-ngo-edits-the-ten-commandments/.

unexpectedly popular.[53] One of NGOs' niches ought to be blogging 'from the field' in a way that communicates the reality of life in developing country communities to people who live elsewhere (mainly in rich countries). In practice, this has proved difficult. If these are crude 'thank you Oxfam for my new goat' type blogs, they probably won't reach many people—nuance and ambiguity is a good thing when trying to describe real life. But some of them can be extraordinarily powerful, like the blogs from Oxfam staffer Mohamed Ali during the Gaza blockade in 2009.[54]

Has Blogging Peaked?

In September 2017, the most widely read of development bloggers, Chris Blattman, announced he was suspending operations.[55] Blattman made his decision due to writing commitments (a new book) and because 'few people read blogs anymore. Including me. I no longer feel the pressure to write often, because the person who comes directly to the page daily or weekly in search of something new is a dwindling breed. Most people reach blogs by Twitter and Facebook'. While it is not obvious why someone reading your post via Facebook should be any more or less of an incentive to keep writing than them coming directly to your website, it is likely that blogging, like other social media platforms, will have a finite lifespan. Bloggers falling by the wayside such as Blattman or Bill Easterly (who gave up blogging in 2011)[56] are not apparently being replaced by new names. Google Analytics suggests traffic to FP2P has levelled off, although it so far shows no sign of falling.

What is not clear, at least to this author, is what will replace it. Content remains king, and blogging generates the content that other social media (Twitter, Facebook) feed off. Possible new platforms to replace/complement written blogs include enhanced use of video and audio podcasts, moving from author-driven blogs to crowd-sourced question and answer formats such as Quora.com,[57] or even a retro return to personal email listserves.

In keeping with the FP2P ethos, I posted a draft of this chapter [58] and received some excellent comments on the current state of blogging. One respondent who asked to remain anonymous observed:

> I share your view that blogging enriches the discussion on development by being direct and conversational while bringing 'substance' and knowledge. In this

[53] Available at https://views-voices.oxfam.org.uk/topic/methodology/real-geek/.
[54] Available at https:// https://oxfamapps.org/fp2p/harrowing-blogs-from-oxfam-staff-in-gaza/.
[55] Available at https://chrisblattman.com/2017/09/06/not-blogging-anymore/.
[56] Available at http://www.nyudri.org/aidwatcharchive/.
[57] Available at https://www.quora.com/.
[58] Available at https://oxfamapps.org/fp2p/bloggings-getting-a-bit-old-whats-next-plus-my-first-vlog-for-your-ridicule/.

> sense, blogging as a 'communication style' or 'modality' will not go away. It has actually contaminated the style of newspapers' articles and even the format of online newspapers—it is evident on media like *The Guardian*. What has however changed since the moment where blogs started to become successful in the mid-2000s is that nowadays the 'transaction costs' to open a blog are quite high. By costs I mean the investment needed to attract traffic to the blog. In a web much fuller of content—in particular commercial content—and where blogging has turned into a profession for some—with increasingly sophisticated strategies—attracting readership is increasingly competitive for new entrants into the market. A blog—just like any other web product—needs a strong branding to be recognizable in the vast jungle of web content. But creating a brand from scratch is a costly endeavour. It is very unlikely that blogs in the future will act as aggregators of a community, like FP2P could do. Rather, a potential blogger now needs to feed off from an existing community or network. Hence the increasing popularity of platforms like Medium[59] that supposedly can help to draw traffic on one's articles by linking up with existing readerships interested in some topics. Overall my point is that FP2P's experience is not easily replicable nowadays. While blogging will not probably disappear soon—and organisations might wish to continue investing in it, exploiting their existing networks, for a number of reasons including those you highlight—individual blogs as platforms are likely to dwindle and maybe disappear.

Other commenters had similar concerns that blogs are losing their human, individual character as they become institutionalized: 'Blogs started off as a platform for individual expression, and are now being used by organisations for marketing (NGOs included).'

Conclusion

Oxfam's continued support for FP2P confirms my own opinion that blogging is a valuable addition to the repertoire of the public conversation on development and aid, enriching arguments and improving impact. It has the potential to put those interested in a given issue in more direct, disintermediated contact with others, while still retaining a place for knowledge and depth of analysis (unlike, say, Twitter). Although institutional cultures, whether in academia or aid institutions, often struggle to adapt to the rhythm and informality required by good blogging, both the wider evidence and my personal experience suggests the effort is worthwhile. I hope that this chapter makes that case, and offers some ideas for ways to strengthen the blogging culture in our organizations.

[59] Available at https://medium.com/.

Acknowledgements

I would like to thank Edward Bourque, Kevin Cook, Tobias Denskus, Alice Evans, María Faciolince, Greta Galeazzi, Matt Haikin, Patricia Lanigan, David Lewis, Amy Moran, Daniela Lloyd-Williams, Lucia Nass, Dennis Rodgers, and Michael Woolcock for their help with this chapter. Any errors are my own.

References

Denskus T. and A. Papan (2013) 'Reflexive engagements: The international development blogging evolution and its challenges', *Development in Practice* 23(4): 455–67.

Eyben, R. (2014) *International Aid and the Making of a Better World: Reflexive Practice.* London: Routledge.

Green, D. (2008) *From Poverty to Power: How Active Citizens and Effective States can Change the World.* Oxford: Oxfam International.

Green, D. (2016) *How Change Happens.* Oxford: Oxford University Press.

Intermedia (2012) *Building Support for International Development.* London: Intermedia.

Lewis, D., D. Rodgers, and M. Woolcock (eds) (2014) *Popular Representations of Development: Insights from Novels, Films, Television and Social Media.* New York: Routledge.

Manning, R. (2014) 'FollowMe,IntDev,Com: International development in the blogosphere', in D. Lewis, D. Rodgers, and M. Woolcock (eds) *Popular Representations of Development: Insights from Novels, Films, Television and Social Media.* London: Routledge, pp. 213–40.

6
Playing for Change
International Development and Digital Games

Jolene Fisher

Introduction

The first international development-oriented video game, *Food Force*, was launched in 2005 by the United Nations World Food Programme. The downloadable PC game, which was aimed at children ages 8–13, took players to a fictitious island to teach them about the challenges of addressing hunger crises through six different emergency-aid missions. *Food Force*, which was downloaded over 6 million times and played by approximately 10 million people, was considered a hit. Since then, over forty digital games have been created specifically as tools for international development.

These digital development games have been designed both to supplement and/or replace on-the-ground development projects in the Global South, and to raise support (both rhetorical and material) for development projects from audiences in the Global North. The latter type of game, which works to teach players what development *is* and *how* it should be accomplished, is especially of interest here. Like other mediated texts about development, these games have the potential to shape public discourse and support around development practice, perpetuating the growth of certain projects and approaches over others. But, unlike other mediated texts, the interactive nature of digital games can be used to allow players to feel they are actually part of the development process. Such was the case in the *Half the Sky Movement: The Game* (hereafter referred to as Half the Sky Game), which not only taught players about issues facing women and girls around the world, it allowed them to directly support various development projects aimed at addressing those issues through gameplay.

The Half the Sky Game, which ran from 2013–16, was one piece of the transmedia project the Half the Sky Movement, based on the book *Half the Sky: Turning Oppression into Opportunity for Women Worldwide*, by journalists and husband and wife team, Nicholas Kristof and Sheryl WuDunn (2009). The book, 'from two of our most fiercely moral voices', according to the jacket description, is a 'passionate call to arms against our era's most pervasive human rights violation: the

Jolene Fisher, *Playing for Change.* In: *New Mediums, Better Messages?.*
Edited by David Lewis, Dennis Rodgers, and Michael Woolcock, Oxford University Press.
 DOI: 10.1093/oso/9780198858751.003.0007

oppression of women and girls in the developing world' (see Half the Sky, n.d.). The authors' goal was to 'recruit' the reader into a worldwide movement to end what they refer to as the key moral challenge of our time.

But although the book reached many people (it was a national best-seller, was included on several 'Best Books of the Year' lists, and received broad mainstream media praise), Kristof and WuDunn wanted to find a way to reach 'beyond the converted'—the non-fiction reading, documentary watching, *New York Times* subscribing audience already alert to and interested in issues of global gender inequality. They found what they were looking for in a Facebook game that could capture a US-based, social-game playing audience, teach them about the issues facing women in the developing world, and present them with solutions that the players themselves could financially support. Over the course of three years, the Half the Sky Game brought in over 1 million players, raised just over US$500,000 in sponsored and individual donations, and received numerous celebrity endorsements and media impressions. But what kind of development project was the Half the Sky Game engaging players in?

This chapter uses the Half the Sky Game as a case study to highlight the ways in which the narrative storytelling and procedural rhetoric of a game are used to frame for players a specific approach to development. In the case of this game, it is an approach based on empowering women in the 'developing world' via microfinance and small-scale business solutions. According to Kristof, bringing women and girls 'out of the margins, into the formal labor force' is the most important thing to do right now, at a global level (Lamont Hill, 2013). An analysis of the Half the Sky Game makes clear how the game works to teach players about the benefits of financial empowerment projects in an effort to turn them into 'hardcore activists' who would support the movement's cause through in-game donations.

But, while such an approach is in line with mainstream neoliberal development logic, it is at odds with feminist and critical development approaches, which argue financial-empowerment projects belie the structural changes necessary to actually end women's oppression and achieve gender equality. By situating this understanding of the game within the historical context of development discourse, it is clear how the game broadens the audience not only for the Half the Sky Movement specifically, but for a neoliberal approach to development more generally. Understanding what audiences are learning and supporting through digital development games like this one is an important area of study, especially as enthusiasm for digital games in international development continues to grow.

Half the Sky Movement: The Game

Nicholas Kristof and Sheryl WuDunn envisioned a digital game about women's oppression as a way to bring the ideas of the Half the Sky Movement to millions of people. According to a member of Games for Change, the New York-based nonprofit that directed the production of the game, Kristof and WuDunn 'kind of got infected with the virus of "Let's do games"'. They thought about it as a cool way to reach 'audiences that may not necessarily watch the [Half the Sky] documentary, or read [Kristof's columns in] the *New York Times*'. A game would enable them to reach 'beyond the converted', as Kristof was fond of saying.

According to a member of the Games for Change team, what Kristof and WuDunn cared about most was reaching an audience in the 'West', because 'the way they think about change is first of all focusing on people in the US and Europe that could influence their government, that could contribute money ... that's the whole way they think about it'. Thus, the game was designed specifically for a US-based audience that could provide both rhetorical and material support for the movement's projects. By designing the game for Facebook, the movement could encourage players to spread the word about what they learned and invite friends to join with them in the game as they take Radhika, the game's main character, on 'a journey from oppression to opportunity' (Half the Sky Trailer, 2013).

The Facebook platform also allowed players to donate directly to the Half the Sky Movement through in-game donations and purchases. The movement's ultimate goal was to convince players to engage in their specific brand of digital activism: 'We wanted to reach the widest audience possible, but turn a small percentage into real activists, into hardcore activists that would really make a difference in the real world by donating money,' said Asi Burak, president of Games for Change from 2010 to 2015 (Gamification Co., 2013).

The Half the Sky Game begins in India, where the player is introduced to the main character, Radhika. As the player progresses through the game, Radhika travels from her home in India to Kenya, Vietnam, Afghanistan, and the United States. In each locale Radhika is introduced to new women and is tasked with helping them address the issues they face. She cannot travel forward in the game until she has unlocked the next location, accomplished via a series of factors that includes play-time and wait-time, task completion, in-game donations, and in-game purchases. After a minimal amount of play, players must either pay (via an in-game purchase) or wait 24-hours before continuing.

As the game progresses, the player has to complete various tasks. Some of these tasks involve built in mini-games, which mimic casual games like *Candy Crush* and ask players to connect a row of similar game pieces together; others involve narrative choices that determine the actions of characters in the game. Regardless of wait-time between sessions, it is often necessary to make in-game purchases (e.g. paying US$2.00-$5.00 to buy energy points) to continue gameplay. Thus, while the game appears to be free to play, only the first location, India, truly is.

The player quickly learns that Radhika is unable to afford medicine for her sick child and needs to find a way to earn money. As the player takes Radhika on her 'journey from oppression to opportunity' she regularly encounters a development narrative of self-help and economic empowerment. Radhika must find ways to earn money and support herself by selling mangoes in the market, applying for a microcredit loan, and buying a goat and selling its milk.

The player gets the chance to see Radhika pursue non-economic activities in India as she works on her reading skills with her children, volunteers at a local clinic, and joins a women's empowerment group; but the game's emphasis quickly returns to the topic of financial empowerment. For instance, the members of the women's empowerment group that Radhika joins are happy to have her there not only because they 'value their time together', but because now they will have the necessary number of people to secure a micro-loan, which Radhika will use to add a room onto her home.

Once Radhika has helped herself, she is able to support other women in her community and beyond. She begins by helping a young woman named Malika avoid early marriage by convincing her to join the women's empowerment group. At her first meeting, Malika is told to go and gather seeds from the forest that she can sell for money. Because Malika has done well, Radhika gives her a gift of money which Malika uses to take computer classes so she can better track her inventory and customers. Once Malika has proven her productive value to her family, they agree to let her postpone her marriage.

Radhika eventually leaves India in order to help women in other countries. In Kenya she helps a group of nurses decide if they will sell mosquito nets or give them away for free. She also works to organize a community discussion on gender and family planning after a local football match, but she is run out of town by an angry mob before the talk can occur. In Vietnam she helps buy back a young woman who was forced into sex trafficking, and she weaves fishing nets to sell to raise money for a community centre for trafficked girls. Interestingly, Radhika must compete against another woman in town who is already making and selling fishing nets in the community. In a meeting between the two women, Radhika gladly takes her on, noting that *her* nets will be the best one can buy. She soon makes a trip back home to India where she joins a friend in a new business venture making beaded clothing. Next, she's off to Afghanistan to help a group of women start a local newspaper and to organize them around a vote for women's right to own property. However, the vote fails and the player learns that political change is a long and cumbersome process.

When a woman back in India asks Radhika how she is able to travel the world and make 'big money', Radhika describes her hard work and sacrifice as 'the only solution'. Radhika is encouraged to run for local office and she tells her friends from the empowerment group that as part of her platform she will work to back micro-finance and micro-saving initiatives in order to 'give everyone the opportunity I was given'. When asked to give a speech at the United Nations, Radhika discusses the oppression she has seen and the opportunities brought about when we invest in women to ensure they are healthier and smarter. While in the US, Radhika learns that sex trafficking is a globally connected issue: not only does she meet victims from the US, she discovers that the girl she helped save in Vietnam has been sent to New York by traffickers. She encourages the victims to learn skills and empower themselves as she did.

As the game progresses, so does Radhika's capacity to solve more problems, both for herself and for others. Throughout the game, Radhika helps a variety of women, and some men, with a range of problems. The solution to these problems generally comes in one of three forms: individual economic empowerment (e.g. sell seeds, start a business); non-financial material resources (e.g. mosquito nets, cook stoves); and cultural or political change (e.g. family planning conversations, a vote to allow women to own property). In the course of the game, however, only the individual economic empowerment solutions and the non-financial material resources solutions prove consistently successful.

Throughout the game there are instances in which Radhika takes a political stance in an attempt to enact broad social change. This is seen specifically in her efforts to host a community conversation around family planning, in her campaign to run for local office, in her support for a law allowing Afghani women to own property, and in her speech at the United Nations. Although the importance of political organizing is presented to players through Radhika's successful run for office, the only outcome of her achievement comes in the form of speeches—one is on the importance of micro-lending practices, the other, at the UN, focuses on her own story of changing her life through hard work. Further, two of these cultural/political change solutions—hosting a community discussion around family planning and birth control in Kenya, and having a vote on women's right to own property in Afghanistan—are total failures. In the first, Radhika is run out of town before the discussion can take place, and in the second the vote does not pass. The player is shown the successful potential of community organizing when Radhika convinces others in her home town to join with her and take to the streets to protest against violence against women, which results in the arrest and imprisonment of a rapist. But more often players see that this approach does not result in successful outcomes.

Alternatively, the scenarios that involve financial empowerment always prove successful and lead to great gain for women at a variety of levels. It is through economic solutions (convincing other women to get a loan, going into business with them, selling a goat to them) that Radhika is able to most effectively help the women around her. While Radhika participates in a variety of activities, some of which bring groups of women together to fight for change in nuanced ways, the moments of actual change in the game—when the female players successfully transition from 'oppression' to 'opportunity'—are predicated on financial gain. Unlocking her own earning potential and building up a small business allowed Radhika to change her own life, and it is the key she presents to others along the way. Whether it is selling one of her goats to a pregnant woman in the market so that she too can make money off of its milk, helping her friend start a business beading clothes and employing other women in the village, or helping a young woman collect seeds and take a computer class to grow her profits, Radhika helps other women move towards the same path to empowerment and opportunity—one focused on individual economic gain via individual effort.

The game provides players with information on global issues the Half the Sky Movement has identified as key to women's oppression, such as the number of women living in poverty and the number of people infected with HIV. Yet there is little given in the way of context: the women facing these issues are in India, Kenya, Afghanistan, Vietnam, and the US, but there is no explanation of regional differences regarding these issues; or of why certain women are in poverty while others are not; or how historical and current political and economic processes have impacted such issues. The player might gain a better sense of scale regarding the issues identified, but what she is unlikely to come away with is an understanding of the role asymmetrical North/South power structures play in contributing to the oppressive reality of women and exacerbating issues of inequality. Moreover, the game fails to provide any discussion of the well-documented negative effects of micro-lending practices, especially as they relate to women, as will be examined in a later section. Instead, micro-lending is presented as a critical component of women's empowerment.

Empowering Players

Thanks to the movement's professional marketing campaign, celebrity endorsements, and help from gaming giant Zygna (which included the game on its scrolling Z-Bar), one month after its release the Half the Sky Game's Facebook page had brought in 1,487,306 views and 547,511 people had installed the game. Although the Half the Sky Game eventually brought in over 1 million players, only a few thousand actually played the game all the way through. Thus, the majority of players only encountered the early storylines in the game, almost all of which are based on economic empowerment. The idea of political organizing and group action for social change, which comes much later in the game, would never be encountered by most. Instead, players would leave the game with a positive narrative of micro-lending and small business ventures as key to women's empowerment.

But money doesn't merely drive the storyline forward—it drives the gameplay itself. Without making a financial contribution via in-game donations or purchases it becomes impossible to continue to play. Players automatically unlock sponsored portions of a US$500,000 donation by Johnson&Johnson and the Pearson Foundation simply by playing the game. But, they are also asked to facilitate the game's so-called 'virtual-to-real-life translation' by contributing personal donations to the game's non-profit partners. For instance, after Radhika prospers from buying a goat and selling its milk, the player is asked to help a woman in real life by purchasing a goat through Heifer International. WuDunn points to this as the 'social impact element' of the game: 'You aren't playing just for fun. You actually can have an impact' (Lamont Hill, 2013). According to WuDunn, the game has 'actually married the problems with the solutions', so players don't simply learn what is wrong in the world, they also learn how to fix it and are given direct access to act on that knowledge (Lamont Hill, 2013). By making a game for Facebook, the movement was able not only to access a new audience; they were able also to use that audience's playtime to generate real funds for their NGO-led projects.

As Kristof emphasized in an interview with HuffPo Live, a Facebook game is 'a very low barrier way to expose yourself to the issues' (Lamont Hill, 2013). The game creates an opportunity for engagement that requires little change in behaviour (in terms of time, money, energy, etc.) on the side of the player. And the players, most of whom were women in the US between the ages of 18 and 34, loved how easy it was to feel like they were doing good simply by playing the game. On Facebook, a player chosen to test the beta version of the game pre-launch wondered if this kind of easy impact could be real. Her post reads:

> Hi guys. Is this for real??? Did I really just do this??? I've read all about the movement, etc. but by me playing a game, a school really receives one book???
>
> Even if I don't have actual money to donate, myself? Sorry for being so skeptical, but it seems too good to be true. If this is the case ... I guarantee you on March 4th, I will be spreading the word about this game.

For many players, the game was all about 'Unlocking donations by playing, and reminding myself how much help others need in the world'. Once players have provided financial support to the movement, either by unlocking sponsored donations through gameplay (which happens early on in the game), or making in-game donations and purchases, they often felt a sense of action and empowerment at having helped a 'real-life woman' in the Global South. As one player said on Twitter, 'I donated a book (for free!) to @RoomtoRead by playing for a short period of time. So empowering'. Other players on Twitter called the game 'an easy and fun way to create change', a way to make a 'real difference', a game that 'Empowers Women & Donates to Charity', a 'great way to make money for social causes', and 'something you can do right now ... to help real-world women'. One player posted a screen shot from the game that read, 'You've reached the rank of community advocate!' with the added text, 'What I achieved last night before bed'.

But even when players didn't expect such direct real world impact, simply playing the game provided a sense of catharsis. In a Facebook post about her favourite in-game quest, saving a girl from a brothel, one player recounts that:

> It was my favorite because those chapters in the book affected me so much. I wanted to help every girl and woman whose stories were told, but I really wanted to go out and rescue every single girl in every brothel and give her shelter and education and love and safety. I know that I didn't actually rescue anyone in the game, but ... I don't know, I just felt better afterwards.

In the end, the opportunity the game presented to easily engage in the development process and participate in empowering women-in-need was well received by players.

The game engaged players in what Dingo (2012) refers to as the 'mega-rhetoric of empowerment'—a mainstreamed, naturalized discourse, in which it is assumed that women's empowerment is equal to women's financial security. Because the player has given money (either by directly donating funds herself or by unlocking material goods and services through gameplay) she can 'simply forget about the broader context of poverty and feel assuaged by his or her action' (Dingo, 2012: 177). But if the solution to women's empowerment is indeed financial support generated through gameplay, there is little reason to consider broader political action once this support has been given. Nor is there reason to critically consider the implications of the player's position within an asymmetrical global system. Instead, the positioning of the game player supports a hierarchy of expertise, power, and agency, which rests with the women who have the access, resources, and skills to play the game, and which constructs them as most capable of directing and impacting the lives of women throughout the Global South. In the game, individual players are asked to join in on the development process by generating the investments that will allow for the empowerment of women and girls in the real world. Players can help Radhika and real women get money and goods by donating directly to the nonprofits featured in the game, or by purchasing in-game goods necessary to continue gameplay. This emphasis on individual aid from those in the Global North aligns nicely with a broader neoliberal development agenda that 'reduces social change to entrepreneurship in a market-based system, and civic involvement and voice to clicktivism' (Wilkins and Enghel, 2013: 169).

The discourse around poor women and market participation that players learn and support through the game is not new. It is, in fact, reflective of the mainstream discourse within both the development industry and the corporate social responsibility field that promotes 'Gender Equality as Smart Economics'. This line of thinking advances a 'neoliberal economic policy agenda characterized by market fundamentalism, deregulation and corporate led-development' (Calkin, 2015; 296), while doing little to question or dismantle global and local power structures that create and reinforce gender inequality. Such a discourse shifts the responsibility of individual, communal, and even national level development directly onto poor women (Wilson, 2015). In this context, challenging issues of gender inequality, specifically the rates of poverty facing women in the developing world, is most effectively achieved through individual effort, self-help programmes, microcredit loans, and small business ventures—all of which the game reinforces.

The problem, of course, is that when the concept of individual empowerment is emphasized above all else, the constraints that social inequalities place on achieving individual success are erased, creating a depoliticized approach that supports a 'neoliberal project, in which market-based exchanges are assumed to be beneficial without serious critique' (Wilkins and Enghel, 2013: 170). To better understand this narrative of financial empowerment and gender equality seen in the game, the Half the Sky Movement must be situated within broader development discourse. The following section outlines the contemporary moment in which the game was conceived, and the historical context of gender and development that led to it.

Women's Empowerment and Neoliberal Development: The Game in Context

When Nicholas Kristof and Sheryl Wudunn published their book, *Half the Sky: Turning Oppression into Opportunity for Women Worldwide* in 2009, it quickly became a best-seller. The book—which highlighted issues facing women across the 'developing world'—received tremendous praise from readers, mainstream media outlets, celebrities, and key names in the world of international development scholarship (see for instance Nussbaum, 2009). The authors also received substantial backlash on a variety of issues, from the book's paternalism to its voyeurism (see North, 2012 for a round-up of critical voices). But praise and book sales outnumbered the critiques, and Kristof and WuDunn became prominent faces in the fight to empower women and girls on a global scale.

The year 2009 also saw the induction of Hillary Clinton as the United States Secretary of State. For Clinton, empowering women and girls was a central tenet of American foreign policy. As Clinton often noted, 'Putting women and girls at the center of our foreign policy is not only the right thing to do, it's the smart thing to do' (Fleischman, 2014). By the mid-2000s, a similar focus was taking shape within a range of US-based social corporate responsibility departments, private foundations, nonprofits, and governmental organizations.

Gender Equality as Smart Economics

Empowering women and girls would come to be seen as key to solving a wide range of development problems, and the approach to empowerment set forth in these programmes—based on skills training, education, and microfinance—created strong ties between development projects and the corporate sector. As a 2013 report by the Association of Women in Development notes, within funding for women's rights three trends have emerged: a focus on empowering women and girls (at least rhetorically); the rapid growth of private corporations and foundations as development funders; and a general corporatization of development agendas (Arutynova and Clark, 2013).

This focus on empowering women and girls built, of course, on decades of work around issues of gender equality within the international development industry. Beginning with the push for the inclusion of women that led to the Women in Development (WID) movement of the 1970s—and later the Gender and Development (GAD) paradigm, a response to and critique of WID—the role of women and girls in international development would become a key point of discussion (although actual support for gender projects would remain limited). By the release of the Millennium Development Goals in 2000 (in which promoting gender equality and empowering women was goal number three of eight) women and girls had become integral to the concept of development.

After years of sharp critique from feminist and other critical scholars on the failures to include women in development planning and projects (Boserup, 1970; Spivak, 1988; Mohanty et al., 1991; Cornwall et al., 2007;) the newfound focus on policy around women and girls would seem to be a victory. However, as Calkin (2015) noted, 'these ostensible gains require close feminist scrutiny because much of the gender equality policy discourse is so closely tied to the advancement of a neoliberal economic policy agenda characterized by market fundamentalism, deregulation and corporate-led development', a process that does little to achieve gender equality, and instead deepens it for its own gain (p. 296).

In 2006, the World Bank unveiled a new slogan for its gender and development approach: 'Gender Equality as Smart Economics.' The slogan epitomizes the framing of women and girls as an 'untapped resource' in development, emphasizing a return on investment in the form of economic growth to be made when women are given the resources necessary to access and participate in the global marketplace. Wilson (2015) argued that the notion of Smart Economics is 'premised on the assumption that women will always work harder, and be more productive, than their male counterparts; further they will use additional income more productively than men would' (p. 807). Thus, investing in women (in the form of skills training and micro-loans to be used towards small business ventures) and young girls (in the form of education as a precursor to employment) is seen as good business.

A range of private corporations and public institutions have since taken up a 'business case for gender equality', and numerous empowerment projects have been created through partnerships between nonprofit organizations and corporations, the numbers of which continue to grow (Calkin, 2015). Two prominent examples are The Girl Effect, launched in 2008 by the Nike Foundation, and the 10,000 Women initiative, launched in 2008 by Goldman Sachs. For large corporations looking to 'do good while doing well', investing in women and girls presents an appealing opportunity: these types of empowerment projects are seen as 'straightforward transactions, a matter of putting money directly into the hands of women and girls, training them in the arts of the market, and watching them flourish as they lift their families, communities, and national economies', all the while creating new markets and new sources of corporate profit (Cornwall, 2014: 131). But linking women's empowerment to women's market participation shifts the burden of responsibility for poverty alleviation onto these women, challenging and oppressing them in new ways, while a global market system deepens the divide between the haves and the have nots (Kabeer, 1994; Alvarez, 1999; Aguilar and Lacsaman, 2004; Karim, 2011; Wilson, 2015).

The Smart Economics approach is fuelled by a discourse on the underutilization of women's entrepreneurial potential. This framing of women is accomplished through 'an assemblage of transnational policy discourses, novel corporate investment priorities, biopolitical interventions, branding and marketing campaigns, [and] charitable events designed to produce a social movement for change and designer goods' (Koffman and Gill, 2013: 84). As outlined in the previous section, the Half the Sky Game works to further this discourse by calling on game players to support, both rhetorically and materially, an approach to women's empowerment built on individual economic gain.

This specific type of empowerment process calls on global corporations and already empowered individuals in the Global North—in this case, the game players—to invest in women and girls. But once they have made that initial investment, 'responsibility shifts entirely onto the individualized figure of the girl, as "she will do the rest"' (Wilson, 2015: 819). Such a framework ensures that critiques of global systems of power, and the disruptions that lead to global economic crises like the one seen in 2008, are made irrelevant (Wilson, 2015). Further, the role of capitalism and globalization in burdening women in the Global South, including the ways in which a focus on women's labour creates the flexible, low-wage labour markets necessary for the accumulation of global capital, is glossed over (Aguilar and Lacsamana, 2004; Pearson, 2005; Wilson, 2015).

The use of micro-finance as a path towards women's market participation is glorified within the game and within the broader discourse around women's empowerment. And yet, an extensive body of academic research illuminates the ways such a system oppresses women in the developing world, often benefiting the middle class at the expense of the poorest (Mayoux, 2010; Karim, 2011; Wilson, 2015). As Wilson (2015: 809) stated, 'microfinance epitomizes the neoliberal focus on the individual, and on moving up hierarchies rather than collectively challenging or dismantling them'. This in turn weakens potential solidarities across class and gender; and reinforces the idea that responsibility for poverty alleviation rests with individual, poor women rather than large institutional bodies and/or the state.

Further, the broad generalizations made about the positive relationship between economic growth and gender equality seen in the Smart Economics discourse is inaccurate at best and dishonest at worst. The relationship between the two is 'mediated by a variety of contextual factors' (Kabeer, 2016: 295). And while there have been numerous studies citing the benefits of gender equality for economic growth, 'reverse findings relating to the impact of economic growth on gender equality are far less consistent', and are found generally only in high-income countries (Kabeer, 2016: 299).

The Smart Economics framework presents a form of empowerment that actively works to 'train and shape bodies for particular forms of economic agency and participation' (Calkin, 2015: 302). It further works to 'actively reinforce and extend, existing patriarchal structures and gendered relationships of power' (Wilson, 2015: 808). As the model neoliberal subject 'is one who strategizes for her/himself among various social, political and economic options, not one who strives with others to alter or organize these options', a discourse like the one seen in the Half the Sky Game is useful for the expansion of a global market-based system, for it teaches players to expect women to work within the system, rather than ask players to critique the system itself (Brown, 2003: 15).

Bringing women and gender into the development discourse has been an arduous task, and the mainstream focus on gender inequality and issues facing women is something to celebrate. However, the current neoliberal discourse around women and girls is used to 'legitimize harmful neoliberal economic policies, empower corporate actors in the governance process, compound the invisibility of social reproduction and close off space for resistance by anti-capitalist feminists' (Calkin, 2015: 305). Such a discourse fails to question asymmetrical North/South power structures and economic flows that contribute to the difficult reality of women in the Global South. Women's inequality, instead of becoming a challenge to a system that is inherently unequal, is depoliticized and used to promote new market subjects (Elson, 1995; Karim, 2011).

Games as Ideological Tools

Through the creation of development oriented games like the Half the Sky Game, organizations are adding a new text to the discourse about development—framing for players how development should be carried out, on whom it should focus, and what the end goal should be. From a game studies perspective, video games are a perfect tool for generating and distributing such a message (Dovey and Kennedy, 2006). In creating the software for games, producers, designers, etc. construct realities for players that are filled with the value systems, world views, and norms of the designer, whether embedded in the games intentionally or not (Flanagan, 2006). The idea that technological systems, devices, and artefacts are value-laden is not new, or exclusive to games (Winner, 1977; Hughes, 1983; MacKenzie and Wajcman, 1985; Latour, 1987). But games are an especially pertinent area of study as game designers, through the production of software, are 'in essence creating worldviews and worlds' that they ask players to interact with (Flanagan, 2006: 493). Further, embedding ideologies in games works well as players are called on to take them up via the specific subject positions constructed through virtual play. These virtual subject positions create a subtle, 'more flexible order where users of their own initiative adopt the identities required by the system' (Dyer-Witheford and de Peuter, 2009: 193).

Considered 'the media of Empire' in the twenty-first century, games often work in favour of global hypercapitalism as digital gameplay 'trains flexible personalities for flexible jobs, shapes subjects for militarized markets, and makes becoming a neoliberal subject fun' (Dyer-Witheford and De Peuter, 2009, xxix–xxx). In the case of the Half the Sky Game, it is about teaching players the benefits of neoliberal development and training them to appreciate and support such projects. In this way, games have the potential to 'shape work, learning, health care and more', including the field of international development (Flanagan and Nissenbaum, 2014: 3).

Game studies scholars argue that a textual, critically oriented analysis of games is necessary (Bogost, 2006; Flanagan, 2006; Flanagan and Nissenbaum, 2014; Fernandez-Vara, 2015). And an analysis of the ideological framing of development in digital games is necessary as a continued critique of the broader international development industry discourse (Escobar, 1984; Wilkins, 1999). Development oriented games, like any other mediated development narrative, work within a broader development discourse to frame our understanding of the field both in terms of the pertinent issues that should be addressed by the development industry and the best (or possible) solutions to them (Arce, 2003). This framing has important implications for the types of development projects carried out, the types of policies supported, and the kinds of solutions that gain acceptance (Hajer, 1995; Cornwall et al., 2007). As Cornwall et al. (2017) argued, 'The struggles for interpretive power are not struggles to get the language and representations right for their own sake, but because they are a critical part in the determination of policy' (p. 17). As seen in the analysis of the Half the Sky Game, digital development games work in favour of particular kinds of solutions, and they engage players in building direct support for them.

While players might have encountered a similar narrative of women's empowerment in other spaces, the Half the Sky Game is the first to present this discourse directly to a social-media gaming audience. Further, it is the first to link gameplay directly to the material support of these types of empowerment projects: players unlock sponsored donations simply by playing and are encouraged to make individual donations as part of the game's so-called virtual-to-real-world translation. Thus the game emphasizes both the importance of economic gain for women in the Global South and the need for economic support from women in the Global North. Approaches to empowerment that focus on financial exchange between individuals in the Global North and Global South reinforce the 'notion of personal agency and monetary exchange over a broader feminist understanding of the transnational contexts that make donations, charity work, and development programs in the first place' (Dingo, 2012: 177).

While the game narrative touches on a variety of gender related issues and presents the player with nuanced moments that begin to hint at the complexity of systemic problems like poverty and gender based violence, the overarching ideology embedded in the game is built on an approach to individual empowerment in which one must overcome structural, cultural, and personal barriers to achieve economic gain. The game was designed specifically to take this message 'beyond the converted'—to bring the issues of the Half the Sky Movement to an audience unfamiliar with them, and to directly connect solutions to problems so that players gain not only an understanding of what is happening in the world, but also a clear sense of what needs to be done to address the issues.

Conclusion

Despite over a decade of use, digital games are represented as innovative, revolutionary tools in popular discussions of development and social change. This framing of games is not unlike the narratives around Information Communication Technologies (ICTs) that positioned them as a 'magic solution' for development (Ogan et al., 2009: 667). Yet little research has actually examined the type of development these games support. As the global Serious Games industry—of which digital development games are a part—continues to grow rapidly (with a projected market value of US$5 billion by 2020) we need to ask not whether development-oriented games are changing the world, but what type of change they encourage.

In the Half the Sky Game, and others like it, players are presented with an opportunity to feel they are engaging directly with the process of development: through gameplay, they learn that important gains are made when women participate in economic activities, and that such participation brings positive outcomes not only for the woman herself but for her community and the world at large. Further, players are able to generate material support for similar real-life projects by unlocking sponsored donations and contributing their own funds to the Half the Sky Movement. As such, the Half the Sky Game presents a novel way both to teach audiences about development and to encourage their participation in the process through individual aid.

However, as outlined in this chapter, the narrative that the game reinforces—a mainstream, neoliberal approach to development that frames poor women as responsible for overcoming social, cultural, and economic obstacles in order to change their lives for the better—has negative implications for poor women in the Global South as it works to erase the root causes of inequality while framing women as an 'untapped resource'. Through the narrative of self-help and individual empowerment, the burden placed on poor women is increased.

Thanks to its Facebook-based game, the Half the Sky Movement was able to extend this narrative to 1 million gameplayers, as well as countless others who read the many media stories about the game. While the game was less than successful in turning gameplayers into 'hardcore activists' who would willingly donate their own money to the cause (only 10 per cent of all donations came from individuals), players were enthusiastic about the opportunity to support this brand of women's empowerment simply by playing.

Future research in this area should continue to give critical attention to the development ideologies embedded in games, as they are a growing channel for distributing development messages to a broad audience. But the political economic implications of the production of digital games for development should be examined as well. Thus far, the majority of digital development games have been created and supported by development institutions and commercial gaming companies situated in the Global North. As smaller game industries emerge throughout the world, it will be necessary to examine the ways in which production, knowledge, and technology hierarchies are disrupted, or reinforced.

References

Aguilar, D.D. and A. E. Lacsamana (2004) *Women and Globalization*. Amherst, NY: Humanity Books.

Alvarez, S.E. (1999) 'Advocating feminism: The Latin American feminist NGO 'boom'', *International Feminist Journal of Politics* 1(2): 181–209.

Arce, A. (2003) 'Re-approaching social development: A field of action between social life and policy processes', *Journal of International Development* 15(7): 845–61.

Arutynova, A. and C. Clark (2013) 'Watering the leaves, starving the roots: The status of financing women's rights organizing and gender equality', AWID Women's Rights' Report from the Association for Women's Rights in Development, available at http://www.awid.org/sites/default/files/atoms/files/WTL_Starving_Roots.pdf.

Bogost, I. (2006) 'Videogames and ideological frames', *Popular Communication* 4(3): 165–183.

Boserup, E. (1970) *Women's Role in Economic Development*. London: Allen & Unwin.

Brown, W. (2003) 'Neo-liberalism and the end of liberal democracy', *Theory & Event* 7(1), https://muse.jhu.edu/article/48659.

Calkin, S. (2015) 'Feminism, interrupted? Gender and development in the era of 'Smart Economics', *Progress in Development Studies* 15(4): 295–307.

Cornwall, A. (2014) 'Taking off international development's straightjacket of gender', *The Brown Journal of World Affairs* 21(1): 127–139.

Cornwall, A., E. Harrison, and A. Whitehead (2007) *Feminisms in Development: Contradictions, Contestations and Challenges*. London: Zed Books.

Dingo, R.A. (2012) 'Turning the tables on the megarhetoric of women's empowerment', in R. A. Dingo and J. B. Scott (eds) *The Megarhetorics of Global Development*. Pittsburgh, PA: University of Pittsburgh Press, pp. 174–98.

Dovey, J. and H. W. Kennedy (2006) *Game Cultures: Computer Games as New Media*. New York: Open University Press.

Dyer-Witheford, N. and G. de Peuter (2009) *Games of Empire: Global Capitalism and Video Games*. Minneapolis, MN: University of Minnesota Press.

Elson, D. (1995) 'Gender awareness in modeling structural adjustment', *World Development* 23(11): 1851–68.

Escobar, A. (1984) 'Discourse and power in development: Michel Foucault and the relevance of his work to the Third World', *Alternatives* 10(3): 377–400.

Fernandez-Vara, C. (2015) *Introduction to Game Analysis*. New York: Routledge.

Flanagan, M. (2006) 'Making games for social change', *AI & Society* 20(4): 493–505.

Flanagan, M. and H. Nissenbaum (2014) *Values at Play in Digital Games*. Cambridge, MA: MIT Press.

Fleischman, J. (2014) 'Why it's time to put women's issues at center of foreign policy', Center for Strategic & International Studies. https://www.csis.org/blogs/smart-global-health/why-it%E2%80%99s-time-put-women%E2%80%99s-issues-center-foreign-policy

Gamification Co. (2013) 'Asi Burak – Half the Sky: Lessons from Games for Change', available at https://www.youtube.com/watch?v=clwRENB4PMQ.

Hajer, M.A. (1995) 'Politics on the move: The democratic control of the design of sustainable technologies', *Knowledge Technology & Policy* 8(4): 26–39.

Half the Sky n.d. 'About', available at http://www.halftheskymovement.org/pages/about-half-the-sky-movement.html.

Half the Sky Trailer (2013) 'Introducing Half the Sky Movement: The Game', available at https://www.youtube.com/watch?v=emmCKa-YmDg&t=34s.

Hughes, T.P. (1983) *Networks of Power*. Baltimore, MD: Johns Hopkins University Press.

Kabeer, N. (1994) *Reversed Realities: Gender Hierarchies in Development Thought*. London: Verso.

Kabeer, N. (2016) 'Gender equality, economic growth, and women's agency: The 'endless variety' and 'monotonous similarity' of patriarchal constraints', *Feminist Economics* 22(1): 295–322.

Karim, L. (2011) *Microfinance and its Discontents: Women in Debt in Bangladesh*. Minneapolis, MN: University of Minnesota Press.

Koffman, O. and R. Gill (2013) "The revolution will be led by a 12-year-old-girl': Girl power and global biopolitics', *Feminist Review* 105(1): 83–102.

Kristof, N. and S. WuDunn (2009) *Half the Sky: Turning Oppression into Opportunity for Women Worldwide*. New York: Vintage.

Lamont Hill, M. (2013) 'Empowering women through Facebook', March 4, available at http://live.huffingtonpost.com/r/segment/half-the-sky-movement/51192ce778c90a5caa0003c5.

Latour, B. (1987) *Science in Action: How to Follow Scientists and Engineers through Society*. Cambridge MA: Harvard University Press.

MacKenzie D. and J. Wajcman (1985) *The Social Shaping of Technology*. Philadelphia, PA: Open University Press.

Mayoux, L. (2010) 'Reaching and empowering women: Towards a gender justice protocol for a diversified, inclusive, and sustainable financial sector', *Perspectives on Global Development and Technology* 9(3–4): 581–600.
Mohanty, C.T., A. Russo, and L. Torres (1991) *Third World Women and the Politics of Feminism*. Bloomington, IN: Indiana University Press.
North, A. (2012) 'The anti-Nicholas Kristof backlash: Criticisms of the way the Times columnist covers women in the developing world, especially sex workers, are mounting. What's the alternative?' October 3, available at https://www.buzzfeed.com/annanorth/the-anti-nicholas-kristof-backlash?utm_term=.dgvXYN9MwG#.ucYLJ6egxN.
Nussbaum, M. (2009) 'Seeing women's rights as a key to countries' progress', *New York Times*, September 7, available at http://nytimes.com/2009/09/08/books/08nussbaum.html?_r=0.
Ogan, C. L., M. Bashir, L. Camaj, Y. Luo, B. Gaddie, R. Pennington, S. Rana and M. Salih (2009) 'Development communication: The state of research in an era of ICTs and globalization', *International Communication Gazette* 71(8): 655–670.
Pearson, R. (2005) 'The rise and rise of gender and development', in U. Kothari, J. Harriss, and R. Chambers (eds) *A Radical History of Development Studies: Individuals, Institutions and Ideologies*. London: Zed Books, pp. 157–79.
Spivak, G.C. (1988) 'Can the subaltern speak?', in C. Nelson and L. Grossberg (eds) *Marxism and the Interpretation of Culture*. London: Macmillan Education, pp. 271–313.
Wilkins, K.G. (1999) 'Development discourse on gender and communication in strategies for social change', *Journal of Communication* 49(1): 46–68.
Wilkins, K.G. and F. Enghel (2013) 'The privatization of development through global communication industries: Living proof?', *Media, Culture & Society* 35(2): 165–81.
Wilson, K. (2015) 'Towards a radical re-appropriation: Gender, development and neoliberal feminism', *Development and Change* 46(4): 803–32.
Winner, L. (1977) *Autonomous Technology: Technics-out-of-control as a Theme in Political Thought*. Cambridge, MA: MIT Press.

7

Women Saving the World

Narratives of Gender and Development on Global Radio

Emily Le Roux-Rutledge

Introduction

According to media scholar Marshall McLuhan, 'radio affects most people intimately, person to person, offering a world of unspoken communication between writer and listener. That is the immediate aspect of radio—private experience ... [It has the] power to turn the globe into a single echo chamber' (1964: 137). Not surprisingly, radio has long been used as a tool for development, including 'big D' development—the intentional practice of intervention in countries to achieve improvements or progress (Hart, 2001). This is true not just in those countries that we today think of as 'developing', but in 'developed' western economies as well. At the beginning of the twentieth century, for example radio was used in the United States to broadcast information to farmers and people in rural areas on topics such as weather, soil conditions, and crop prices (Hilliard, 2003), just as in the UK the BBC radio drama *The Archers* was used to deliver educational information to farmers in the 1950s about how to increase food production in post-war Britain.[1]

Radio and Development

Although most radio stations in high-income countries today are primarily devoted to playing popular music in order to attract an audience and sell advertising, in low and lower-middle income countries radio is still a vital source of information (Hilliard, 2003; Locksley, 2009). It is more readily available than other forms of media; it is pervasive, portable, inexpensive, and efficient; and, unlike the internet, it can be easily understood by those with low levels of literacy (Manyozo, 2009). At least 75 per cent of households in so-called developing countries have

[1] Available at http://www.bbc.co.uk/programmes/articles/5xGwGj4NgfGRJ1B2mFqg6QM/frequently-asked-questions.

Emily Le Roux-Rutledge, *Women Saving the World.* In: *New Mediums, Better Messages?.*
Edited by David Lewis, Dennis Rodgers, and Michael Woolcock, Oxford University Press.
 DOI: 10.1093/oso/9780198858751.003.0008

access to radio,[2] making it a preferred communication channel for organizations undertaking communication for development in many parts of the world.

Not all radio has equal reach, however. Radio stations range from the local to the global. At the local level, community radio is one kind of radio that has been particularly embraced by international development organizations and practitioners. It first took off in Latin America, later gaining ground in South East Asia and Africa (Manyozo, 2009). Indeed, since the 1990s, the number of community radio stations in the non-industrialized countries of Latin America, Africa, South and South East Asia, and the Pacific has exploded, with community radio growing faster than either state or commercial radio. In Africa, for example it grew, on average, 1,386 per cent between 2000 and 2006 (Myers, 2011).

Community radio is radio produced by a community, for a community, with 'community' meaning either a geographically bounded community, or a community of interest. Community radio stations are supposed to be not-for-profit, located within the communities they serve, and owned by those communities. Typically, community members who have been trained in radio production produce most of the content, and audience participation features prominently (Myers, 2011). Community radio stations are, however, often set up and funded by international NGOs, giving such NGOs a stake in the stations and the content they broadcast (Manyozo, 2009). Many stations even devote a portion of their broadcast to pre-packaged content made directly by international NGOs (LeRoux-Rutledge, 2007; LeRoux-Rutledge et al., 2011). These stations must walk a fine line between pleasing their NGO funders, and pleasing their local audiences (Manyozo, 2009; LeRoux-Rutledge, 2020). Because community radio has been seen by NGOs as a tool for development, it has been the subject of much scholarship and scrutiny within the international development field (UNESCO, 2001; Fraser and Restrepo-Estrada, 2002; Manyozo, 2009; Myers, 2011).

Far less attention has been paid, however, to global radio—transnational, publicly funded radio services, such as the BBC World Service or Voice of America, designed for an international audience (Street and Matelski, 1997). This may be because such radio services are not seen as actively contributing to 'big D' Development—although parts of them do. BBC Media Action, the BBC's international NGO, for example, has an explicit 'big D' Development remit to produce programmes on particular development issues in particular countries (Skuse et al., 2011).[3] However, much of what the BBC World Service and other transnational radio services broadcast is not designed to actively achieve development goals.

It would be wrong, however, to assume that global radio conveys no messages about development. The premise of this volume is that knowledge about

[2] Available at http://www.unesco.org/new/en/unesco/events/prizes-and-celebrations/celebrations/international-days/world-radio-day-2013/statistics-on-radio/.

[3] See BBC Media Action, available at https://www.bbc.co.uk/mediaaction/.

development takes different representational forms, and that often overlooked forms are worth exploring in order to better understand development as a complex global system of institutions and ideas. As such, this chapter will focus on the relatively unexplored format of global radio to see what insights it can yield about development—specifically, about women and development.

Focusing on Women

Some of the most crucial constituents of 'big D' development are women. Gender equality and women's empowerment have been at the top of the international development agenda for decades. In 1995, at the conclusion of the Fourth World Conference on Women in Beijing, the United Nations adopted the Beijing Declaration and Platform for Action—a global blueprint containing strategic objectives to advance gender equality and women's empowerment.[4] In 2000, 189 countries agreed on a set of Millennium Development Goals,[5] and gender equality and women's empowerment were among the goals (United Nations, 2000); and when the Sustainable Development Goals replaced the Millennium Development Goals in 2015, gender equality and women's empowerment were again among the goals, as were a range of other gender-related targets.[6]

Radio, as a medium, has long been associated with the achievement of such goals (Hilliard, 2003). It has been regarded by international development organizations as a particularly good way to reach and empower women in rural areas, who may have little education and limited access to other forms of media. Echoing this idea, media scholars have pointed out radio's 'transgressive power', highlighting 'the subversive potential of unseen voices [to challenge] ... conventional social norms' (Hilmes and Loviglio, 2001: xiii). Feminist scholars have similarly highlighted the medium's potential to contribute to a feminist public sphere, in which the 'private' sphere—traditionally associated with women—can be made public, women's interests can be represented and transformed, and forms of resistance and oppositional discourse can be set up (Jallov, 1992; Baehr and Gray, 1995; Mitchell, 1998, 2000). This feminist argument generally hinges on the idea that women can easily be both producers and consumers of radio (Mitchell, 1998). Indeed, the barriers to contributing on radio are rather lower than for television, film, or text-based media, and radio is easier to consume, as one can listen while devoting one's attention to other tasks. This is, perhaps, why radio has been seen as a good vehicle for bringing development issues concerning women to the fore (UNESCO, 2001; Gatua et al., 2010; Myers, 2011).

[4] Available at https://www.un.org/womenwatch/daw/beijing/platform/declar.htm.
[5] Available at https://www.un.org/en/development/devagenda/millennium.shtml.
[6] Available at https://sdgs.un.org/goals.

Women and Local Radio

One of the preferred ways of using radio to foreground development issues concerning women has been, unsurprisingly, at the local level, through the establishment of women's community radio stations. UNESCO has been a leader in this endeavour, establishing various women's community stations—such as Radio *Muye* in the Caribbean—as part of its *Women Speaking to Women* project (2001). Other examples of women's community radio include *Moutse* Community Radio in South Africa (Gatua et al., 2010) and *Mama* FM in Uganda (Khamalwa, 2006)—and similar examples exist in Burkina Faso, Cameroon, Niger, Nigeria, DRC, Ghana, Senegal, Mali, Jordan, Algeria, Indonesia, Fiji, India, Mexico, Haiti, and Peru (Solervicens, 2008). Even those community stations that are not run by and for women often see the inclusion of women's voices as key to their operation. Many community radio stations have at least one women's programme, and encourage women to become community journalists. Internews-funded community radio stations in South Sudan, for example, train female journalists and broadcast women's programmes (LeRoux-Rutledge, 2016), while Bush Radio in South Africa has a policy of not running training programmes in radio production for new community journalists unless at least 50 per cent of the trainees are women (UNESCO, 2001).

Various research has explored the context, content, and impact of these kinds of community stations in low and lower-middle income countries (Jallov and Lwanga-Ntale, 2007; Kamal, 2007; Musubika, 2008; Manyozo, 2009; Myers, 2011; Sow, 2014; LeRoux-Rutledge, 2016, 2020). Such research details examples of how local community radio can provide a forum for public dialogue, in which powerful local actors can be held to account over issues that women deem to be a priority (Jallov and Lwanga-Ntale, 2007; Solervicens, 2008; Sow, 2014). For example, according to UNESCO, in Budikote, India, women were able to hold local authorities to account over broken water pipes impeding the village water supply by voicing their complaints on community radio. The pipes were promptly mended. Community radio can also provide a forum in which gendered narratives and norms in particular local contexts—on issues such as girls' and women's education, women's leadership, and violence against women—can be discussed and challenged (Myers, 2011; Sow, 2014; LeRoux-Rutledge, 2016, 2020). For example, in Tanzania, a woman who shared her story of domestic violence on community radio engendered a lively debate on air, and received an apology from her husband (Jallov and Lwanga-Ntale, 2007), while, in South Sudan, patriarchal gender narratives were recast in creative ways on community radio to argue for gender and development goals (LeRoux-Rutledge, 2016). At the same time, the constraints of community radio are well documented, including financial constraints (Musubika, 2008; Manyozo, 2009), restrictions on freedom of speech (Ibrahim, 2009), and tensions that may arise when women attempt to challenge the status quo (Kamal, 2007). While illuminating, this research is limited in scope, as it looks at radio content with a specific women and development remit, aimed at a local audience in a so-called 'developing' country.

Women and Global Radio

Far less research has looked at radio content about women and development that does not have a specific development remit, and is aimed at a global audience. Why would such content be of interest? As previously mentioned, feminist scholars have highlighted the potential of radio to contribute to a feminist public sphere (Jallov, 1992; Baehr and Gray, 1995; Mitchell, 1998, 2000)—and that sphere is undoubtedly global as well as local. Indeed, as the McLuhan quote at the beginning of this chapter points out, radio has the 'power to turn the globe into a single echo chamber' (1964: 137). Moreover, global radio is less driven by 'big D' development processes, and so might reveal new insights into how we understand and represent women's role in development.

To that end, this chapter seeks to explore representations of women and development in a hitherto underexplored format: the global radio series. In order to understand what such a format tells us about representations of women and development, we will consider a relatively new, but far-reaching, global radio series that deals with women and development: the BBC's *100 Women* series.

The BBC's *100 Women* Series

Selected as the exemplar of a global radio series because of its large international audience, the BBC's *100 Women* is a radio series that goes out for two weeks, towards the end of the year, during what is called the BBC's 'women season'. It aims to reflct women's experiences around the world, and to celebrate their achievements. The series was launched in 2013, following the infamous gang rape of a female student on a Delhi bus, which, in the words of series editor Fiona Crack, 'prompted me and many other journalists to think about how we cover news stories about sexual violence and other issues that particularly affect women'.[7] The *100 Women* series became, Crack says, 'a season inspired by our female audience who told us they wanted more voices like theirs to be heard on the BBC and for their experiences to be better reflected'. While a list of 100 Women is put out by the BBC at the start of each season, the *100 Women* series does not limit itself to their life stories, but rather covers a broad range of themes and issues that affect the lives of women around the world.

[7] Available at https://www.theguardian.com/women-in-leadership/2013/oct/31/bbc-100-women-series.

Content goes out on various platforms—most notably the BBC World Service, a radio station that reaches a weekly global audience of 269 million people, or 4 per cent of the world's population, 75 million of whom listen in English.[8] This audience is diverse and international, and by no means confined to low or lower middle-income countries, with the USA and Canada among its top ten markets. The *100 Women* series is also available as a podcast. By July 2017, forty episodes were available on iTunes, from both the 2015 and 2016 seasons, which constitute the data for this chapter.

The *100 Women* series does not focus exclusively on women from so-called developing countries. It includes interviews with the likes of Hollywood actor Hilary Swank, American musician Alicia Keys, and American gymnast Simone Biles. However, many of the episodes and stories do look at the lives of women in, or from, low and lower middle-income countries—as defined by the World Bank.[9] Out of the forty aforementioned episodes available on iTunes, exactly half mention a low, or lower middle-income country in either their programme title or description. These episodes were analysed in detail. The countries mentioned were: Bangladesh, El Salvador, The Gambia, Ghana, India, Kenya, Kosovo, Morocco, Nigeria, Pakistan, Somalia, South Sudan, Syria, and Uganda. How is the BBC World Service's *100 Women* series representing women in and from these countries, and does it tell us anything about women's role in development that is potentially new?

Analysing Media Content

When analysing media content media scholars often draw on the concept of *framing*. A media *frame* can be understood to be 'a central organizing idea or story line that provides meaning to an unfolding strip of events' (Gamson and Modigliani, 1987: 143). In other words, a frame is the *narrative* given to a sequence of events. Narratives play a powerful role in our culture, because they help us to construct meaning (Bruner, 1990). Media scholars Tewksbury and Scheufele (2009) point out that frames, or narratives, are often drawn on unconsciously by those who produce media content: 'Journalists, by definition, are working within the culture of their society and will therefore rely unconsciously on commonly shared frames' (Tewksbury and Scheufele, 2009: 24). The importance of such frames is that they suggest to an audience how to think about an issue (Tewksbury and Scheufele, 2009). As such, in analysing the content of the *100 Women* series, a narrative analysis was conducted, focusing explicitly on what Pan and Kosicki call 'script

[8] Available at http://www.bbc.co.uk/mediacentre/latestnews/2017/global-audience-measure.
[9] Available at https://datahelpdesk.worldbank.org/knowledgebase/articles/906519.

structures' (1993) or what Schank and Abelson call 'story skeletons' (1995), to see if one more media frame could be identified.

Two Narratives about Women: Local Phenomenon and Global Success

The analysis suggested that two media frames, or narratives, about women and development were prominent in the BBC's *100 Women* series. In the first, a woman was depicted as a *local phenomenon* and in the second she was depicted as a *global success.*

Local Phenomenon Narrative

In the *local phenomenon* narrative, a young woman, or group of young women, from a low or lower middle-income country, motivated by a desire to forge their own path in the world, to help their family and to make a positive contribution to society, embark on a quest for employment or entrepreneurship in their country, in a traditionally male-dominated field. They work extremely hard, and are supported along the way by older female role models from their country, who have themselves been pioneers for gender equality in the chosen field. They are also helped by the private sector, and by supportive male partners, who believe in gender equality. They are not helped by the government, and must overcome this hurdle. At first, men in their society discourage them, then are astonished by them, and finally afford them a measure of respect. As their quest progresses, they grow in self-confidence and self-esteem. Their goal, although seemingly at odds with traditional views of femininity and motherhood, turns out to be entirely compatible with such views. The outcome of their quest is uncertain, but ultimately, they have laid the groundwork for the women of their country who will come after them.

An example of this frame, or narrative, can be found in the *100 Women* podcast *Young, Geeky and Black: Kampala.* The podcast is about 'girls, women, coding and development', and in the podcast a group of 'bright young women' in Kampala, whose 'enthusiasm is infectious' and who are 'brimming with ideas' for apps and tech start-ups, pitch their ideas at an event organized by a consortium of African and global universities. One group is designing an app that will tell farmers 'what to grow, how to grow it ... how to breed animals, and about the market conditions in the different markets in Uganda'. Another group is developing an app for mothers, which 'diagnoses pneumonia in young children at a very early age'. A third group, called Afrigirl Tech, is developing an app for 'diagnosing sickle cell anaemia'. The male presenter of the programme explains that, 'for these coders, the motivation to help is often personal', and demonstrates with a story told by Afrigirl Tech's founders:

> We had a friend who we lost, who had sickle cell anaemia, and he found out late that he had the disease. So if he had found out earlier and managed it earlier he would have lived longer ... Our dream is to take this application to the health centres in the rural areas ... [s]o at least a bigger percentage of the people will have access to this diagnosis.

What we see here is that girls are presented as passionate, altruistic saviours who are driving the development of their country. Indeed, when the presenter asks, 'What value do you [girls] bring to the coding scene?' the girls reinforce this vision of themselves, stating that girls 'really do things ... which are not really for getting money, but for improving the community where they live'. They then go on to detail the 'hours of sacrifice' and personal financial investment they have put into developing their app.

The programme also interviews the female Director of Innovation for the consortium of universities hosting the tech start-up event. She is positioned as a mentor for the girls, saying:

> We've called them to pitch because we believe in what they have to say. We need to get more girls switched on in terms of the change they themselves can create, believing they can solve their communities' problems.

The private sector is likewise positioned as a supportive partner. In a voice over, the presenter explains:

> If there's external support, it's often in the form of prizes in innovation, competitions supported by international tech firms. Afrigirl Tech gets hardware and software support from Microsoft.

This support is not forthcoming from the government, however. The girls from Afrigirl Tech describe the government as having 'too much red tape' and ask rhetorically, '[W]hat happens when [the money doesn't] come in? Does that mean you don't start?'

The programme then moves on to discuss what men think. 'I have been to hack-a-thons where I'm the only girl present', one member of Afrigirl Tech relates:

> I remember at one hack-a-thon, I heard them discuss, 'No, no, no, you know, when you put a girl on a team she won't actually do anything.... [Then] they found out that I could actually do something, and then they were looking at themselves and laughing at themselves.

She is quick to point out, however, that being a coder is not at odds with traditional views of femininity:

> [T]his doesn't mean that you lose out the feminine side of you. You're still the lady who you are. If it means heels, you put them on, and go out show the world what you can actually do.

When the presenter asks:

> We all live in a culture where there's a lot of pressure on you as women to get married, have a baby. Ten years from now, do you think you will have time for all of this? Or will you be making babies and cooking for your husband instead of coding?

The Afrigirl Tech member replies:

> [I]t should not get in the way of our dreams and our prospects, yeah? If you can get that partner who can support you, and they understand that you love coding, and this is what made you who you are—if you get a partner who's supportive, I think it's easy to balance.

The presenter concludes the story on a hopeful but uncertain note, saying, 'The girls have big ambitions, but, like many start-ups in Uganda, lack experience'. He ends the programme with the following reflection:

> [D]uring my time in Uganda the thing that impressed me most was the energy, inspiration and effort young people are directing towards solving problems that matter ... [E]ven if this generation of start-ups are not the ones who go on to bigger success, they are laying the groundwork for the future.

The same *local phenomenon* story structure is evident in the *100 Women* podcast *Jobs for the Girls—Part 1*, set in India. This programme follows the lives of not one, but several, women in India who are pursuing careers in traditionally male-dominated fields, working as mechanics, bouncers, pilots, computer gamers, firefighters, driving instructors, and taxi drivers. They are usually presented as either trying to forge their own path in life, or help their families, or both. For example, a female gamer interviewed for the programme talks about how gaming is her 'passion,' saying 'I will do anything that I have to do ... cause [gaming is] the most important thing [to me]', while a female driving instructor's story is related thusly:

> [S]he was a housewife when her husband was alive, and then in 2009 he died ... [S]he sat at home for ... six months thinking about her life, and she came to the

> decision that she needed to support her children, of course—bring them up—but [also] she needed to do something for which she can be proud. She didn't want to be dependent on others. She didn't want to live on charity... [S]he wanted to get into a respectable and respectful job.

All of the women—regardless of whether their motivation is presented as primarily personal or family-oriented—are described by the female presenter of the programme as making an important social contribution, by 'stepping outside the box, defying gender stereotypes, and breaking down barriers in the world of work'. Moreover, for some, the social benefit of their work is stressed even further. For example, the female bouncers are credited with 'helping with security and safety' while the female firefighters are described by their training director as 'most dependable ... [They don't even] bother for their life'. Their heroism and altruism is further emphasized in the following tale, related by the presenter:

> [One of the female firefighters] is saying that—my God this is such a dare devilry it's is giving me goose bumps to hear what she's recounting—she's telling me about this huge factory fire in Jaipur ... [T]he focal point of the fire was on the third floor of the building, and three women and three children were trapped inside and they were howling and shouting and screaming for help ... [T]hey [the female firefighters] were outside on ladders and they thought, 'well it's either rescuing these women or we might even die', and they were prepared for that. And they finally tried to open the windows by breaking them and a lot of smoke came out ... but finally they were able to make their way inside and rescue all six people. And that was really very, very satisfying.

Many of the tales recounted in *Jobs for the Girls—Part 1* position other, older women, as trailblazers and mentors. The segment on drivers includes an interview with 'the first female taxi driver in Rajasthan' and the 'first female driving instructor' who paved the way for others to follow. Similarly, the 'first woman firefighter in Rajasthan' relates her story:

> When I first came here [to the government training institution] they refused to admit me. They said it was a hard job and a girl couldn't do it. They kept saying the Rajasthan [government] might have advertised posts for women firefighters but that we women couldn't be trained in Rajasthan. So I kept coming and pestering them and finally they gave in to my perseverance. I said that if men can do it, why can't women? You give me a chance and I'll prove it to you.

She is credited with 'convincing this institute [to open] training for firefighting to women'.

Again, commercial partners, like the Indian aviation industry, which hires 'a good percentage of female pilots' and the nightclub industry, which hires 'lady bouncers', are credited as being supportive, while the government is seen as bureaucratic and slow to change. Moreover, it is pointed out in the programme that many of the women profiled have supportive male partners. For example, the husband of the female mechanic interviewed is:

> [V]ery happy that his wife helps him and ... very proud of the legacy that they have built, with educating their children, building a house of their own and then marrying them off—everything that the Indian social ladder kind of wants.

This husband is quoted as saying: 'Why should I feel any shame? She is my wife and we do everything together. I think of her as my equal.' Likewise, one of the female bouncers, whose sister is also a bouncer, explains:

> [M]y husband has never restricted me, nor my sister's [husband]. We've both got very supportive husbands. They believe that we will always do the right thing. In fact my husband helped me to finish my school education, something my family did not.

As for other men in society, they may take time to come around, but are ultimately persuaded of the value of the women's work. The female gamer says:

> At first it used to be like, 'Oh my God we have a girl; we're going to lose the game', and they were like, you know, 'Why is she even here? Go make a sandwich ...' [but] recently one guy came and said that, 'I saw so many portfolios and I chose you because you knew how to game', and that was the day I was like, 'I own my respect'.

Similarly, the presenter describes how 'it took a bit of time for men to get used to the women firefighters, but they performed as well as the men and that helped them gain respect'.

Moreover, it is stressed throughout the programme that the work the women do builds their confidence. 'When she was at home she felt she was nobody, but when she started doing this, she's now very proud of the path that she's chosen for herself', the presenter says of one of the female bouncers. Similarly, the story of a female taxi driver is summarized as follows:

> [S]he used to earlier feel very scared of what the family [her in-laws] would think, so whatever she wanted to do there were always restrictions that the family imposed about how she should dress, where she should go, how many hours of the day can she spend outside ... what she can do for her children. But now she says

> that, 'I have realized that ... these are my own two hands, my own two legs, my own eyes and my own mind. I'll do what I want to do for my children and I'll dress the way I want to'.

Having said that, the programme again takes pains to imply that the work the women do is not incompatible with their traditional roles as wives and mothers. For example, one of the bouncers is described as being 'like any other traditional housewife: a mother who takes care of the house, a husband and her children'. Similarly, when the presenter asks the other bouncer:

> [Y]ou have really sweet daughter here who is drinking water from her bottle ... [S]he's probably not even a year old, a little baby, so how do you manage with the children? Who takes care of the children when you go out [at] these odd hours at night to work?

The bouncer explains (interpreted by the presenter):

> [A]ctually [she says] the job helps her take care of her daughter, because [she] is home during the day, so it's only a few hours at night when she needs someone to take care of the child, and her husband does that, which really helps. And she's decided not to do any other work during the day so she can be with the children.

Ultimately, while the programme acknowledges that there are still not many women in the professions it has showcased it implies that the women it has profiled are breaking ground for those who will follow.

Overall, one of the key features of the *local phenomenon* narrative is the extent to which it positions women as 'saviours' who simultaneously care for others, and drive development and social change. This will be discussed further in the concluding section of the chapter. Other examples from the BBC's *100 Women* series that use the *local phenomenon* frame—either entirely or in part—are *Jobs for the Girls—Part 2; Young, Geeky and Black: Accra; Business: India's changing gender balance; When Wangari Maathai Won the Nobel Peace Prize;* and *Interview: Sania Mirza—Tennis Player.*

Global Success Narrative

In the second frame, or narrative, a woman is depicted as a *global success.* In this narrative, a young woman from a low or lower middle-income country chooses to leave, or is forced to leave her country. She makes her way to a developed country, where she is startled to experience racism and prejudice. Nevertheless, through sheer determination, she excels in her education and goes on to pursue a career in a field that is male-dominated or not typical for those of her nationality or ethnicity. In the course of her career, she encounters prejudice, but achieves considerable professional success by working extremely hard. However, she never forgets the country of her birth, and—motivated by altruism and a sense of justice—she ultimately finds a way to help the people of her country.

A good example of this narrative is *Shriti Vedara: The 100 Women Interview*. In this programme, Shriti Vedara, chair of the UK's Santander bank, is interviewed about her life. 'Exiled from [her] country following Idi Amin's expulsion of all of Uganda's Asians', a voice over tells us at the beginning of the programme, she 'settled into a new home in India' and then, 'at the age of fifteen ... asked to be sent to school in England to avoid ... the risk of an arranged marriage'.

When she arrived in England, however, she explains she was:

> ... a little shocked and not entirely happy, it's fair to say. It was, you know, it was a lot more racist than it is now, and I hadn't really thought about that properly and sort of expected it and anticipated it.

As a consequences, she say 'I've never worked so hard [in school] ... because I felt I had the weight of a nation, and I had to prove it for the nation, not just for me'. Similarly, as an Asian woman in the banking sector, she says:

> For the early part of my career I spent so much time trying to be like a man, better than a man. I just had to work harder, be better, be tougher, be more determined—and you know, I'm talking about the city [of London] in the 1980's ... Ugh, I just worked so hard. I didn't show any vulnerability. I just had to do every single little thing better, just because that was the only way to prove that you could, you should be there.

The female presenter clarifies that the city of London—the heart of London's banking industry—was, in the 1980s 'a very sexist world ... [with] very few women around, very few black faces around'.

Through her hard work and determination Shriti Vedara apparently achieved considerable professional success. According to a voice over, she gained 'a reputation as a dynamic and influential economist. UK Prime Minister Gordon Brown, when in office, had her at his top table', and she is now 'a leading voice in British business'.

In her own words, however, it's never been about 'succeeding; it's about 'I need to fix that. I need to make that problem go away'.' As such, Shriti Vedara echoes the idea, present in the *local phenomenon* narrative, that women are saviours who altruistically drive change. This is evidenced by a story she tells from her childhood:

> I remember one of my earliest memories ... is of my carer crying ... [S]he was an amazingly wonderful ... black woman ... And I remember her crying because ... she couldn't get her children, who were my friends by the way, into school, because she couldn't pay for them. And I think I understood some basic economics at the time, and [I] sort of said, 'I think my grandmother has money, so you know ... we'll go and ask her'. And my grandmother didn't want to give her the money because her husband would drink and gamble it away, and I remember sitting there thinking, 'well that's not right, and we'll get them to school, and we'll take the money with us and we'll give it to the school at the time'. And so we used to go every month with my grandmother to pay the school fees for my [carer]'s children.

This kind of 'outcome' orientation is, Shriti Vedara claims, a trait particularly common among women:

> I think ... quite a lot of women are outcome focused. Why else would I take ... [a] tiny fraction of what I was earning in the city, and go and do something [in the government]? Because I believed it; because I wanted to change it; because I wanted to make it better.

She goes on to opine that women leaders today:

> [H]ave a core [that] I think a lot of women have, which is to focus more on the outcome than on their own political positioning, their own power, where they are on the corporate ladder. I think that women focus on outcomes more.

In her case, she ultimately used her success and influence to address the issue of universal education in Uganda. Picking up from her childhood story, she explains:

> I remember when—oh gosh how many years later ... I don't know. Thirty? ... advising the treasury on debt relief for all developing countries, mainly in Africa. And the then-chancellor Gordon Brown was very interested in that subject—that's actually how I met him—and we gave one hundred percent debt relief. And the first country that was picked was Uganda, because it had got itself organized. But everybody was concerned that they would take the money and use it ... for corrupt things, so the deal that I was asked to negotiate with them is that they would spend every penny that was released to get every child into school for free. And I remember standing in the back of the hall in the IMF meetings, with that being announced, thinking 'what a strange world. Everything has come around full circle'.

A second example of the *global success* narrative can be seen in the programme *Interview: Alek Wek—Model.* Alek Wek is described as 'a New York based supermodel who spent years of her childhood fleeing from civil war'. A voice over explains how:

> At the age of nine she walked for weeks through the bush in Southern Sudan with her family when her hometown was overrun by militia and government forces [and] sought asylum in London as a teenager.

In London, Alek Wek says, it was:

> Very, very challenging. Children at school are not very pleasant. You know, they can be bullies. 'Midnight black' and, you know, 'long, skinny, lanky'. I got called everything ... But I just threw myself into school.

She started working as a model at a time when, according to a voice over, 'dark skinned models were rare, and her debut was received with some enthusiasm and a lot of scepticism', but again, she threw herself into the work:

> I was going back and forward [from] London [to New York] ... I was travelling tremendously, every week or two ... six, seven, eight hours in flight. That was really, really exhausting ... [but] it was very crucial at the beginning to make sure that I was consistent, because ... if you work, and then you do very well, and then you leave, you come back [and] it may not be the same. And then you can just be a one hit wonder. I knew, and I felt, that whatever I was going to choose, and do, and have a profession in—I better take it serious. I better work hard at it.

Today, according to the programme, she has 'revolutionised the way beauty is defined'. However, she apparently never forgot her home country of South Sudan and a voice over tells us that 'the plight of her people prompted Alek to become a global advocate for refugee rights, as one of the UN refugee agency's goodwill ambassadors'. When questioned about this by the presenter, Alek Wek explains:

> To destroy a family and a community, [it] is very hard to put back together .... I got involved with the UNHCR, I would say, just witnessing it first hand. When the civil war broke out [in South Sudan] they were the ones that were there and helping save lives, giving ... the basic necessities that a human being needs: shelter, food, safety you know. UNHCR [is] the biggest refugee agency in the world and they are in places that no one wants to go into.

She concludes, '[S]o much more [has] to be done to just help [refugees] because the refugees are like me and you'.

What we see is that, as with the *local phenomenon* narrative, the *global success* narrative positions women as saviours driving development and social change. Other programmes that use the *global success* frame—either entirely or in part—are: *Interview: Fatou Bensouda—Prosecutor, International Criminal Court; Health: Dr Comfort Momoh, midwife and FGM campaigner;* and *Rachida Dita: the 100 Women Interview.*

The Problem With These Narratives

How does this analysis of the BBC's global radio programme *100 Women* inform our understanding of the ways in which women's roles in development are presented for a global audience, and does it yield any new insight into our understanding of women and development? The first thing that comes across clearly is that both the *local phenomenon* and *global success* frames position women as 'saviours'.

The positioning of women as saviours in international development discourse has a somewhat complicated history. Academic literature on gender and development suggests that women in so-called developing countries have traditionally been presented as 'victims'. This depiction had its roots in colonialism, and was prominent in pre-1970s development discourse. At the time, the role that women played in international development was largely ignored, and development tended to be gender blind (Misra, 2000). When women were discussed, it was as recipients of welfare (Rowlands, 1997). Although other presentations of women within international development gained ground over subsequent decades, they never truly supplanted this one, which retained its prominence largely because of its ability to pull in financial resources (Win, 2004). For example, at the Fourth World Conference on Women in Beijing in 1995, the 'feminization of poverty' claim, which asserted that 70 per cent of the world's poor were women, became a rallying cry that arguably galvanized the international development community to devote significant resources to women (Chant, 2015).

The problem with this presentation of women as 'victims', however, is that, in drawing attention to the structural inequalities they face, it arguably downplays their agency, and can thus be viewed as post-colonial and patriarchal (Mohanty, 1988; Cornwall and Anyidoho, 2010; Grosser and van der Gaag, 2013; Chant, 2016). Moreover, it homogenizes women in development contexts, representing them as a single, powerless group, and ignoring profound differences in their realities and experiences (Mohanty, 1988).

The alternative that emerged in the 1970s was the 'saviour' depiction, which presented women as hardworking agents, central to development. This idea took off after Ester Boserup critiqued the pre-existing discourse about women, and encouraged policymakers to incorporate women into the development process (1970). In the 'saviour' story, women are seen as an untapped resource, which need only be invested in by NGOs and development agencies. Because of their intrinsic community-mindedness and altruism, women will, with a little bit of investment, lift themselves, their families, and their communities out of poverty—so the story goes (Chant, 2016).

This presentation of women, while perhaps responding to some of the critiques of the 'victim' presentation, is also problematic, according to post-colonial feminist scholars. The problem lies in the fact that, in positioning women as saviours, it instrumentalizes them as tools for development, and suggests they are all inherently noble and self-sacrificing (Cornwall *et* al., 2007; Chant, 2016). It also appears to let men off the hook, as men are not perceived to have the same altruistic qualities as women, and therefore cannot be expected to work collaboratively towards poverty alleviation (Chant, 2016). The depiction further positions women as active choice-makers, ignoring many of the structural barriers—such as cultural norms and practices—that restrict their choices (Cornwall and Edwards, 2010); and last, it ignores a more human-rights-based rationale for equality between men and women, which briefly gained ground in the 1990s before being watered down in favour of an instrumentalist argument for women's empowerment (Cornwall et al., 2007; Cornwall, 2014; Chant, 2016).

In addition, both depictions have been criticized for ignoring women's actual voices and the diversity of women's experiences. This is part of a general critique of international development, which has been seen as a top-down process, far removed from the everyday realities of women's lives (Wallace and Porter, 2013).

So, how transformative is the BBC's *100 Women* global radio series as a medium of representation for stories of women and development? One thing it arguably does well is foreground women's voices—a trait it shares with community radio. Admittedly, they are not always the voices of the most marginalized women in society, but women are at the centre of the story. Interestingly, this, at times, makes the 'big D' Development initiatives undertaken by formal international development institutions seem almost irrelevant. The BBC's *100 Women* series actually changes the 'saviour' narrative somewhat, largely eliminating the role of development organizations, so that women become the engines of 'small d' development—a broad, historically complex process of change, naturally occurring under capitalism.

And yet, despite decentralizing development institutions in the narratives it presents, the BBC's *100 Women* series still depicts women as saviours. It thus appears that, in this instance, global radio, far from being a 'transgressive power' with 'the subversive potential' to challenge conventional social norms (Hilmes and Loviglio, 2001: xiii), merely reproduces many of the existing tropes about women and development. It seems that both the journalists creating the *100 Women* series, and the women themselves, have been influenced by commonly shared narratives about women—leading to stories in which women are presented as altruistically driving development for the benefit of society.

Potentially problematic is the seeming ease with which the women in the series are depicted taking on new economic roles and responsibilities, while simultaneously managing old. Nowhere is there an acknowledgement of the double burden this places on women to continue their unpaid domestic labour while taking on paid work—something feminists have long commented on (Hochschild, 1989; Väänänen *et al.*, 2005).

Also potentially problematic is the way in which men in the series are depicted, either as supportive male partners—who are ostensibly just waiting around for empowered women to view as equals—or as patriarchal gatekeepers—who are eventually brought around by women's outstanding performance in traditionally male dominated fields. Both of these depictions suggest that women's fates ultimately hang on the grace and favour of men.

Finally, potentially problematic is the way in which multinational corporations and the private sector are positioned in the series as the ideal institutional partners for women undertaking development. Organizations such as Microsoft are portrayed as philanthropic benefactors, seeding innovation. This is a trend that has been noted in the literature, as international development has, in general, seen a shift in emphasis from the nation state to the private sector over the last 20 years (Cornwall and Edwards, 2015). This too has been critiqued by post-colonial feminist scholars. According to Chant (2016: 14), it represents:

> [A] disturbing deflection of the spotlight from market enterprises ... which have played a major part in entrenching and intensifying poverty in the Global South ... Instead, through their ostensibly philanthropic gestures, corporates have managed, on the surface, to rise to the exalted rank of 'saviours' dedicated to liberating girls.

Conclusion

Despite laudable aims, the *100 Women* series does not appear to have majorly subverted the tropes about women and development currently prevalent in today's development discourse. Rather, it has reproduced the 'saviour' narrative about women and development currently in vogue, along with a number of other accompanying problems.

What does this mean for the potential of global radio to replicate some of the successes of community radio, and contribute to a feminist public sphere? As previously noted, community radio provides a public forum for community members to air their problems and concerns, and to hold powerful local actors to account. Community radio, which is situated in the community it serves, often with a 'big D' Development remit, has the power not only to *represent* women, but also to spur communities to *action*. Global radio series like the BBC's *100 Women* series, while similarly representing women, are farther removed from local communities, and do not have a 'big D' Development remit. As such, they may lack the capacity, or the concern, to spur people to action in quite the same way.

One could, however, imagine a scenario in which global radio spurred its audience—the *global* community—to action, and was able to hold powerful *global* actors to account. According to feminist theory, such an outcome would be possible if the series set up forms of resistance and oppositional discourse that could act as a rallying cry for the global community; however, herein lies the paradox. While, on the one hand, the series *has* set up oppositional discourse in relation to context specific narratives about the kinds of jobs women can do, the kinds of successes they can achieve, and the kinds of leadership positions they can hold in particular local cultures, it has, on the other hand, reproduced and reified a larger global meta-narrative about gender and development, prominent in international development discourse. By continuing to produce stories depicting women in 'saviour' roles, it may therefore be undermining its ability to say something truly transformational in the global feminist public sphere.

References

Baehr, H. and A. Gray (1995) *Turning It On: A Reader in Women and Media*. London: Hodder Education.

Boserup, E. (1970) *Woman's Role in Economic Development*. London: Allen and Unwin.

Bruner, J. (1990) *Acts of Meaning*. Cambridge, MA: Harvard University Press.

Chant, S. (2015) *The 'Feminization of Poverty': A Reflection 20 Years after Beijing*. Geneva: United Nations Research Institute for Social Development (UNRISD).

Chant, S. (2016) 'Women, girls and world poverty: Empowerment, equality or essentialism?', *International Development Planning Review* 38(1): 1–24.

Cornwall, A. (2014) 'Taking off international development's straight-jacket of gender', *Brown Journal of World Affairs* 21(1): 127–39.

Cornwall, A. and N. A. Anyidoho (2010) 'Introduction: Women's empowerment: contentions and contestations', *Development* 53(2): 144–9.

Cornwall, A. and J. Edwards (2010) 'Introduction: Negotiating empowerment', *IDS Bulletin* 41(2): 1–9.

Cornwall, A. and J. Edwards (2015) 'Introduction: Beijing+20: Where now for Gender Equality?', *IDS Bulletin* 46(4): 1–8.

Cornwall, A., E. Harrison, and A. Whitehead (2007) 'Gender myths and feminist fables: the struggle for interpretive power in gender and development', *Development and Change* 38(1): 1–20.

Fraser, C. and S. Restrepo-Estrada (2002) 'Community radio for change and development', *Development* 45(4): 69–73.

Gamson, W.A. and A. Modigliani (1987) 'The changing culture of affirmative action', in R. G. Braungart and M. M. Braungart (eds) *Research in Political Sociology*. Greenwich: JAI Press, pp. 137–77.

Gatua, M.W., T. O. Patton, and M. R. Brown (2010) 'Giving voice to invisible women: "FIRE" as model of a successful women's community radio in Africa', *Howard Journal of Communications* 21(2): 164–81.

Grosser, K. and N. van der Gaag (2013) 'Can girls save the world?', in T. Wallace and F. Porter with M. Ralph-Bowman (eds) *Aid, NGOs and the Realities of Women's Lives: A Perfect Storm*. Rugby: Practical Action Publishing, pp. 73–87.

Hart, G. (2001) 'Development critiques in the 1990s: Culs de sac and promising paths', *Progress in Human Geography* 25(4): 649–658.

Hilliard, R. (2003) 'Farm and rural radio in the United States: Some beginnings and models', in B. Girard (ed.) *One to Watch: Radio, New ICTs and Interactivity*. Rome: Food and Agriculture Organization (FAO), pp. 201–8.

Hilmes, M. and J. Loviglio (eds) (2001) *Radio Reader: Essays in the Cultural History of Radio*. New York: Routledge.

Hochschild, A.R. (1989) *The Second Shift: Working Parents and the Revolution at Home*. New York: Viking.

Ibrahim, M. (2009) 'Rebel voices and radio actors: in pursuit of dialogue and debate in Northern Uganda', *Development in Practice* 19(4-5): 610–20.

Jallov, B. (1992) 'Women on the air: Community radio as a tool for feminist messages', in N. Jankowski, O. Prehn, and J. Stappers (eds) *The People's Voice: Local Radio and Television in Europe*. London: John Libbey, pp. 215–24.

Jallov, B. and C. Lwanga-Ntale (2007) 'Impact Assessment of East African Community Media Project 2000–2006: Report from Orkonerei Radio Service (ORS) in Tanzania and Selected Communities, unpublished report commissioned by SIDA Department for Democracy and Social Development, Birgitte Jallov Communication Partners.

Kamal, S. (2007) 'Development on-air: Women's radio production in Afghanistan', *Gender and Development* 15(3): 399–411.

Khamalwa, D.J.W. (2006) *African Media Development Initiative: Research Summary Report*. London: BBC World Service Trust.

LeRoux-Rutledge, E. (2007) 'Afghan Women's Hour: Psychological Empowerment Using a Mass Media Approach', unpublished MSc dissertation, London School of Economics and Political Science.

LeRoux-Rutledge, E. (2016) 'Public Narratives as Symbolic Resources for Gender and Development: A Case Study of Women and Community Radio in South Sudan', unpublished PhD dissertation, London School of Economics and Political Science.

LeRoux-Rutledge, E. (2020) 'Re-evaluating the "traditional": How the South Sudanese use established gender narratives to advance women's equality and empowerment', World Development, 132, available at https://doi.org/10.1016/j.worlddev.2020.104929.

LeRoux-Rutledge, E., G. Power, and C. Morgan (2011) 'Telling other people's stories: Cultural translation in drama for development', in A. Skuse, M. Gillespie, and G. Power (eds) *Drama for Development: Cultural Translation and Social Change*. Thousand Oaks, CA: Sage, pp. 116–34.

Locksley, G. (2009) *The Media and Development: What's the Story?*, World Bank Working Paper Number 158, Washington, DC: World Bank.

McLuhan, M. (1964) 'Radio: the tribal drum', *AV Communication Review* 12: 133–45.

Manyozo, L. (2009) 'Mobilizing rural and community radio in Africa', *Ecquid Novi African Journalism Studies* 30(1): 1–23.

Misra, J. (2000) 'Gender and the world-system: Engaging the feminist literature on development', in T.D. Hall (ed.) *A World-Systems Reader: New Perspectives on Gender, Urbanism, Cultures, Indigenous Peoples, and Ecology*. Lanham, MD: Rowman & Littlefield, pp. 105–27.

Mitchell, C. (1998) 'Women's (community) radio as a feminist public sphere', *Javnost-The Public: Journal of the European Institute for Communication and Culture* 5(2): 73–85.

Mitchell, C. (ed.) (2000) *Women and Radio: Airing Differences*. London: Routledge.

Mohanty, C.T. (1988) 'Under Western eyes: Feminist scholarship and colonial discourses', *Feminist Review* 30: 61–88.

Musubika, J. (2008) 'Women's potential and challenges in community radio: the case of Mama FM', *Agenda* 22: 127–34.

Myers, M. (2011) *Voices from Villages: Community Radio in the Developing World*. Washington, DC: Center for International Media Assistance (CIMA).

Pan, Z. and G. M. Kosicki (1993) 'Framing analysis: An approach to news discourse', *Political Communication* 10(1): 55–75.

Rowlands, J. (1997) *Questioning Empowerment: Working with Women in Honduras*. Oxford: Oxfam GB.

Schank, R. and R. Abelson (1995) 'Knowledge and memory: The real story', in *Knowledge and Memory: The Real Story, Advances in Social Cognition, Vol. 8*. New York: Psychology Press, pp. 211–26.

Skuse, A., M. Gillespie, and G. Power (eds) (2011) *Drama for Development: Cultural Translation and Social Change*. Thousand Oaks, CA: Sage.

Solervicens, M. (ed.) (2008) *Women's Empowerment and Good Governance through Community Radio: Best Experiences for an Action Research Process*. Montreal QC: World Association of Community Radio Broadcasters (AMARC).

Sow, F. (2014) 'Women's Community Radio in Africa: The Case Study of Gindiku FM in Senegal', unpublished PhD dissertation, University of Oregon.

Street, N.L. and M.J. Matelski (eds) (1997) *Messages from the Underground: Transnational Radio in Resistance and in Solidarity*. Westport, CT: Praeger.

Tewksbury, D. and D.A. Scheufele (2009) 'News framing theory and research', in J. Bryant and M. B. Oliver (eds) *Media Effects: Advances in Theory and Research* (3rd edn). New York: Routledge, pp. 17–33.

UNESCO (2001) *Community Radio Handbook*. Paris: United Nations Educational, Scientific and Cultural Organisation (UNESCO).

Väänänen, A., M. V. Kevin, L. Ala-Mursula, J. Pentti, M. Kivimäki, and J. Vahtera (2005) 'The double burden of and negative spillover between paid and domestic work: Associations with health among men and women', *Women Health* 40(3): 1–18.

Wallace, T. and F. Porter with M. Ralph-Bowman (eds) (2013) *Aid, NGOs and the Realities of Women's Lives: A Perfect Storm*. Rugby: Practical Action Publishing.

Win, E.J. (2004) 'Not very poor, powerless or pregnant: The African woman forgotten by development', *IDS Bulletin* 35(4): 61–4.

8

'Being in the spotlight is not something we are used to'

Awkward Encounters in *The Guardian*'s Katine Initiative

Ben Jones

Introduction

The Katine initiative was a major development initiative that ran from 2007 to 2011. It was located in Katine sub-county in eastern Uganda and sponsored by readers of *The Guardian* and Barclays Bank and implemented by the non-governmental organization (NGO) AMREF (African Medical Research Foundation). Over four years, more than £2.5 million was channelled into development work in the sub-county. Journalists from the newspaper—sports writers, feature editors, staff from the health and environment desks—went to Katine and described what they saw. The sub-county was also visited by politicians, business leaders, development experts, and even the English Premier League Trophy (as part of a football tournament). The novelty of the partnership was recognized for the way it brought development to a wider audience, and the website won the 2008 International Visual Communications Association's Clarion award and the 2008 One World Media 'new media award'. *The Guardian*, Barclays, and AMREF also won the 2010 Coffey International Award for Excellence recognizing the positive impact the project had had in promoting the United Nations (UN) Millennium Development Goals.

This public recognition needs to be understood against what turned out to be a difficult relationship. The initiative trained a spotlight on the NGO, and this was often an uncomfortable experience for those involved. Parts of the project were picked apart by journalists and bloggers. In some cases, the NGO changed its approach because of the focus of a particular reporter, with new elements being introduced because they worked in media terms. *The Guardian* was both funding and reporting on the project, and so the words of journalists, and what appeared on the website, influenced the way the project worked out on the ground. A senior manager at AMREF told me that 'being in the spotlight is not something we are

Ben Jones, *'Being in the spotlight is not something we are used to'*. In: *New Mediums, Better Messages?*. Edited by David Lewis, Dennis Rodgers, and Michael Woolcock, Oxford University Press.
 DOI: 10.1093/oso/9780198858751.003.0009

used to' and described the experience as a 'healing process'.[1] A fieldworker commented that 'with this project every small bit of what you do in the community is on the website' and that 'a newspaper is always on the watch, twenty-four hours ... they see what you are implementing, [if] you try to divert a bit there is a big question'.[2]

This particular chapter looks at examples of this scrutiny and how this was difficult for the NGO to deal with. I give examples of what happened when stories of things going wrong appeared on the website and of commentators questioning the competence and ethics of the NGO. I also show the relative power of journalists and how this shaped aspects of the project—an example that runs counter to much of the literature on journalism and NGOs (where NGOs are assumed to have the upper hand) (Cottle and Nolan, 2007; Franks, 2008; Polman, 2010; Powers, 2013). Amid these discussions of conflict in the project, I also point to the ways the relationship grew more settled at higher levels and, in some ways, less critical over time. Over the course of the project, managers at the NGO got better at dealing with the demands of *The Guardian*, a change that can be read against a broader story of AMREF becoming more interested in the field of advocacy. A change that also shifted power towards those parts of the non-governmental organization dealing with media and policy work.

Before looking at the project in more detail, I discuss some of the assumptions that characterize studies of NGOs and journalism. I then introduce the Katine initiative and my own relationship to the project, before moving on to examples from the field.

NGOs and Journalism

Until very recently, NGOs have exercised a good degree of authorship over how their work appears in mainstream media.[3] In many of the places where they work, they are assumed to be the good guys in contexts where most of the actors are a problem: corrupt governments, militias, armies, big business. While academic work has been critical of NGOs, the sector has been given a relatively easy time by mainstream journalism. As Polman (2010) argues, 'journalists scarcely question aid organizations' and often struggle to see the work of NGOs in a critical light. Lugo-Ocando and Nguyen, in a harshly worded critique of the way journalists work with the development sector, suggest that 'not much has been done to

[1] Interview with management, Kampala country office, 1 July 2010.

[2] Interview with field staff, Katine office, 5 July 2010. By 'divert', the respondent meant 'diverge' from the project place, rather than anything that might imply corruption.

[3] The crisis that came to the fore in 2018 surrounding the use of sex workers by OXFAM staff in Haiti—and other stories of abuse and corruption in the sector—illustrates how 'shocking' this sort of behaviour appears when set against the more usual way the work of non-governmental organizations working in humanitarian situations is reported.

investigate how the media and aid agencies ... interact with each other in shaping the agenda on international development' and that the current state of affairs is 'opaque, superficial and ideologically biased ... an example of a failure of transparency and accountability' (Lugo-Ocando and Nguyen, 2017: 71–3). Rothmyer (2011: 4) goes as far as to suggest that reporters writing about the developing world can be found 'routinely following the lead of press-savvy aid groups on topics such as war victims and refugees'.[4] NGOs are often presented as skilful in managing journalists, while journalists reporting on development issues come across as both dependent and sympathetic in their dealings with NGOs.

In the following section, I develop these ideas and discuss both the increasing sophistication with which NGOs approach their work with the media, and look at the ways in which scholars have understood the position of journalists reporting on development issues. I also question assumptions made above about the dependence and sympathy of journalists or the apparent sophistication of 'press-savvy' NGOs. The relationship between *The Guardian* and AMREF was not really a story of vulnerable journalists being taken in by a press-savvy NGO, or of an aid organization charming a particular journalist into producing uncritical or unquestioning reporting. Even when the outcome is relatively uncritical, this is not always arrived at unquestioningly or easily.

Publicity is at the heart of the NGO enterprise, and good publicity is important for obvious reasons—fundraising, awareness, market share (Smith and Yanacopulos, 2004; Powers, 2013, 2016; Van Leuven and Joye, 2014). Smaller NGOs often concentrate publicity around raising money; larger international NGOs rely on publicity for awareness raising and campaigning and policy work (Yanacopulos, 2005).[5] As Powers observes, the identity of larger international NGOs is increasingly tied to their interest in global policy agendas (Powers, 2016) and campaigning NGOs like OXFAM and ActionAid have professional press and publicity divisions, with journalists on the staff, where success is measured, in large part in media terms (Jones, 2016). NGOs are involved in a more complex 'production and reception of development's public faces' beyond the image of the starving child or the empowered mother. In many ways NGOs have become more like media organizations.

This leads to a first set of observations around the sophistication of NGOs in their relationship to the media. Kimberly Abbott of the International Crisis Group has argued that 'NGOs are taking on more and more functions of news

[4] Scholars working in the NGO sector have noted examples of NGOs being criticized by the media, although this is more than outweighed by accounts that are largely supportive (cf. Lewis, 2007: 10–12).

[5] This shift towards advocacy took on particular importance in the late 1990s and early 2000s as many international NGOs pulled out of direct 'in-country' work, instead preferring to subcontract their work to local civil society organizations working on development issues (Watkins and Swidler, 2012: 199).

media in their capacity to gather and manage foreign news'(2009).[6] NGOs produce press releases and media packages, and, in many cases, are behind the stories that appear in the mainstream media (Rothmyer, 2011; Powers, 2016). Suzanne Franks (2008: 31), a former BBC producer, makes a point about the 'growing media sophistication of NGOs', who 'send out well-trained staff—some of them former journalists—to produce well-edited packages and then offer them' to media organizations. Powers (2016: 12) writes of NGOs with 'sizable public relations departments whose primary task historically has been to pursue media coverage'. A number of NGOs can be thought of as 'expert news source organisations' ready with 'background information and reliable eyewitness accounts' (Van Leuven and Joye, 2014: 160). Wright (2015) makes an interesting argument about the way digital technologies make it easier for NGOs to produce carefully constructed pieces in an effort to have their copy picked up by cash-strapped news organizations.

In the above, there is something close to Nick Davies's (2008) argument that newspaper reporting has become a form of 'churnalism', with journalists simply cutting and pasting press releases. A 2014 study of reporting on development issues in the Belgian press, for example, found that media reporting on development issues depended mostly on NGO press statements, while a later study looking at media coverage of the UN's Millennium Development Villages project found that most of it was 'derived from press releases' (Schiffrin and Ariss, 2017: 76).[7] The picture is of journalists recycling press releases and media packages, even though few organizations have the sort of media outfits available to only the larger campaigning NGOs such as OXFAM or Save the Children that dominate accounts of development and its public faces.

The second set of observations concerns what Powers (2016) has termed the 'social proximity' of journalists and NGO workers; that is to say, the fact that NGO workers and journalists often see themselves as 'natural allies', sharing similar outlooks and values. There is a sense in both professions—particularly those doing humanitarian work—that they are responding to what are often acute crises and where it is important to quickly assemble some facts (cf. Hoijer, 2004; Cameron and Haanstra, 2008). Although Powers is more interested in the way this closeness encourages NGOs to focus their media strategies on mainstream news outlets (rather than alternative media sources), his work points to a broader set of similarities between the professions. As one respondent, a media officer from International Crisis Group told him, 'they're sharing planes, they're sharing cars, and they're sharing food. They're living together in many cases' (Powers, 2016: 13). Wright

[6] See http://www.niemanlab.org/2009/11/kimberly-abbott-working-together-ngos-and-journalistscan-create-stronger-international-reporting/.

[7] The attraction for NGOs in this sort of coverage is relatively clear. A much-cited study suggested that for every *New York Times* article a disaster-stricken country would receive an extra US$600,000 in US humanitarian aid, while each additional death would only increase the amount by an additional US$400 (Drury et al., 2005: 465).

(2015: 14), in a discussion of freelance journalists and the role they play in producing the media content of many NGOs, found one respondent describing their work as that of an 'activist', seeing this both as a way of making sense of the blurred boundaries between the professions and the emergence of a category of journalist that increasingly relies on commissioned work (see also Dichter, 1999).

This leads to what can seem like a given when it comes to writing about NGOs and journalists—the 'media sophistication' of NGOs. There is a persistent lack of questioning on the part of journalists, and the sense of alliance between the professions. The case material below shows a slightly different situation where questions were asked, where distrust was part of the mix, and where the NGO often felt fairly unsophisticated when it came to dealing with a much more sophisticated media organization. AMREF was on a learning curve, as one of the senior managers explained to me:

> In the past we let the work speak for itself. But we saw the opportunities with this [project] to send across some messages on development issues. We also saw that we did not have the big media outfit that other NGOs had, the OXFAMs, the CAREs.

One of the managers in the Uganda country office spoke of a process of adaptation: 'We have to adapt to respond to the frequent calls, the frequent visitors, the calls for information' (see note 3). AMREF was becoming used to being a different sort of organization, one where there was more responsiveness around how it profiled and presented its work.

I use evidence from the Katine initiative to point to the amount of work that went into what was to become a more settled relationship between *The Guardian* and AMREF. Any relationship between an NGO and a media organization comes out of what are often complex sets of interactions, negotiations, and compromises, and it is helpful to observe these interactions in the making (cf. Wright, 2015). The more settled relationship occurred in a context where AMREF, like many other international NGOs, was increasingly trying to fashion itself as a campaigning, advocacy organization. In a sense, the case material suggests a situation of an NGO becoming more like a media organization. Before discussing some of these interactions and the context in which they took place, a few more words on the project and the source material that forms the basis for the analysis.

The Katine Initiative

The Guardian's Katine initiative grew out of a desire to form new partnerships and an interest in making sense of new media technologies (Lewis et al., 2008;

Franklin, 2014; Conrad, 2015; Pew Research Centre, 2016).[8] The key impetus came from *The Guardian*'s then editor, Alan Rusbridger, who wanted to use 'all the possibilities of the web to give maximum exposure to the challenges of development'.[9] It is worth remembering just how little web-based technologies had been used up to that point and how different the media landscape has since become (Fenton, 2009). Facebook had 20 million subscribers in 2007, and Twitter, Snapchat, and Instagram had not yet been invented or were not yet widely used. Katine moved coverage away from one-off stories or the time-bound reporting that traditionally profiles major crises in the developing world—what Cottle and Nolan (2007) refer to as the 'fleeting coverage' of much development journalism (p. 863; see also Schiffrin and Ariss, 2017). In place of one-off stories, there would be an account of development work in something close to real time.[10] It was this sort of long-form reporting that resulted in the Katine initiative winning a number of media awards.

Katine should also be seen as a response to the structural changes affecting newspapers themselves. It came at a time of 'dwindling profitability, technological transformation, audience fragmentation' and less coverage of international affairs in the newspaper sector as a whole (Powers, 2013: 6; see also Hannerz, 2004: 23). The project was part-funded by Barclays Bank and *The Guardian* was coming out of a period of staff retrenchment. For younger staff at the paper, Katine offered a relatively safe space to continue in journalism at a time the sector as a whole was struggling (cf. Waisbord, 2011). The initiative also helped *The Guardian* link up to a number of other actors—development agencies, micro-finance institutions, universities, pharmaceutical companies, government ministries—who used the website as a space for discussion and publicity, and the newspaper was thinking about drawing in new sources of funding.[11] *The Guardian*'s 'Global Development' website, which is in many ways the successor to Katine, relies on financial support from the Gates Foundation (along similar lines to *The Guardian*'s Cities website which has funding from the Rockefeller Foundation).[12]

[8] The Pew's State of the News Media 2016 report noted the precarious situation of newspapers in the United States, with delinking advertising revenue in both print and online versions (down 8% from the previous year).

[9] Interview with Alan Rusbridger, 22 June 2010.

[10] It is perhaps worth saying that ordinary readers of the newspaper seemed to have little interest in the project. Although I was never able to get a precise sense of overall traffic to the micro-site, I was told by one of the website editors that it was 'very, very small'. Much of the sustained interest in Katine came from the media divisions of larger NGOs, and I was told by one of the editors that these divisions wanted to know 'how we are using the internet, Twitter, blogging and videos to talk about development and how we can engage people ... how you can have those "north-south dialogues" on the blog'.

[11] It also made sense of *The Guardian*'s commitment to campaigning journalisms—I was told by one of the reporters on the project that it was an opportunity for journalists to take a very specific situation 'and see if it is happening in the rest of Uganda, the rest of Africa'.

[12] A relationship between news journalism and financing from foundations such as Rockefeller and Gates that is growing. A report found that 'between 2009 and 2011, 1012 foundations in the United States made 12040 media related grants', totalling US$1.86 billion (Bunce, 2016: 3).

A number of NGOs responded to *The Guardian*'s original call for expressions of interest. AMREF's winning proposal was an 'integrated rural development project'—somewhat out of fashion in development circles at the time—that made investments in health, education, governance, livelihoods, and water and sanitation in a single location. AMREF was chosen, I was told, because Katine was rural; it would be a place that readers could identify with in thinking about development in Africa. Katine was uniformly poor, its rural setting meant it seemed like a more bounded space than the urban locations proposed in at least one of the other two bids. AMREF was also chosen because it had a different profile from the more famous or visible international NGOs, and Alan Rusbridger noted in an introductory piece on the website that the staff were '97% African' with headquarters in Nairobi.[13] Of the three shortlisted organizations bidding, the other two appear to have been by major, UK-based, international NGOs.

When I spoke with staff at AMREF, they told me they did not have the 'big media outfits' of larger international NGOs, that Katine had been a 'sharp learning curve'.[14] AMREF's earliest iteration was as a Flying Doctors service in the 1950s, with most of its money coming from a small but consistent pool of donors. They had arrived fairly late to the sort of media work that defined the operations of many large, campaigning international NGOs, and AMREF's background in health also meant it was a slightly unprepared choice to run a rural development project (*Guardian* staff would later wonder whether the 'top down' approach of AMREF was due to this medical background—many senior staff are doctors) (AMREF, 2001, 2012). AMREF, like many smaller development NGOs, lacked the sorts of elaborate press and media outfits that dominate accounts of aid organizations working with the media. When I spoke with staff members early on there was a mixture of inexperience and curiosity reflecting back on what it meant to work with *The Guardian*: 'within AMREF we had a lot of discussions, we saw both sides; working with the media was a significant area of interest, it also taught us a lot'.[15]

By now it should be clear that the sort of 'natural alliance' between NGOs and journalists, with the NGO in the stronger position, was not a perfect description of the Katine initiative. In many ways, neither party was entirely clear how things would work; AMREF lacked much of the media sophistication of many other NGOs, and for *The Guardian* it was their first time doing anything like this. As one journalist told me, 'none of us were development experts'.[16] AMREF staff were not prepared for the type of critical publicity that came with the project.

[13] Available at https://www.theguardian.com/katine/2007/oct/20/about. Many of the comments posted at the foot of Rusbridger's initial piece received were critical of the 'Middle Ages' tag (although it is, perhaps, worth noting that Rusbridger was himself paraphrasing the development economist Paul Collier and his view that many poor people live in, 'a reality that is the 14th century').

[14] Interview with management, Kampala country office, 8 July 2010.

[15] Interview with management, Kampala country office, 9 July 2010.

[16] Interview with *The Guardian* journalist, 22 June 2010.

Many working at lower levels felt that they were in a fairly weak position, both in relation to journalists visiting the project and in relation to their own senior management. Field staff spoke of the disorienting experience of journalists visiting the subcounty, asking questions and raising expectations in the community. These visits often involved AMREF managers coming along as well.

Katine was launched through a *Guardian* Christmas appeal back in 2007. Interested readers could give a one-off donation or commit to a monthly sum. They could also track the progress of the project on the website and in the newspaper. Barclays Bank made an initial donation of £500,000, part of which helped meet the costs of setting up the website, and contributed a further £1 million in match-funding, much of which was directed to the village savings and loans associations that formed the 'livelihoods' part of the project. AMREF's London office set up a dedicated staff team to work on the project, to manage the relationship with the project donors—the *Guardian* and Barclays—and to provide separate administrative support to manage the donations. The Uganda country office in Kampala took responsibility for overseeing the implementation of the project on the ground (with a greater degree of oversight than is typical, in my experience). There were also two types of project evaluation, one commissioned by AMREF, the other commissioned by the *Guardian*, as well as 'progress reports' every six months. Evaluators gave ongoing feedback as the project progressed and these reports were shared not only with the funders, but also with those following the project online. In many ways the project was remarkable for the amount of documentation made available on the website—budgets, surveys, evaluations—and the website was open to comment from interested members of the public. As well as visits by *Guardian* journalists, the newspaper also employed two Ugandan stringers to provide a steady supply of news from the field.

The project got off to a slightly bumpy start with a piece by *The Guardian*'s then editor, Alan Rusbridger: 'Can we, together, lift one village out of the Middle Ages?'[17] The article captured both the optimism surrounding the project in the newspaper (and the awkwardness that finds its way into many mainstream media representations of Africa). The piece also pointed to an inherent tension between *The Guardian*'s position as a journalistic enterprise, committed to professional standards of reporting, and a more paternalistic role as a funder: 'can we, together'.

Methods

My understanding of the stresses and strains of the project came from my involvement with the project over its full life, and in this sense can be considered part

[17] Available at https://www.theguardian.com/katine/2007/oct/20/about.

of what Mosse (2006) has written about as the type of analysis that comes from being partly an 'insider'. I authored one of the early blogs on the site (about the history of the region) and also conducted a review of the project at the end (I have published a number of articles and a book on the Teso region where Katine sub-county is located—see for example, Jones, 2009). For NGO workers in Katine, there was weariness and wariness when I met them, particularly when the project was coming to a close. They regarded my review of the project as one more thing that might provoke criticism. Journalists were more open in conversation, and I remember one particular instant where a reporter told me of both the simultaneous achievements of the initiative and the 'blurred' boundaries that emerged.

The chapter draws on semi-structured interviews with *Guardian* journalists, AMREF staff, and people living in Katine. I spent time at *The Guardian*'s London headquarters, visited AMREF's country offices in London and Kampala, and participated in some of the public events that *The Guardian* organized around Katine. I have anonymized sources, and the quotes used are illustrative of what a number of respondents told me about an issue. Journalists often repeated the same points, while project staff often had a similar experience of the project and the relationships involved. A total of twenty-two interviews were conducted: eight with journalists and staff employed by *The Guardian* and fourteen with AMREF staff (of which four were with senior managers in London and the Uganda country office and eight with AMREF staff in the Katine office).

In what follows, there are two examples of the relationship between AMREF and *The Guardian*. The first looks at the public scrutiny that surrounded the early phases of the project and the building of a primary school. I show how this coverage was disorienting for staff at the NGO and points to the ways in which scrutiny was very different from the sort of publicity the NGO hoped for. The second looks at the health strand of the project and shows journalists influencing the project on the ground. In this instance, journalism reoriented the NGO's work. I also suggest that as the project evolved these disorienting/reorienting moments became fewer, and that the relationship grew more settled and established at higher levels, at least. In other words what may be thought of as the relatively uncritical relationship between NGOs and journalists is not always arrived at easily (cf. Lugo-Ocando and Nguyen, 2017). A final section looks at how the case can be read as part of a larger story of AMREF becoming more of a media organization.

'It was insulting of AMREF': Disorienting Scrutiny

In the early part of the project, the main effect of *The Guardian*'s spotlight on Katine was to show up the sizable gap between the public face of the NGO and the way it went about its work in the field. This was not a particularly comfortable experience for AMREF. NGOs are usually able to control the differences between what turns out to be fairly messy work on the ground and presentational aspects of their work: a leaflet, a web campaign, or a policy paper (Lewis, 2007: 165). AMREF staff were less practised in dealing with criticism than their counterparts in some of the bigger, more high-profile NGOs. Criticism focused on the details of a single project, rather than the generalities of the NGO, and could be levelled against individual staff as well as the NGO as a whole. Commentary on the website was often sharp in tone. There were concerns that some of the construction work was over-budgeted and of poor quality, that the NGO was spending too much money on trainings and workshops, that the relationship between the NGO and the local population was less than the stated ideal of 'participation'.

Take what was, perhaps, the most complicated story told on the website—that of the building of Amorikot Primary School. Over the course of two years, *Guardian* journalists and members of the public documented the mixed and uneven experience of Amorikot. AMREF adopted an approach that differed from the usual 'community-supported' model used by other NGOs in the Teso region. They brought in a contractor from Kampala, the capital city, and the school was put up quickly, and there was a sense that things were not quite right. A quick rundown of what appeared on the website demonstrates just how contested, problematic, and long-running was the story of building the school:

8 September The new school opens.[18] Alam Construction refurbished seven classrooms in Amorikot. These classrooms were budgeted at 18.7 million Ugandan shillings. Katine also provided Amorikot Primary School with 126 desks and a number of new textbooks.

The same month there were reports that Alam were delaying their work.[19]

The budget for Amorikot is questioned by journalists and bloggers. Richard Kavuma noted that the government spends only 14 million Ugandan shillings per classroom. 'Ugandalife', who regularly comments on Katine blogs and who runs a project in Masaka district in Uganda, said that he had built classrooms for only 9.5 million Ugandan shillings.[20]

9 March Katine staff defend their approach by stating that their work was of better quality than government contracted school buildings and done more quickly.

17 June AMREF take legal advice over delays in school building work, claiming that Alam construction have defaulted in their work.[21]

[18] Available at http://www.guardian.co.uk/katine/2008/sep/16/education.news.
[19] Available at http://www.guardian.co.uk/katine/2008/sep/22/education.news.
[20] Available at http://www.guardian.co.uk/society/katineblog/2008/sep/29/education.
[21] Available at http://www.guardian.co.uk/katine/2009/jun/17/kadinya-school-construction.

23 June *Guardian* journalist Madeleine Bunting reviews the project and questions the education budget.[22]

9 July Joseph Malinga, a stringer employed by The Guardian, reports that the number of desks accounted by Katine staff contradicted the actual number of desks found in the schools. AMREF suggests that this report was inaccurate.[23]

12 October Joseph Malinga, reports on the unhappiness of locals, schoolteachers included, with the work of AMREF. After trying to end the contract with Alam Construction, AMREF is obliged to let them resume work on another primary school in Katine.[24]

30 November Concerns among parents and teachers are reported, particularly over the question of whether Amorikot will become a registered government school.[25]

The last piece, by Anne Perkins from November 2009, suggested that the confident exterior of the new school at Amorikot threatened to become a 'shell', with declining local support, no money from the district education office, unused textbooks, and a shortage of teachers.[26] While there were a number of more positive, descriptive pieces elsewhere on the website—'training to make a difference', 'primary schools get health kits'—the dominant story of Amorikot was of the unevenness of AMREF's work and the poor design of the project. This was all a long way from the idea of Katine as an opportunity for AMREF to advertise its work.

Getting schools built in Uganda is a difficult business, relying, as it does, on a range of actors—contractors, NGOs, district officials, Parent-Teacher Associations, School Management Committees—where corruption and mismanagement are common problems (*The Monitor, 2002*). The quality of the build at Amorikot would not have come as a surprise to people living in the area, but what was unusual was that it happened on a website in something close to real time, in ways that risked damaging the reputation of an NGO. The reporting focused on whether or not the NGO was competent in its work.[27] The following comment posted by 'Ugandalife' challenged AMREF's decision to use outside contractors in school building work:

[22] Available at https://www.theguardian.com/society/katineblog/2009/jun/23/education-amref-review?CMP=gu_com

[23] Available at http://www.guardian.co.uk/katine/2009/jul/29/school-desks-textbooks.

[24] Available at https://www.theguardian.com/katine/2009/oct/12/education-amref.

[25] Available at http://www.guardian.co.uk/katine/katine-chronicles-blog/2009/nov/30/amorikot-school-government-failure.

[26] Available at http://www.guardian.co.uk/katine/katine-chronicles-blog/2009/nov/30/amorikot-school-government-failure.

[27] In this, there is a slight difference to the more recent scandal that engulfed OXFAM in the spring of 2018. In the case of OXFAM, the scandal focused first on the personal actions of staff members—the use of prostitutes—and only later focused on broader governance questions.

> It was insulting [of AMREF] to suggest that local builders could not build a quality school ... Was the community informed that 173 million (£52,424) was being spent on a school? Not likely. There were no specifics about what the community involvement was ... Of course the people would be happy with what they got. An oversized tent could have been erected and they would have been happy.[28]

This sort of criticism proved difficult for AMREF staff and was a long way from the sort of publicity that NGOs desire. The article on school desks, for example, carried a strong whiff of corruption (suggesting that the NGO was budgeting for items it was not delivering). Moreover, this sort of critical piece got more reaction than articles of the more anodyne type: 'opening new doors at Katine primary school'.[29] This all took place in a context where the journalists were also, in the thinking of the NGO, part of the funding architecture of the project. An evaluation of the project conducted at the half-way stage noted that project staff had little idea of what blogging might mean in terms of opening up their work to scrutiny and that staff 'go to work anticipating what they might see on the website', which makes them feel 'upset, sometimes confused and angry'.[30]

As the project moved along, however, it was possible to see a more established relationship between managers at AMREF and the newspaper. This was for a number of reasons. First, interest in the website fell away, and the comments of critical bloggers such as Ugandalife grew less frequent (the early hopes that such 'crowd sourced knowledge' could influence the implementation of the project proved unworkable). *The Guardian* and AMREF had become more used to each other and were more conscious of the sorts of difficulties that might arise when stories appeared. Second, while Katine never achieved the sort of easy 'alliance' described in much of the literature, AMREF managers nonetheless developed mechanisms for dealing with their relationship with the newspaper (journalists often told me that they felt managed by the NGO). AMREF's country office in Uganda exercised a good degree of control over interactions between staff on the ground and visiting journalists, and field staff told me they resisted engaging with the website, in part, because they felt they had to spend time checking what they said with those higher up. Journalists spoke of the 'top down' style of AMREF's managers. In a description of a later workshop, one of the *Guardian* journalists present wrote of the way 'the agenda was tightly controlled' and that AMREF 'left no space for people'.[31]

[28] Available at http://www.guardian.co.uk/society/katineblog/2008/sep/29/education.
[29] Available at http://www.guardian.co.uk/katine/2008/sep/16/education.news.
[30] Available at http://www.guardian.co.uk/katine/2009/sep/03/mid-term-review-report.
[31] Available at https://www.theguardian.com/society/katineblog/2009/sep/29/amref-exit-strategy. Although, in a sign of uneasiness that this sort of reporting was produced, there was a follow-up piece where participants at the workshop stated uniformly that they were happy with what had gone on.

On a more prosaic level, the relationship itself grew more routine and the personalities involved got used to each other. The possibility of financial mismanagement hinted at in the pieces on school desks and in the contracting of the school building work was never really followed up, nor was there much discussion in the life course of the project of the close and problematic relationship between AMREF, the Ugandan government, and the corporate sector (a relationship that many Ugandan friends of mine have pointed out as at odds with AMREF's profile as a crusading NGO). This was not because journalists were not concerned with the way the project was being implemented or the way AMREF managed its relationship with others (I was told later on by one of the journalists involved that there was more to the story of poor contracting and possible 'shadow work' within the project).[32] It was rather that such stories, if published, had the potential to add more stress and strain to a set of relationships that needed Katine to be a success.

'No drip, no oxygen mask, no injections, no resuscitation': Reorienting Journalism

> Journalists, they come to Katine and interview staff. It raises expectations in the community. When they [community members] see a white person they express their needs. Journalists are not experts in development, but people go to them and complain to them and say 'ask AMREF. You gave them the money' ... that has been very challenging.[33]

The above was a comment from one of AMREF's employees working in Katine. The experience of having journalists turn up and ask questions raised expectations among locals, and for many in Katine, journalists were regarded as donors and sponsors of the project. *The Guardian* was not just reporting on Katine, it was, in a very real sense, a funder, and the tensions that surrounded this dual role remained throughout the project. While some journalists claimed a fairly clear distinction between their work and the work of AMREF—'we made a decision to do fundraising and then report on it'—others spoke of the blurring of boundaries and the awkward sense that journalists were the 'white people' who had 'given the money'.[34]

One area in which the decisions of journalists made a tangible difference was in the field of health. As time moved on, coverage of health focused a lot of attention on issues of drug delivery and the poor state of the local government health centre. This differed from the approach AMREF had taken in the project design,

[32] Interview with journalist in Katine, 7 July 2010. 'Shadow work' meaning work that is billed for but does not take place.

[33] Interview with field staff, Katine office, 7 July 2010.

[34] Interview with *The Guardian* journalist, 22 June 2010.

which had been more interested in preventive measures and community initiatives, and was at some distance from working directly with clinics and hospitals (AMREF, 2007). In the original design of the health programme, Katine concentrated the majority of its efforts on prevention rather than treatment. The focus was on having a public health strategy—immunization, mosquito nets, trainings, clean water, village health teams—rather than investing too heavily in the sub-county's medical infrastructure. AMREF was reluctant to involve itself in the work of the government-run health centre. Their position was that the obvious failings of the health centre—the lack of drugs and absence of qualified medical personnel—were matters for the government; the most that the NGO could do was to raise awareness of these issues. AMREF focused instead on community-level health work including the training of village health teams alongside the provision of clean water and mosquito nets. Journalists, however, increasingly turned their attention on the eye-catching problems of the health centre.

A series of articles on *The Guardian*'s website put the failings of the medical system in human terms In December 2008, a piece asked 'why is there no medicine in the dispensary?'.[35] The author, Sarah Boseley, questioned why other aspects of life in Katine had seen 'modest but significant improvements' when the health centre still lacked drugs. In May 2009, Boseley reported on the death of a woman at the health centre. The piece was titled 'I watched a woman die' and documented the story of a woman who had haemorrhaged after giving birth:

> I counted the seconds ticking away while nothing was done. No drip, no oxygen mask, no injections, no resuscitation. They [the medical staff] had seen it too often before. They knew there was nothing they could do.[36]

The piece makes clear the lived experience of what it is like to turn up to a health clinic in Uganda: 'it has an operating theatre, but nobody qualified to do surgery, and hardly any drugs, let alone a blood bank', and connected the story to wider developments such as the UN's Millennium Development Goals, the International Day of the Midwife, and the work of charities such as Merlin International. This was later referred to in the newspaper as one of the most powerful pieces to appear on the website.

AMREF's Uganda country director Joshua Kyallo was asked directly whether 'health initiatives ... could hope to succeed when the drug stores were empty?'[37] He had to defend AMREF's approach by saying that drug provision was not within their remit and that the best the NGO could do was to lobby 'hard at both national

[35] Available at https://www.theguardian.com/society/katineblog/2008/dec/02/health-centre-drugs.

[36] Interview with *The Guardian* journalist, 22 June 2010.

[37] Available at https://www.theguardian.com/society/katineblog/2008/nov/21/joshua-kyallo-drugs-and-cattle.

and district level to try to improve this situation'. This sort of public questioning was a challenge for the NGO, and AMREF staff explained to me their frustration about the way the health programme was being shifted from what was originally proposed in the project outline. One manager said that 'the project was not to change the system established by government ... staff and drug distribution are issues we were not involved in', but that there had to be changes because 'what comes through the newspaper acts to modify our activities'.[38] These sorts of interactions moved AMREF towards a more active role in making drugs widely available in Katine and in lobbying to upgrade the facilities at Tiriri health centre. This move was pushed by AMREF managers but was difficult for field officers, who were better described as community health workers. By the end of the project, the NGO was giving village health teams drugs to distribute, while Tiriri health centre had a supply of drugs, solar power, a newly built laboratory and had, for a time at least, piped water and a resident doctor, all consequences of AMREF's work in the area. This was not something originally envisaged in the project proposal, nor was it something AMREF staff were supportive of, at least in the initial phase.

In all of this, there is a departure from the usual narrative of NGOs successfully managing journalists, of NGOs having the upper hand. There is also a departure from the sense that journalists and NGO workers are natural allies. This explains why AMREF managers spoke of a process of 'adaptation' and 'healing', of turning the project to some of the issues raised by journalists. A 'management forum' was set up, where 'on a monthly basis we [project managers] are on call to discuss issues related to the project'. From a managerial perspective the forum was a success as it resulted in 'far less issues and far fewer challenges than we did in the past'.[39] In working through these stresses and strains there is also a larger story of the evolution of a middle-sized international NGO in how to work with the media.[40]

Becoming the 'voice on health in Africa': Media and Managerialism

The easing of the relationship between journalists and NGO workers was more apparent at the level of management than on the ground. Senior managers pointed to the awards and the recognition they received among other NGOs and in the

[38] Interview with management, Kampala country office, 1 July 2010.

[39] Interview with management, Kampala country office, 1 July 2010.

[40] It is perhaps worth noting that although AMREF staff sometimes felt pushed around by what appeared on the website, there is also a sense that, as the project evolved, those working in the NGO became better at resisting or postponing what was asked of them. While the health programme was reoriented, there were examples of project elements moving forward in ways that many journalists regarded as unsatisfactory. The governance strand, for example, was described to me by journalists as something they had never really 'got their head around', and although they were critical of AMREF's approach to empowerment, AMREF made few changes.

wider policymaking community, as a way of showing the difference Katine had made to AMREF. I was told of the way Katine had made it possible for AMREF to make good on a broader strategy of becoming the 'voice on health in Africa', that it

> is good for publicity ... A lot of feedback is got through the feedback that comes through the newspaper and that acts to modify our activities, to modify our behaviour as development workers. It brings us more into focus with our objectives.

There is a lot in the above, including the claim that journalists help to change the project. During the course of the project AMREF, as a whole, was coming to look more like an advocacy NGO. Its website had improved, and published material—AMREF's annual reports, campaign material, media applications, imagery—had grown more elegant. AMREF, like many aspiring international NGOs, had started producing 'media content' presenting development issues in ways that mirrored the sort of reporting that appeared on the Katine website (in the hope that this might get picked up in the mainstream media).

Take for example, a piece of commissioned journalism on AMREF's website concerning the 2011 drought in the Horn of Africa:

> For as far as the eye can see, the area surrounding Wajir town is covered in a carpet of loose red soil, dotted with a stubble of hardy thorn trees and leafless bushes. July is the 'winter' season in this arid district of northern Kenya, and while the mornings are relatively cool, the temperature rises quickly and by mid-afternoon, it is 36 degrees centigrade and rising (AMREF, 2011).

The posting offers a personalized and complex account of a drought.[41] As with coverage of health issues on *The Guardian*'s Katine site the piece relates personal narratives to context, and explains the lives of those profiled in relation to health services in the region. In this we can see a more professionalized approach to writing about development, away from the more sensationalist use of images and text criticized by earlier scholarship looking at NGOs and their use of media (Cameron and Haanstra 2008). We can also see a less well-known international becoming more like a campaigning and media organization able to participate in global policy work, and further and further from its original mission as a Flying Doctors

[41] The piece on Wajir town is also noteworthy for the absence of any mention of AMREF, and goes on to mix the stories of individuals, with facts and figures, conveying the way people in the area are coping, or not coping, with the ongoing drought in north-eastern Kenya. The report describes the pressure this places on local government officials and health centres. It begins with a description by Steven Mwangi, a nurse in charge of the maternity ward of the district hospital, of the problems with anaemia among expectant mothers.

service. One of the most important benefits of Katine for senior managers, I was told, was the way the partnership with *The Guardian* opened doors to some of the big global health forums.

This turn toward media and advocacy work had effects on the inner workings of the NGO. An emerging theme in AMREF's work in Katine was the way staff on the ground were pushed around by the demands of media officers and higher up managers. Just as the relationship between AMREF management and *Guardian* staff grew more relaxed, the relationship between field staff and officials in Kampala and London grew more tense and managerial. As one field officer observed:

> It can make you divert from what you had planned. You had planned A but are forced to do B because at the end of it all the demands are different, the expectations are different.[42]

The 'it' he was speaking of was senior management taking too much of an interest in turning the project in directions that worked in media and advocacy terms, but had less relevance for field staff on the ground. In the case of Katine, field staff felt more managed than they had in the past, and their sense of what was worth doing on the ground was second-guessed by those with an awareness of what was, or was not, working in media terms. This was partly due to the relationship with *The Guardian*. But it was also due to larger changes in the sector. As AMREF's 2012 Annual Report makes clear there was a growing commitment to 'raising the organisation's profile and positioning it as an authoritative voice on health in Africa' (AMREF, 2012: 28). The report mentions media-based innovations: not only AMREF's work with *The Guardian* but also a BBC Radio 4 spot, a Facebook application, an event with GlaxoSmithKline; and a Coffey award for their work on the Katine project.

Conclusion

Katine was unusual. A British newspaper, with funding from its readers and Barclays Bank, put more than £2.5 million into a rural sub-county in Uganda over the course of four years and worked in close collaboration with an NGO. The particulars of the initiative, of a newspaper funding a development project, and reporting on it on an almost daily basis was a one-off, and the dynamics outlined in this chapter are in some ways peculiar to Katine.[43] In other ways, though, Katine can be seen as part of a broader trajectory in the relationship between NGOs and the media. In seeking out new partners and in wanting to have a media profile 'like

[42] Interview with AMREF project staff, conducted at Katine, 8 July 2010.

[43] The closest example I could find was Save the Children's Kroo Bay project, set in a slum in Freetown, Sierra Leone. This project also had its own blog and micro-site, although the initiative was more straightforwardly a public relations and media exercise; Save the Children managed the content and coverage.

the OXFAMs', AMREF is emblematic of the changing landscape of international NGOs. NGOs increasingly value those parts of their work that mean something in media terms, and the decision to work with *The Guardian* was part of a broader trajectory of AMREF's in terms of moving into advocacy and public policy work.

At the same time, Katine is also something of a synecdoche for the changing face of the news media more generally. It was possible because *The Guardian* was seeking out new sorts of partnerships and revenue streams. The involvement of Barclays Bank was central to the financial model of Katine, and the initiative also allowed for visits by the CEO of GlaxoSmithKline and a number of development experts and philanthropists. What can be thought of as the successor to Katine, *The Guardian*'s 'Global Development' micro-site, receives financial support from The Gates Foundation, and many of the journalists involved in Katine went on to play a key role in setting up this new micro-site.[44] This is part of the slow evolution of newspapers where they become platforms for issues that might be of less interest to their regular readership, but of particular interest to wealthy sponsors (I was told that 'traffic' on the Katine website was very small). This model of funding journalism repeats itself with the Rockefeller-funded 'Cities' microsite.

This chapter also nuances some of the more general statements made about the relationship between NGOs and journalists. The standard view in the literature is of journalists and NGO workers as natural allies, with NGOs feeding stories to journalists. The case shows that this sort of alliance is not always easy. In the Katine initiative, there was scrutiny and criticism, and we have also seen the ways in which journalists were in a position to influence the work of an NGO in ways that were direct and substantive. Katine also reminds us that while many NGOs are not always 'the OXFAMs with their big media outfits', the landscape inhabited by international NGOs is increasingly defined by the ability to achieve relevance in media and policy terms, of getting used to being in the spotlight.

Acknowledgements

I would like to thank Penny Plowman, Martin Scott, Kate Wright, and Dan Wroe, as well as the editors of this volume, for comments on earlier drafts. The interviews that provide quotes for the chapter came out of a review of the Katine Initiative funded by *The Guardian* and administered by the School of International Development at the University of East Anglia. Other material was taken from the website, available at http://www.guardian.co.uk/katine. This research received financial support from the 'Academic Review' of the Katine Initiative outlined in the methods section commissioned by the *Guardian* News and Media (UEA Project Ref no. D00435).

[44] Browne questions claims that this sort of 'foundation funded journalism' promotes some sort of unitary public interest, suggesting instead that it introduces new types of censorship and self-censorship in what should be the public square (Browne, 2010 see also Scott et al., 2017).

References

Abbott, K. (2009) 'Working together, NGOs and journalists can create stronger international reporting', *NiemanLab*, 9 November, available at www.niemanlab.org//kimberly-abbott-working-together-ngos-and-journalists-can-create-stronger-international-reporting.

AMREF (African Medical Research Foundation) (2001) *AMREF Annual Financial Report 2001*, Nairobi: AMREF, available at https://amref.org/wp-content/uploads/2017/05/Annual-Financial-Report-2001.pdf.

AMREF (African Medical Research Foundation) (2007). Putting African Communities First: Strategy 2007-2017, Nairobi: AMREF, available at https://paperzz.com/doc/7020764/amref-health-africa-s-current-ten-year-strategy--2007.

AMREF (African Medical Reseach Foundation) (2011) Wajir: bearing the bring of the drought in Northern Kenya, Nairobi, AMREF, available at https://reliefweb.int/report/kenya/wajir-bearing-brunt-drought-northern-kenya.

AMREF (African Medical Research Foundation) (2012) *AMREF Annual Report 2012*, Nairobi: Colourprint, available at https://amref.org/wp-content/uploads/2017/05/Annual-Report-2012.pdf

Browne, H. (2010) 'Foundation-funded journalism: Reasons to be wary of charitable support', *Journalism Studies* 11(6): 889–903.

Bunce, M. (2016) 'Foundations, philanthropy and international journalism', *Ethical Space* 13(2-3): 6–15.

Cameron, J. and A. Haanstra (2008) 'Development made sexy: How it happened and what it means', *Third World Quarterly* 29(8): 1475–89.

Conrad, D. (2015) 'The freelancer–NGO Alliance: What a story of Kenyan waste reveals about contemporary foreign news production', *Journalism Studies* 16(2): 275–88.

Cottle, S. and D. Nolan (2007) 'Global humanitarianism and the changing aid-media field', *Journalism Studies* 8(6): 862–78.

Davies, N. (2008) *Flat Earth News: An Award-Winning Reporter Exposes Falsehood, Distortion and Propaganda in the Global Media*. London: Chatto & Windus.

Dichter, T.W. (1999) 'Globalization and its effects on NGOs: Efflorescence or a blurring of roles and relevance?', *Nonprofit and Voluntary Sector Quarterly* 28(1): 38–58.

Drury, A.C. R. S. Olson, and D. A. V. Belle (2005) 'The politics of humanitarian aid: U.S. foreign disaster assistance, 1964–1995', *Journal of Politics* 67: 454–73.

Fenton, N. (2009) 'Has the internet changed how NGOs work with established media? Not enough', *NiemanLab*, 23 August, available at https://www.niemanlab.org/2009/11/natalie-fenton-has-the-internet-changed-how-ngos-work-with-established-media-not-enough/.

Franklin, B. (2014) 'The future of journalism: In an age of digital media and economic uncertainty', *Journalism Practice* 8(5): 469–87.

Franks, S. (2008) 'Getting into bed with charity', *British Journalism Review* 19(3): 27–32.

Hannerz, U. (2004) *Foreign News: Exploring the World of Foreign Correspondents*. Chicago, IL: University of Chicago Press.

Hoijer, B. (2004) 'The discourse of global compassion: The audience and media reporting of human suffering', *Media, Culture & Society* 26(4): 513–31.

Jones, B. (2009) *Beyond the State in Rural Uganda*. Kampala: International African Library for the International African Institute, Edinburgh University Press, and Fountain Publishers.

Jones, B. (2016) 'Looking good: Mediatisation and international NGOs', *European Journal of Development Research* 29(1): 176–91.

Lewis, D. (2007) *The Management of Non-Governmental Development Organisations*. London: Routledge.

Lewis, J.A., B. Williams, and R. A. Franklin (2008) 'Four rumours and an explanation: A political economic account of journalists' changing newsgathering and reporting practices', *Journalism Practice* 2(1): 27–45.

Lugo-Ocando, J. and A. Nguyen (2017) *Developing News: Global Journalism and the Coverage of "Third World" Development*. London: Taylor and Francis.

The Monitor (2002) 'Schools collapse in Teso' by Ongom Komakech. Available at: http://allafrica.com/stories/200211250758.html (accessed 15 March 2018).

Mosse, D. (2006) 'Anti-social anthropology? Objectivity, objection, and the ethnography of public policy and professional communities', *Journal of the Royal Anthropological Institute* 12(4): 935–56.

Pew Research Center (2016) 'The state of the news media', available at https://assets.pewresearch.org/wp-content/uploads/sites/13/2016/06/30143308/state-of-the-news-media-report-2016-final.pdf/.

Polman, L. (2010) *The Crisis Caravan: What's Wrong with Humanitarian Aid?*. New York: Metropolitan Books.

Powers, M. (2013) 'Humanity's publics: NGOs, journalism and the international public sphere', unpublished PhD Thesis, Department of Media, Culture and Communication. New York: New York University.

Powers, M. (2016) 'NGO publicity and reinforcing path dependencies: Explaining the persistence of media-centered publicity strategies', *The International Journal of Press/Politics* 21(4): 490–507.

Rothmyer, K. (2011) *They Wanted Journalists to Say "Wow": How NGOs Affect U.S. Media Coverage of Africa*, Public Policy Discussion Paper Series no. D-61, Cambridge, MA: Joan Shorenstein Center on the Press, Politics and Public Policy, Harvard University, available at https://shorensteincenter.org/wp-content/uploads/2012/03/d61_rothmyer.pdf.

Schiffrin, A. and A. Ariss (2017) 'News coverage of foreign aid: A case study of the millennium villages project in African, US and UK media', in J. Lugo-Ocando and A. Nguyen (eds), Developing News: Global Journalism and the Coverage of "Third World" Development. London: Taylor and Francis, pp. 70–88.

Scott, M., M. Bunce, and K. Wright (2017) 'Donor power and the news: The influence of foundation funding on international public service journalism', *The International Journal of Press/Politics* 22(2): 163–184.

Smith, M. and H. Yanacopulos (2004) 'The public faces of development: An introduction', *Journal of International Development* 16(5): 657–64.

Van Leuven, S. and S. Joye (2014) Civil society organizations at the gates? A gatekeeping study of news making efforts by NGOs and government institutions. *The International Journal of Press/Politics* 19(2): 160–80.

Waisbord, S. (2011) 'Can NGOs change the news?', *International Journal of Communication* 5: 142–65.

Watkins, S.C., and A. Swidler (2012) 'Working misunderstandings: Donors, brokers, and villagers in Africa's AIDS industry', *Population and Development Review* 38: 197–218.
Wright, K. (2015) "'These grey areas": Freelancers and the blurring of INGOs and news organizations', *Journalism Studies* 17(8): 989–1009.
Yanacopulos, H. (2005) 'The strategies that bind: NGO coalitions and their influence', *Global Networks* 5(1): 93–110.

PART III
ENGAGEMENT

9

Allah megh de

Culture and Climate Struggles in Bangladesh

Shahpar Selim

Introduction

The Ganges Brahmaputra Meghna basin is home to Bangladesh, a predominantly agrarian country with rivers flowing down its flat and low topography towards the Bay of Bengal. These features not only define its culture, economy and society, but also make it one of the world's most climate vulnerable countries. Sea level rise, increased soil salinity, devastating tropical cyclones, storm surges, flash floods, torrential rains, monsoon floods, extreme temperatures, and droughts have all impacted people's health, well-being, and economic security. In their book *Bangladesh Confronts Climate Change*, Roy et al. (2016: 26) develop the argument that this country on the front line of climate change has made impressive (and perhaps surprising) progress with adapting to climate crisis, influencing and also regularly challenging assumptions made by outside experts and development professionals. Taking a historical perspective, they make a case that 'climate change will not create new problems for Bangladesh but it will exacerbate many of the existing problems'. Such a perspective highlights the ways in which the country's natural ecology has over many generations helped to equip people with many of the capacities to deal with the risks arising from environmental instability and that this experience may offer useful resources for the future.

Bangladesh Responds to Climate Change

Building further on these arguments, this chapter considers the role of cultural resources as useful sources that can inform climate policy and programming. In doing so, the chapter also engages with wider discussions about the neglect of the arts in engaging with climate change. The novelist Amitav Ghosh's *The Great Derangement: Climate Change and the Unthinkable* (2016) draws attention to what he sees as the mysterious silence of contemporary arts and fiction in relation to climate crisis and policymaking. Since climate impacts on cultural life why has

Shahpar Selim, *Allah megh de*. In: *New Mediums, Better Messages?*. Edited by David Lewis, Dennis Rodgers, and Michael Woolcock, Oxford University Press. © Shahpar Selim (2022). DOI: 10.1093/oso/9780198858751.003.0010 this been the case, and is there anything that policymakers can learn by paying more attention to culture? In the first part of the chapter the relationship between culture and environment in Bengal is discussed and explored in general terms. Despite some continuing tendencies for a preference in policymaking for western scientific knowledge over local cultural knowledge, this is a cultural resource that has had positive though largely indirect influence. In the second part, a case is made for making more of the potential value of cultural resources in climate policy and development intervention, drawing on the case of Bangladesh and its *pot gan* tradition of community theatre. By discussing selected policy documents and a number of practical examples the chapter suggests that Bangladesh's relative success in this field—such as being selected to host a major international conference on climate change innovation—makes clear that the integration of both 'formal scientific' and 'local contextual' approaches to knowledge is both highly desirable and demonstrably possible.

The Environment, Culture, and Bengal

Samovar and Porter (2003: 8) define culture as 'the cumulative deposit of knowledge, experience, beliefs, values, attitudes, meanings, hierarchies, religion, notions of time, roles, spatial relations, concepts of the universe, and material objects and possessions acquired by a group of people in the course of generations through individual and group striving'. Strongly influenced by its geography, Bangladesh has a rich cultural tradition of songs, poems, seasonal rituals, folk theatre, and painting that speaks to environmental issues, of which two main strands relevant to our discussion are discussed in this section.

First, central to the identities of the people of Bengal (which includes both Bangladesh and West Bengal, India's fourth most populous state) are romanticized images of rural beauty, farming, harvesting, and fishing. The deification of nature and a softness in its expression are hallmarks of Bengali romanticism. For example, Nobel laureate Rabindranath Tagore's (1864–1941)[1] seasonal songs praised Bengal as 'the land of six seasons' (*shoro rhitur desh*). The Bangladeshi national anthem, *Amar Shonar Bangla*, written by Tagore, is a love song to the many seasons that bless 'My Golden Bengal'. The national anthem refers to the shade and the beauty of the countryside as the seasons change. It describes the end of a mother's sari spreading itself over the landscape containing riverbanks and banyan trees. In a nod to Bengal's vulnerability to the vagaries of nature, there is a line saying that when anything affects the beautiful countryside, the protagonist is in tears. Bengalis in the West Bengal town of Shantiniketon, the cultural centre associated with the Tagore family, have celebrated the *Poush Mela* since 1891, a festival held every

[1] Available at https://www.nobelprize.org/prizes/literature/1913/tagore/biographical/.

December celebrating the harvest season with Bengali folk songs and tribal dances. In Bangladesh, every year at the start of the monsoon, Dhaka hosts *Borshamongol* evenings where cultural groups perform Tagore's monsoon songs, dances, and poems.

Jibanananda Das (1899–1954), another of the many writers of Bengal, wrote *Dhanshirir Deshe* which depicts the region's rolling bountiful paddy fields and in which he nostalgically describes wanting to return to the 'most beautiful and compassionate place in the world', time and time again, to the riverbanks covered in green grass. Every *Pohela Boishakh* (Bengali New Year) there is a national holiday in Bangladesh that marks the start of the Bengali calendar year and is celebrated nationwide with processions highlighting rural symbols of identity and celebration (for example, clay dolls depicting agricultural scenes, family life, harvests; and animals commonly featured in folklore, most popularly the Royal Bengal tiger). Food is a vital part of Bengali culture and the harvest season is marked with special sweets called *pithas*, made with fresh ingredients from the harvest and *pitha* fairs are held every winter.

Second, alongside the harmonious vision of an abundant natural world there can also be found imagery of a far darker kind—of emaciated, malnourished, destitute villagers walking through a derelict landscape while vultures loom. Such images are drawn from the still-recent experiences of famine, such as the terrible 1943 outbreak when up to 3 million people died from starvation. Calcutta and its surrounding areas were filled with villagers who had escaped to the city in the hopes of finding relief, only to die there. As Sunderason (2017:7) writes

> Rather than food riots or resistance from a starving mass, the monumentality of the famine lay in its spectres of suffering, as city streets bore the macabre sight of starvation deaths, piled up dead bodies in street corners, people and dogs struggling over morsels from city bins ... This visceral presence of sights of emaciation and death as part of the everyday cityscape made famine imagery a staple of artists, writers and performers.

The 1940s therefore saw the emergence of a more realistic depiction of nature and the political system. Realist painters such as Chittaprosad Bhattacharya (1915–78), Zainul Abedin (1914–76), Govardhan Ash (1907–96), Somnath Hore (1921–2006), and Gopal Ghose (1930–80) responded to both famine and political unrest by departing from earlier forms of Bengali romanticism. Paintings, songs, and poems visualized hunger and death as testimony. Art transcended the cultural and became political.

Frequent experiences of environmental distress also pushed artists towards more activist positions. For example, the singer and composer Abbasuddin Ahmed's (1901–59) iconic *bhawaiya* folksong goes: *Allah megh de, pani de, chaya de re tui, Allah megh de*. It describes a farmer begging his creator for clouds, water, and shade, as he stands on a hot sand riverbed contemplating his extreme thirst. Poet Laureate Jasimuddin (1903–76) was another particularly powerful voice who depicted the challenges of the climate vulnerable life. In his poems we find rural beauty and struggle coexisting, each drawing the other out in sharp relief. His work reveals rural Bengal not only as an idealized space of unbroken bounty, but also as a place of bitter survival. Peasants are depicted as tilling the hard land as a symbol of humanity's attempt to wrestle with nature and fate. One of his most famous poems, *Asmani*, was written about a little girl he had met in Rasulpur.[2] Her frail body is wracked with malaria, and her existence is as fragile as her hut made of leaves. In the last few lines, he contrasts her life with those who were born into more fortuitous circumstances, and asks the reader to decide who deserves more compassion. Another poem by Jasimuddin, *O Bajaan, Chol Jai Chol*, is about a farmer made destitute due to chronic drought. The farmer's wife has committed suicide because of hunger, and he has buried her. Now the farmer is doggedly ploughing deep into the field, not because he hopes for a good harvest, but because he is hoping for his mortality to give him relief. In the poem he says that he must plough, for then he might see his wife again. The fragility of lives—and farmer suicide mentioned in the poem—brought on by old agricultural practices and natural disasters, is a form of realist visualization that is a hallmark of Bengali climate consciousness.

Unsurprisingly, the natural disaster that has most prominently caught the imagination of artists was the 1970 Bhola cyclone. A Category 4 cyclone with wind speeds of up to 155 miles per hour, this was the world's deadliest tropical cyclone on record and hit coastal Bangladesh (then East Pakistan) on 12–13 November, demolishing much of the coastal area and causing the loss of around 300,000 lives.[3] The painter Zainul Abedin visited the cyclone site and almost overnight completed a major work in the form of a 30-foot scroll—using Chinese ink, wash, and wax on paper—that depicted the devastation he witnessed there.[4] The scroll, which he named *Monpura '70* after the island where the cyclone hit, was itself an act of resistance (Sunderason, 2017). The loss and desperation of the islanders shook him from within, and he gave it an expression that had the same idiom as the climate trauma felt by Jasimuddin and others.

[2] Available at http://sos-arsenic.net/lovingbengal/jasi-poems.html.

[3] Available at https://public.wmo.int/en/media/press-release/wmo-determines-highest-death-tolls-from-tropical-cyclones-tornadoes-lightning.

[4] 'Monpura '70', 1973, Ink, wash, and wax on paper, 105×960 cm (scroll), Bangladesh National Museum, available at https://www.bcssolutionbd.com/bangladesh/শিল্পাচার্য-জয়নুল-আবেদিন/ for an image.

The Challenge of Participatory Policy Intervention

From the mud and soul-soaked fields of Bengal we now turn to the much drier world of climate policymaking and project design. The Bangladeshi government's overall climate strategy has been to build institutional strength and capacity, mainstream climate thinking across sectors, and reach out to the most climate vulnerable population with climate adaptive solutions. Policy responses have certainly been designed in ways that keep in mind local cultural contexts, but technical specialist knowledge has always held priority. While these wider cultural ideas and values doubtless have an influence on everyday identities, it is not surprising that they have only been weakly reflected within official climate policymaking, project design, or implementation discourses.

Understanding why local vernacular expressions of culture, whether in the form of folk songs or religious values, tend to be sidelined within climate policy processes in favour of western scientific knowledge and prescription requires us to consider development as a system of knowledge, practices, technologies, and power relationships that have ordered, accelerated, and limited climate action. Arturo Escobar's (1995) work, drawing on the work of Michel Foucault, analyses development discourses and practices, can be analysed as instruments through which western countries and technical specialists place themselves in positions of power over aid-recipient countries. Development agencies tend to produce 'depoliticized' knowledge while offering technical solutions to development problems.

Second, such power structures instrumentalize knowledge systems that use dehumanized language and methods to frame the climate crisis and its solutions. For example the Intergovernmental Panel on Climate Change (IPCC) has privileged western science in its production of the technocratic knowledge system that underpins most field-level intervention (see for example reports by the United Nations Office for Disaster Risk Reduction,[5] the Global Platform for Disaster Risk Reduction,[6] and the EU's Climate Adaptation Support Tool[7]). Climate experts and disaster risk reduction (DRR) experts mostly attempt to explain adaptation in climate risk assessments using the natural hazards-based approach, and these tend to characterize risk as a function of three variables: the climate hazard, the vulnerability of the exposed population to the hazard, and the coping capacity linked to the reduction, mitigation, and resilience of the community exposed to the hazard.[8]

[5] Available at https://www.unisdr.org/we/inform/publications/48588.

[6] Available at https://www.preventionweb.net/globalplatform/2007/first-session/docs/session_docs/ISDR_GP_2007_3.pdf

[7] Available at https://climate-adapt.eea.europa.eu/knowledge/tools/adaptation-support-tool.

[8] Available at https://www.ipcc.ch/site/assets/uploads/2018/03/WGIIAR5_SPM_Top_Level_Findings-1.pdf.

Lack of cultural knowledge dehumanizes such insights. In practice, in the context of community coping capacity intervention, women are often extremely difficult to reach as beneficiaries or participants, with women's responses to natural disaster affected by a conservative patriarchal culture and entrenched class structures (Howell, 2003). Local 'community elites' tend to be over-represented in local participatory consultations and this may result in biased accounts of climate struggles, skewed project designs, and unreliable end of project evaluation (Cooke and Kothari, 2001; Kirkby et al., 2018). Thinking about how climate challenges are articulated and how solutions are produced and considered will be influenced by diverse and potentially conflicting values, priorities, and perspectives—not only within the community, but also between the different community groups, government agencies, and non-governmental organizations (NGOs) involved. Certain stakeholders may not be interested in participating at all, while for others the extent of their participation will depend on how far they see it as a personal priority (Mansuri and Rao, 2013). Climate development tools have a long way to go to address these gaps and tensions.

Third, development work on the ground depends not only on stimulating local involvement but also on the important challenge of mediating and translating between different interests. The role of 'knowledge brokers' therefore becomes important in producing project realities. This role is at the interface where 'technical expertise' meets 'local knowledge and beneficiaries' (Mosse and Lewis, 2006). Knowledge brokers 'translate' information between the social, professional, and geographical spheres that they inhibit. For example research on agricultural extension projects in India shows how the construction of identity among technical specialists and farmers, who were suspicious of the extension workers, impacted outcomes because knowledge is not a neutral product (Desai, 2006). Similarly, a study of local Bangladeshi development workers shows how climate change is used as a 'spice' to make project intervention more attractive to donors, at the expense of local concerns or preferences for a different kind of intervention. Furthermore, local realities that do not jeopardize state politics and/or prescribed project legitimacy logic are 'safe' to be included. Knowledge production is thereby politicized by the local brokers through a process of 'climate reductive translating'. Project designs are produced by multilevel consultations which generate and stabilize mutually supported interpretations and representations, in a way that matches climate realities to project design (Dewan, 2020).

Finally, this is not a system that can be simplistically reduced to the instrumental rationality of western science-driven prescription and the automated machinery of development. It reflects collaboration of central level policymakers, mid-level bureaucrats, international climate negotiators, development partners, western-educated consultants, Bangladeshi development practitioners, implementing partners, and 'beneficiaries' who participate in the system of laws, jurisdiction, the rules of business within institutions, and agreed outcomes of successful climate programming, all the while working within their spheres of agency and power, as skewed as it may be. Recognizing the interaction between these different actors in climate development is important if we are to understand the balance needed between science-based prescription, community-based adaptation models, and the scope for mutual improvement. An understanding of cultural resources from a grassroots perspective can usefully inform climate resilient development at the central level.

However, this is not to say that the importance of planning adaptation around societal values is unacknowledged in current development discourse. The rise of participatory approaches in relation to development intervention, including in the field of climate adaptation, has to some extent opened the door to more positive representations of local knowledge and culture. For example, according to the IPCC:

> Assessment of risks in the WGII AR5 relies on diverse forms of evidence. Expert judgment is used to integrate evidence into evaluations of risks. Uncertainties about future vulnerability, exposure, and responses of interlinked human and natural systems are large (high confidence). This motivates exploration of a wide range of socioeconomic futures in assessments of risks ... Adaptation planning and implementation at all levels of governance are contingent on societal values, objectives, and risk perceptions (high confidence). Recognition of diverse interests, circumstances, social-cultural contexts, and expectations can benefit decision-making processes.[9]

These kinds of insights have begun to open up more opportunities for bottom-up approaches that are effective. For example the Bangladesh government's Community Risk Assessment (CRA) tools developed within the donor-supported Comprehensive Disaster Management Programme allows planners to learn more about rural conditions, and decision-making elites to engage and create plans based on more local consultation. The CRA approach acknowledges that if a disaster strikes, local communities are the first responders, that each community has unique strengths, weaknesses, and needs, and that they should have an important voice in how to react during a disaster. CRA tries to shift the role of planning and decision making, traditionally taken by experts within the government system, further towards the community.

CRA has also become a knowledge brokering tool that uses scientific data and disaster forecasting institutional mechanisms to find out the actions that communities need and wish to take. Inclusivity and community 'buy-in' are acknowledged as important preconditions for an effective disaster response. It engages with local

[9] Available at https://www.ipcc.ch/site/assets/uploads/2018/03/WGIIAR5_SPM_Top_Level_Findings-1.pdf.

government structures in the form of the Union Parishad Disaster Management Committee (UPDMC), which sets up consultations with both communities and experts designed to take into account locality, livelihoods, environmental risk perceptions, and priorities alongside local preparedness and existing coping strategies. The principle is that it is the local community that assesses the hazards, vulnerabilities, risks, and ability to cope, and then prepares a tailor-made coping strategy with help from the experts.

However, the critical literature on participation has long challenged the idea that participation is a straightforward goal (the more the better), given the unequal power being exercised and the differentiated communities that are consulted (Cooke and Kothari, 2001; Dewan, 2020). While the deconstructive criticism of development (for excluding the 'subaltern') has led to more attention being paid to participatory approaches in the institutional methodology of project design, participatory advocates were also criticized for overplaying the role of local knowledge and naively rejecting scientific knowledge and technological opportunities. Olivier de Sardan's (2015) distinction between *ideological populism*, which he suggests is a naive simplification contained in the idea of 'alternative approaches to western solutions', and *methodological populism*, a more nuanced approach in which local perspectives are engaged with critically, is helpful here. While development gradually makes space for more informed bottom-up participation, the roots of development discourse still have their base in western science. Until South–South learning becomes more broad based, western science will continue its hold.

Climate experts often assume that adaptation will proceed under more or less optimal conditions of implementation if tools such as CRA are used. Even though Bangladesh is now rightly hailed as an example of effective disaster response and management, it still has a way to go in understanding and addressing these complexities. An important example of how culture and our values impact our seemingly 'non rational' responses to climate projects, comes from disaster management. Risk perception is one of the core elements of a well-functioning early warning system, but provides a good example of how even with proper risk information, monitoring, dissemination, and response capacities, response priorities will emerge differently among various groups due to their differences in risk perception, and this is directly related to culture. For example, early warning practitioners are starting to recognize that the community's perception of risk may not be the same as that of local disaster management officials (Cowan et al., 2014).

Research from Bangladesh shows how ordinary people may engage with scientific information about climate disasters such as cyclones through the frame of pre-existing cultural and folklore-based narratives around climate events, which may be different from the 'rational' responses assumed by policymakers. For example such cause and effect models fail to explain why in May 2019, despite getting adequate early warning to vacate to cyclone shelters when Cyclone Fani was approaching, some Bangladeshi families living close to the shelters were reluctant to evacuate their homes, resulting in unnecessary deaths in the Borguna area.[10] Similarly during Cyclone Amphan, which hit Bangladesh May 2020, the government ordered 2 million people to evacuate to cyclone shelters. Ground reports suggest that many people were reluctant despite the highest signal level being communicated by the Bangladesh Department of Meteorology.[11]

Patriarchal cultural norms mean that some women feel reluctant to go to cyclone shelters in a conservative culture where they are generally not seen outside their homes without male relatives (Howell, 2003). Inhabitants of the particularly vulnerable *char* areas tend to be more religious and likely to view cyclones as divine punishment. Prayers and penance are their preferred disaster responses, as there is a deeply held belief that everyone's death is preordained. Low levels of literacy also make villagers more likely to feel alienated from formal scientific warnings, which underscores the importance of humanizing climate science jargon and using vernacular terms. Research by Akter et al. (2017) on maize farmers in the coastal areas found that climate fatalism affects farmers' interest in crop insurance. Most farmers were risk insurance averse, and their understanding of climate change risks, and not only the design of insurance schemes, impacted on their likelihood of insurance adoption. How people 'connect to' a particular climate problem, how they feel about a regulatory directive, and how they 'take up' scientific information is ultimately filtered through their cultural values.

Going Further—the Need for Hybrid Approaches, Drawing More on Culture

Engagement between culture and climate policy and intervention is deepening and this may be part of the explanation as to why Bangladesh continues to do well in disaster preparedness and adaptation both domestically and on the international policy stage. Conversation between different forms of knowledge will doubtless continue to develop, and there is a need to learn from a hybrid approach to climate knowledge that draws as much as possible on both local and wider culture and arts.

For example, climate crisis issues are finding their way more prominently into popular culture. The 1970 Bhola cyclone lives on in contemporary imagination, within new novels by Amitav Ghosh (*Gun Island*, 2019) and Arif Anwar (*The Storm*, 2018). A 2009 tropical cyclone named *Aila* was the inspiration behind a

[10] Available at https://bdnews24.com/bangladesh/2019/05/04/fani-1.3m-people-take-refuge-in-cyclone-shelters, and https://thefinancialexpress.com.bd/national/two-die-as-they-stay-at-home-refusing-to-go-to-cyclone-shelter-in-barguna-1556961857.

[11] Available at https://www.deccanherald.com/international/world-news-politics/bangladesh-orders-overnight-evacuation-of-vulnerable-people-as-cyclone-amphan-approaches-839611.html.

recent movie called *Shunte Ki Pao*, which tells the story of a family made destitute by the cyclone which then strives to stand on its own and live a dignified life.[12] Bangladesh's Deepto television company released a 3D animated short film on climate change called *Tomorrow*, intended for a young audience, which was released in November 2019.[13] The plot centres on a young boy called Ratul who learns about rising sea levels and the threats to his family. He starts a global movement to tax fossil fuels, and helps combat greenhouse gas emissions.

Climate change is also leading to new cultural rituals that reflect adaptations to changes in people's lives. Not only are farmers having to shift away from traditional agricultural practices towards climate smart technologies, seed varieties, and practices, they are following different patterns of consumption. Rural rituals are also changing. For example, every year on the eleventh night in the *Bhadro mash* (month) of the Bengali calendar (which roughly falls between August and September), indigenous populations in the north-eastern belt of Bangladesh hold the *Karam* festival and offer prayers to the agricultural deity of Karam in one of many rituals celebrating relationship with the natural environment. In the summer of 2019 Bangladesh experienced unseasonable amounts of rains and riverine flooding, which affected around a million people in the area.[14] Crops were lost, livelihoods were disrupted, and embankments were weakened. In the flash flood ravaged Sylhet region, a new prayer was included for the enactment of laws to protect local environment and culture.[15]

One innovative approach tries to bridge the gap between culture and climate development by using Bangladesh's rich cultural traditions and expressions as a direct resource to advocate for adaptive behavioural change at the local project level. Folk songs and street theatre have long been part of the cultural repertoire of NGOs undertaking awareness raising work in rural areas. Organizations such as Bangladesh Rural Advancement Committee (BRAC), CARE Bangladesh, Save the Children, and UNICEF have each used cultural performances to convey social messages to local communities using expressions of local values and ideas. Topics have included cyclone preparedness, prevention of child marriage, changing agricultural practices, dealing with wild life, drinking water, and migration rights. Such interventions usually centre on forms of expert technical knowledge being translated into messages through interactive performances by actors or singers. The objective here is to convey ideas by translating scientific jargon into culturally relatable messages to potential participants. The message and the messaging

[12] Available at https://www.imdb.com/title/tt3313734/

[13] Available at https://www.dhakatribune.com/showtime/2019/12/22/animated-film-tomorrow-available-for-streaming-online.

[14] Available at https://reliefweb.int/report/bangladesh/bangladesh-monsoon-floods-2019-final-report-n-mdrbd022

[15] Available at https://www.thedailystar.net/arts-entertainment/event/news/karam-utshab-concludes-sylhet-1798678.

cannot be assumed to be free from the knowledge brokering or climate translation discussed earlier.

The *pot gan* theatre tradition consists of short performances using folk music and illustrative scrolls. The tradition combines elements of deep religious faith and the struggle with natural forces for survival and this makes *pot gan* popular in rural Bangladesh. For example, *Gazir Gaan* are songs about a folk hero called *Gazi Pir*,[16] who is believed to control animals and particularly tigers. Stories from his life are presented in illustrated scrolls, often depicting his battles with natural forces, and his friendship with Raja Dakshin Rai, who lived in the mangroves and battled with the goddess of snakes. The overall message is one of mutual respect and tolerance alongside recognition of people's interdependence with nature, and these ideas can be expressed through songs and dance.[17] This type of performance has long been incorporated into the activities of local social and cultural organizations. For example, an NGO called Rupantar has made it its mission to deploy folk culture—including *pot gan*—within its grassroots work to build awareness and coping capacities in relation to gender issues, natural disaster, conservation and climate change impacts, and is believed to have reached around one quarter of Bangladesh's population with its messages (Ahmed, 2016).

Development agencies have also begun to use *pot gan* theatre performances as interactive events, usually held at a venue and time to maximize attendance by the community, as a way to engage and challenge audiences with information linked to experiences that relate to their own lives. The script is usually written by the performers, who have been briefed by development experts on the issues, interacting with community members. The script for a *pot gan* therefore comes directly from stories told by the subjects themselves, as in the case of one particular initiative of the theatre department of the University of Dhaka in collaboration with Manchester University's Global Development Institute. Following two years of field research on urban climate change migrants in the slums of Dhaka they created an interactive *pot gan* called 'The Lived Experience of Climate Change'.[18] This depicted real stories of the climate migrants who had settled in Dhaka's slums, with stories of urban flooding, health risks from dirty water, lack of sanitary facilities, group struggles in challenging circumstances, and discussion of the socio-political relationships in these communities that impacted on efforts to bring about change. A documentary produced on the *pot gan* work shows how the play made the slum

[16] A *pir*, sometimes translated in English as 'saint', is a Sufi spiritual guide.

[17] Avaialable at https://www.thedailystar.net/supplements/naboborsho-special-1422/gazir-gaan-representation-tolerance-and-social-equality-77169?amp.

[18] A performance filmed at the Independent University of Bangladesh is available at https://www.youtube.com/watch?v=kD5NDoP0R7E&index=4&list=PL3ua0MTzoi86zUZf5gAytXBt5Xg5ZHyiL.

audiences feel heard. Performances in Dhaka reached over 7,000 people including the slum dwellers, policymakers, practitioners, academics, students, and the general public.[19]

There is no denying the efficacy of such interactive and culture specific formats in connecting with the audience on climate change when we compare it to dry technocratic language. When compared to attending a lecture or seminar on climate issues, community audiences for street theatre and *pot gan* report much higher retention. Post-event dialogue with the audience, training the performers (foundational courses) on an ongoing basis, preparing the 'life journey' mapping of the audience ahead of the script writing, and more structured interactions over ongoing awareness raising would help build social capital that could result in deeper climate advocacy. Exploration of innovative ways to advocate for climate action can be found in other countries as well.

In 2019, Germany's international broadcaster, Deutsche Welle, in collaboration with local NGOs, started a project called Eco Islam in Indonesia and Pakistan.[20] The project aimed to communicate the environment-friendly messages of Islam as widely as possible, and to encourage clerics to become involved and take up the cause. In the same year artists and performers in St+Art India held a 'Climate Art Project' in Delhi to raise awareness among citizens about air and water pollution.[21] Moving to the Global North, climate artists including painters, playwrights, photographers, dancers, and sculptors have each tried to find ways to bridge the gap between the sciences and arts, and to use their work and performances as a catalyst to inspire audiences to make eco-friendly life changes.[22] Even though these life changes are radically different and considerably easier to make than those required of the climate vulnerable people of Bangladesh's *chor* lands, the underlying mechanism for translating hard sciences into human emotions remains essentially similar.

Blending Scientific and Cultural Knowledge

Bangladesh's response to climate crisis draws on longstanding cultural traditions that have helped to mediate relationships between its people and the environment. These have evolved over thousands of years and continue to do so in the face of new more recent pressures brought about by global heating. The challenge

[19] Available at https://www.gdi.manchester.ac.uk/research/impact/the-lived-experience-of-climate-change/.

[20] Available at https://www.dw.com/en/why-religious-narratives-are-crucial-to-tackling-climate-change/a-51384374.

[21] Available at https://homegrown.co.in/article/803479/fighting-climate-change-with-art-be-a-part-of-indias-first-climate-parade-in-delhi.

[22] Available at https://www.artsy.net/article/artsy-editorial-10-artists-making-urgent-work-environment.

now is to continue to draw even more effectively on these resources to develop constructive strategies to manage the climate crisis and ensure sustainable and viable livelihoods for Bangladesh's people. Of course, culture, indigenous knowledge, and local participation are not a substitute for scientific knowledge, technical innovation, international cooperation, or upstream policymaking—but they may contribute a relevance and a resilience to development processes that are sorely needed.

So far we have talked about folk performances as tools, but those are rather limited in their reach back into the highest spheres of policymaking unless they are used differently. Art that carries climate messages offers a powerful tool for climate advocacy not only within vulnerable rural and urban communities but also among wider audiences. The *pot gan* format can be used to draw the attention of policymakers and public office holders to climate issues, resource inequalities, gender, power, and social hierarchy dynamics and to help build situated responses. In this case, the messaging and agency must come from the field, not as passive participants but as active creators of mutually agreed upon, internally shared discourse. If climate art is used outside of the context of a project design situation, then perhaps we can hope for a clearer bell ringing out to the policymakers at the national and international level.

Additionally, ethnographic modes of cultural inquiry can be undertaken during programme or project design assessment through forms of immersive collaboration with stakeholders to understand how global processes (such as unseasonable heatwaves) are expressed in local languages or reflected in changing cultural practices. By engaging with how far people are noticing changes in nature, how they are judging the risks associated with these changes, and the extent to which this is driving changes in production and consumption behaviours as well as cultural practices, it is possible to gain a more nuanced understanding through the use of cultural perspectives. For example, a discussion with village elders on how certain seasonal markers, such as bird migration or markings on tree barks have changed over time, would contextualize climate adaptation more closely to the Bangladeshi context. Such 'companion modelling' can be used to explore knowledge systems in ways that can better integrate 'traditional' and 'scientific' perspectives on adaptation in ways that can help with the design of better adjustment management plans (Adger et al., 2013).

There is much more that can be built upon in this vein. Folk expressions of climate change could be used by policymakers to build deeper and more human connection with people living on the razor's edge of climate change, and vice versa, used by scientists and experts to communicate more accessibly with ordinary people. Climate arts can offer powerful advocacy tools at national and international levels, for example the use of epic scrolls such as the *Monpura*, and murals and performances in installation spaces. Collective interactive performances could be interspersed with climate information in entertaining ways, giving urban audiences another perspective on the climate problems that they only see on the news happening to people who live far away from them.

While significant challenges remain, Bangladesh's capacity to build on this longer-term history and culture has contributed to its growing profile on the international stage. For example, the country hosted the 2019 Global Commission on Adaptation (GCA) conference in Dhaka, where Ban Ki-Moon noted that Bangladesh had become a global leader in adaptation to climate change, with many valuable lessons to offer to others.[23] The GCA's 2019 report *Adapt Now: A Global Call for Leadership on Climate Resilience* applauded Bangladesh's achievements in reducing cyclone and flood mortality rates through the use of improved early warning systems, the raising of public awareness, the construction of a network of cyclone shelters, and the development of effective recovery services.[24] The report cites Bangladesh as a success story for placing the locus of adaption at both the sub-national and national scales, and for its use of participatory, transparent, and gender-inclusive approaches. The report recognizes Bangladesh for these achievements, and notes a reversal of its earlier subordinate role in global development relationships:

> Bangladesh, once only the recipient of development solutions, is now hailed as an example that can be learnt from. In June 2020 Bangladesh assumed once again the presidency of the Climate Vulnerable Forum made up of forty eight countries (which it previously chaired from 2011–13 and established the CVF's first trust fund) along with the Vulnerable 20 group of Ministers of Finance from those countries most threatened by climate crisis.

Conclusion

Climate change has shaped our lives, will continue to do so and increasingly challenge us. In responding we will need to combine many strands of thinking—at the policy level, at the scientific level, at the community level, and at the personal level—and we will need to continue to hark back to earlier experiences through which we have over a long period attempted to navigate climate challenges. However, current discourses of climate crisis, backed by scientific risk predictions and prescribed adaptation and mitigation priorities, may still limit our imagination and crowd out the full range of possible responses. What is also needed are local, national, and global climate dialogues that can help determine what a 'good'

[23] Available at https://www.dhakacourier.com.bd/news/Reportage/Climate-Change:-Adaptation-action-to-be-accelerated-in-South-Asia/2848

[24] Available at https://cdn.gca.org/assets/2019-09/GlobalCommission_Report_FINAL.pdf. https://gca.org/reports/adapt-now-a-global-call-for-leadership-on-climate-resilience/

intervention looks like: the types of questions that need to be asked, the types of answers that need to find space in accepted narratives, the kinds of expertise that are deemed necessary, which sections of the population need support, and who has the necessary institutional power and legitimacy to govern the change that's needed. Dominant technocratic and scientific orthodoxies tend to depict climate change primarily in technical and economic terms. But if we are to act effectively, we will need also to talk about power, inequality, and injustice and we will be unable to do this if we tune out local experiences, informal expertise, and diverse forms of knowledge.

What are the lessons that emerge? First, policymakers should be wary of listening only to 'expert' narratives in relation to dealing with climate change, privileging only certain kinds of voices, or designing projects with only a particular 'rational response' in mind. The design of implementable and measurable interventions that can contribute usefully towards adaptation or mitigation will become more plausible if policymakers and technical experts can engage with the broadest possible understandings of what climate change means at the community level. Second, the case of Bangladesh demonstrates that culture offers potentially powerful avenues for enhancing local participation and as a tool for advocacy. A broader recognition and application of this insight can not only help to improve intervention in Bangladesh but also inform work in other climate vulnerable countries.

The way we imagine climate change and its outcomes has profound cultural implications, and our expressions of the climate struggle will need to bear witness to our longer climate history. The challenge for an authentic climate culture is to approach the world in a subjunctive mode, to imagine it as though it were other than what it is—to imagine new possibilities, forms of governance and legislation, and to rethink our own consumption behaviours. The world will come to Bangladesh to learn about climate adaptation, according to Bangladeshi climate expert Dr Saleemul Huq.[25] Our collective cultural experience is a resource that helps us to testify to our past and will enable new possible solutions to share with the world.

References

Adger, W., J. Barnett, K. Brown, N. Marshall, and K. O'Brien (2013) 'Cultural dimensions of climate change impacts and adaptation', *Nature Climate Change* 3: 112–7.

[25] Available at https://www.dhakatribune.com/opinion/op-ed/2019/09/15/leading-the-way-in-adaptation?fbclid=IwAR1WoilliLC5eUh4XUdpHlb2M_wsS29ueOJGYWGh8BEBg8UkCNSPspcPDk8.

Ahmed, S. J. (2016) 'Applied theatre and climate change in Bangladesh: indigenous theatrics for neoliberal attacks', in J. Hughes and H. Nicholson (eds) *Critical Perspectives*anam *on Applied Theatre*. Cambridge: Cambridge University Press, pp.150–71.
Akter, S., T. J. Krupnik, and F. Khanam (2017) 'Climate change skepticism and index versus standard crop insurance demand in coastal Bangladesh', *Regional Environmental Change* 17(8): 2455–66.
Anwar, A. (2018) *The Storm*. New York: Atria Books.
Cooke, B. and U. Kothari (2001) *Participation: The New Tyranny?*. London: Zed Books.
Cowan, Y., E. O. Brien, and R. Rakotondrandria (2014) *Community-based Early Warning Systems: Key Practices for DRR Implementers*. Harare: Food and Agriculture Organization (FAO).
Desai, B. (2006) 'Inside out: Rationalizing practices and representations in agricultural development projects', in D. Lewis and D. Mosse (eds), *Development Brokers and Translators: The Ethnography of Aid and Agencies*. Bloomfield, CT: Kumarian Press, pp. 173–94.
Dewan, C. (2020) 'Climate change as a spice': brokering environmental knowledge in Bangladesh's development industry', *Ethnos* DOI: 10.1080/00141844.2020.1788109.
Escobar, A. (1995) *Encountering Development: The Making and Unmaking of the Third World*. Princeton, NJ: Princeton University Press.
Ghosh, A. (2016) *The Great Derangement: Climate Change and the Unthinkable*. Chicago, IL: University of Chicago Press.
Ghosh, A. (2019) *Gun Island*. London: John Murray.
Howell, P. (2003) *Indigenous Early Warning Indicators of Cyclones: Potential Application in Coastal Bangladesh*, Disaster Studies Working Paper 6, London: Benfield Hazard Research Centre.
Kirkby, P., C. Williams, and S. Huq (2018) 'Community-based adaptation (CBA): Adding conceptual clarity to the approach, and establishing its principles and challenges', *Climate and Development* 10(7): 577–89.
Mansuri, G. and V. Rao (2013) *Localizing Development: Does Participation Work?*, Policy Research Report, Washington, DC: World Bank.
Mosse, D. and D. Lewis (2006) Theoretical approaches to brokerage and translation in development', in D. Lewis and D. Mosse (eds) *Development Brokers and Translators: The Ethnography of Aid and Agencies*. Bloomfield, CT: Kumarian Press, pp. 1–26.
Olivier de Sardan, J-P. (2015) 'Methodological populism and ideological populism in anthropology', in J. P. Olivier de Sardan and A. Tidjani Alou, *Epistemology, Fieldwork, and Anthropology*. New York: Palgrave Macmillan, pp. 133–165
Roy, M., J. Hanlon, and D. Hulme (2016) *Bangladesh Confronts Climate Change: Keeping Our Heads above Water*. New York: Anthem Press.
Samovar, L. and R. Porter (2003) *Communication between Cultures*. Canada: Thomson Wadworth.
Sunderason, S. (2017) 'Shadow-lines: Zainul Abedin and the afterlives of the Bengal famine of 1943', *Third Text* 31(2–3): 239–59.

10

Contemporary Arts Festivals in Nigeria and Nepal

Reclaiming and Reimagining Development Discourse

Caroline Sage

> Our stories provide us with a reflection of who we are as a nation or community. It is like holding a mirror up to ourselves, reflecting who we are, where we have been and how we would like to be different. Our stories allow us to not only value our own histories, but also to help us define our own futures.
>
> Nigerian author

Introduction

The past few decades have seen a proliferation of contemporary arts festivals in the so-called Global South or developing world.[1] Many situate themselves within global movements, such as the Arts Biennale movement or the more recent 'Creative Cities Network' supported by UNESCO. Since the first African Arts Biennale in Dakar Senegal in 1990[2] over a dozen regional, national, and city-based Art Biennials have been established in the Africa region alone. Even those events that are not part of these transnational movements tend to identify themselves with the wider world of 'contemporary' arts and, as such, the 'modern' world. Such events often engage directly with familiar development narratives, focusing on

[1] I recognize the incongruence of relying on the same language and framing that I am seeking to lay bare as cultural constructs—such is the power of our language and the discourses we operate within. At this point in time I can only say that I recognize the contradictions at play, that like Escobar who could never escape the discourses of development with his focus on 'unmaking development', I have found no linguistic or imaginative solutions. But as I strongly believe in the power and real life impacts of particular discourses and framings, recognizing the challenges that developing world actors, actions and narratives can pose to these ideas is one way of perhaps helping change their shape or the impacts they have on how the development industry operates in the world.

[2] Dak'Art: African Contemporary Art Biennale based in Senegal was founded in 1990 by the Senegalese Ministry of Culture and Listed Heritage. While the nature and scale of the event has changed over time, it has consistently aimed to create a platform to showcase, analyse, and debate contemporary African art.

Caroline Sage, *Contemporary Arts Festivals in Nigeria and Nepal*. In: *New Mediums, Better Messages?*.
Edited by David Lewis, Dennis Rodgers, and Michael Woolcock, Oxford University Press. © Caroline Sage (2022).
DOI: 10.1093/oso/9780198858751.003.0011

issues such as inclusion and social and political change, as well as the creative industries as drivers of economic development. In other ways, however, such events often pose direct challenges to dominant development discourses through both the 'contemporary' global framing, and the articulation and promotion of alternative conceptualizations of value and priorities for social change. The concept of 'contemporary' in these contexts displaces linear notions of development and processes of social change, while highlighting existing value, capabilities, and notions of identity and self-representation. As such, these events should not only be valued for their potential contribution to development—more importantly, they provide spaces to gain different perspectives on dominant development discourse as well as different discourses of development altogether.

While all societies are necessarily in a state of constant change, the dominant premise, discourse, and practice of 'global development' posits societies along a particular path towards some imagined 'modern' or 'developed' ideal. While this critique is hardly new, and widely acknowledged even among development practitioners, such discourses are remarkably enduring in their framing and practice. International development, with its continued privileging of economics (growth and poverty reduction) on the one hand and human capital (as the basic human needs of health, education, and jobs) on the other, provides little space for alternative values and priorities. It is true that the more recent cultural turn in development has focused more attention on issues such as cultural heritage and related social and cultural capital, however much of this work has continued to focus on the economic value of heritage—through creative economies or tourism, and has privileged historical and tangible notions of culture and identity, often reinforcing a colonial framing of 'traditional' societies.

Even within this cultural turn, the 'contemporary art' scene sits uncomfortably. In contrast to historic sites or 'traditional indigenous practices' which are increasingly understood to have value for both local economies and as global public goods, contemporary art practices are often not seen as related to development at all. Contemporary arts festivals further complicate their relationship with development discourse through their challenge to national and local boundaries, and their inherent global links and imaginings. They are spaces where alternative narratives about identity, place, value, and thus ultimately the very nature of development are imagined, created, and disseminated. As the first president of Senegal, Leopold Sédar Senghor—who launched the precursor to the Dak'Art Biennale, the 'First World Negro Arts Festival', in 1966 in Dakar—once opined, 'We are all cultural hybrids'.[3]

Contemporary arts festivals in the developing world can be seen as examples of Senghor's 'cultural hybrids' or Arturo Escobar's 'hybrid cultures' in the 'Third World periphery', where Escobar (1995: 225) argues one might find 'innovative

[3] Cited in Mbengue (1973: 12).

visions and practices' that could lead to the 'unmaking of development'. Yet the divide between global development discourse and local identities or critiques of such discourse is rarely so simple. Much of the individual and collective action that is behind and visible in contemporary festivals in the Global South is inseparable from the development discourses that they are challenging or supplanting. They provide spaces for local voices and self-determination, but they are also places where the interaction between the global and the local are debated, contested, and reimagined; where the multilayered connections between place, culture, history, and particular movements or groups of people are explored and reconstituted. More than unmaking development, they provide spaces for reimagining it.

This chapter aims to highlight the ways in which contemporary arts festivals can be seen as both a challenge to global development discourse and a distinctive source of information, data, and even inspiration. In the cities and communities where they occur, they are increasingly important spaces for debate on key social issues, where leading thinkers present, contest, and debate the pressing issues facing communities. They provide spaces for the deliberation of ideas among not only the intellectual class but also, importantly, the political elite—who (for various reasons) frequently attend such events. Moreover, the very public, often performance-based nature of such events necessarily increases their reach and influence within the broader community, providing alterative narratives to the seeming 'poverty or inequality traps' or dystopian futures faced by many, and thereby enabling the 'capacity to aspire' (Appadurai, 2004) to something better. While one cannot ignore the power of development discourse in shaping ideas, events, and practices in both the Global North and Global South, it is possible for practitioners to engage more productively with alternative narratives which would allow for more genuine 'co-creation'[4] of programmes for change. Interestingly, as noted above, these festivals also do something that mainstream development already cares deeply about: in Nigeria, contemporary arts festivals support and promote a vibrant, growing arts market, and in Nepal they are an important element of the tourism industry.

I do not claim to be providing a rigorous study of the range, depth, and aims of the multifaceted festivals that have emerged across the developing world in recent years. Rather, I present a snapshot of experiences, images, and learnings from a small sample of arts festivals in Nigeria and Nepal—in particular, in Nigeria, the *Ake Arts and Book Festival, Art X,*[5] and *Lagos Photo*; and in Nepal, the *Kathmandu Photo, The Kathmandu International Film Festival,* and the *Kathmandu*

[4] Co-creation is generally understood as a form of collaborative innovation or joint creation of an activity or product together with multiple stakeholders. Co-creation in the development space would recognize the knowledge, capabilities, and views of those whose lives organizations are working to change and would include them in the design, implementation, and evaluation of such processes.

[5] While in fact the first West Africa Arts Fair, I have included Art X in the groups of art festivals because the inclusion of a range of festival-like events and discussions, etc., and its lively and important contribution to the discourse and visibility of art in Nigeria and Africa, make it more similar to a festival than many of the more established purely market-focused Art Fairs.

Triennale—all of which I have had the pleasure to attend and in some cases collaborate with in small ways. Needless to say, this sample does not do justice to the variety of festivals in each country, even within my explicitly narrow focus on those festivals that self-consciously and explicitly define themselves as contemporary, international, and connected to a global arts scene.[6]

The chapter explores four different elements at play in each of these festivals: *Representation and the Reclaiming of 'Third World' Narratives*; *Deliberation and Contestation on Value, Politics and Identity*; *Market Relations, Livelihood Strategies and Promotion*; and *Reimagining Development*. I am in no way intending to imply that these elements are separable; indeed, it is the recursive interplay between perceived and real socio-political realities and the imagined and/or real potential for change that is more often than not what gives contemporary art its power: it is this that draws the audience into the dialogue and ultimately to defining revised, public discourse. As such, my aim is to spark debate and interest in the importance of such festivals to development discourse and practice and, much like the editors of the present volume, I hope this may spur on and legitimize more research in this area.

Representation and the Reclaiming of 'Third World' Narratives

While clearly very different countries, both Nepal and Nigeria are places that have to constantly grapple with the way they are defined by the outside world; the dominant narratives about each country, often taken up and perpetuated internally, undermine people's abilities to define themselves in an empowered and 'contemporary' way. For its part, Nigeria is known for endemic corruption, dirty oil wars, 419 scams,[7] violent international drug syndicates, and—perhaps worst of all for the imperial gaze—as the home of arrogant, self-confident Africans. In contrast, the story of Nepal is the story of the remnants of an ancient kingdom—a veritable lost Shangri-La—that is now hemmed in between two of the world's emerging powers: China and India. These interrelated lenses—a romantic fading world or

[6] There is an undeniable narrowness to my focus; this is an inherently urban—some would say middle-class—movement which is drawing on global as much as local ideas and influences. In many ways it could be told in relation to the current focus on 'creative' or 'global' cities, and indeed this is an important part of the story. But by lumping all our analysis into 'cities' as drivers of development, we often seem to miss the constituent parts that shape the development of these cities as inhabited spaces, as well as how such spaces help to define new narratives of a national image and ultimately a 'more developed' imagined community.

[7] '419 scams' is the name given to the advice-fee scams usually involving the promise of large rewards or returns on investment for small—or sometime not so small—up-front payments. The number '419' refers to the section of the Nigerian Criminal Code dealing with fraud, the charges and penalties for offenders.

relatively insignificant country at the mercy of powerful neighbours—allow little space for Nepali agency or a modern Nepali voice to emerge.

While stereotypes often have some geneses in real events or experiences, I would argue that the relationships between these narratives and the majority of people's lived realities in either place are at best limited. They do, however, reflect ongoing world views and framing of many international players or so-called development partners in each place, which in turn shapes development practice. In line with dominant development narratives across the developing world, both places are defined by the deficits and their invariable lack of specific capacities that the development industry hopes to 'fix'.[8] Yet, as in all parts of the world (and previous historical moments), people and communities resist the framing of those who seek to define and control them, and find ways to express their own voices in their own way.

In the last decade or so, a range of innovative contemporary arts festivals in Nigeria and Nepal are providing new spaces and platforms for communities to express alternative representations and narratives of their lives. As is so often the case, forms of artistic expression and engagement serve to challenge stagnant or oppressive ways of thinking and open up new imagined possibilities. In his two-volume exploration of the birth and the remaking of the modern world, Bayly throws light on the roles the arts has played in political, social, and economic life over the last two centuries.[9] While Bayly examines the ways in which the arts reflected and often served to propagate dominant political and economic ideals, he argues that 'at the same time the artistic imagination threatened continuously to subvert these trends'.[10] With Fascist dictators recognizing the power of art as much as revolutionary heroes, the history of various arts movements reads as a history of contestation and cultural reimagining, in which art and literature play a central role in the evolving narrative, or as Bayly reflects, in the twentieth century it 'signally contributed to the remaking of the human person'.[11]

The Power of Representation: Changing Narratives, Changing Lives

While I would challenge any framing of Nigeria that locates blame for many of the country's challenges on something inherent to Nigerians, it remains true that

[8] It would take another paper to explore the drivers and incentives for the perpetuation of such narratives within the international community and many, such as Arturo Escobar cited above, have written scathing critics of the project of development. Others have critiqued the primacy given to economic models of development that prioritize certain elements of societal life over others. Needless to say, for local communities and the overall development of these countries, the framing is not only inherently partial, crowding out other voices and perspectives, it is also in both cases fundamentally disempowering.

[9] See Bayly (2004, 2018).

[10] Bayly (2004: 366).

[11] Bayly (2018: 228).

Nigeria is a country about which it is hard not to despair. An almost textbook case of a resource cursed state,[12] Nigeria is one of the few countries in the world that has gone dramatically backwards on human development indicators since the 1970s. Economic diversification has shrivelled, poverty and inequality continue to spiral upwards, while violent conflict plagues the North and continues to threaten resurgence in the South. The negative reputation of Nigeria and Nigerians globally and within the Africa continent is hard to ignore. Images of conflict and devastation—the bloated starving children of the Biafran war; the oil covered, burning communities of the Niger Delta; the extrajudicial killings and human rights violations of military rule; the notorious violent street gangs of Lagos; to the more recent rise of so-called terrorism in the North—continue to shape the international image of Nigeria as a violent and dangerous place. Stories of international internet scams, global money laundering rings, and Nigerian drug syndicates promote images of Nigerians as predatory even beyond their borders. Internally, the bleak discourse of Nigeria's corrupt state and incessant negative stereotyping from both beyond and within fuels despair—and arguably promotes cycles of conflict and disadvantage—thereby undermining the ability of the next generation to imagine, and aspire to, a more positive future.

But alternative narratives continue to resist the dominant stories of deprivation and predation, and most Nigerians will still defend their peoples as a vibrant, creative, resilient lot. Creative and alive are words I have come to associate with Nigeria and Nigerians. Art, music, fashion, and performative ways of being have always been central to community life in Nigeria. Even in the poorest communities, people take pride in the aesthetics and embedded traditions of what they wear, how they live, what they eat; music, dancing, and performance are an ever-present part of everyday life, bringing not only joy and a deep sense of belonging to communities but enabling people to collectively understand and reflect on their lives and processes of change. For Nigerians these connections stretch well beyond local communities, with an active creative diaspora that moves with pride between the hustle of Lagos, the culturally saturated roots of their hometowns or villages, and the global creative capitals such as London, New York, and Dubai. Leading Nigerian writers, such as Teju Cole and Chimamanda Ngozi Adichie, may live most of their lives in the Global North they still write about Nigeria and Nigerians in both worlds—and in-between. The first theatrical performance of *The Secret Lives of Baba Segi's Wives* by Lola Shoneyin that I saw at the first Ake Arts and Book Festival in Nigeria in 2013 was reproduced for sell-out shows in London a few years later.[13]

[12] Zubikova (2017).

[13] Available at https://www.theguardian.com/stage/2018/jun/14/the-secret-lives-of-baba-segis-wives-review-arcola-london.

Those who run festivals are often acutely aware of the importance of images and owning their stories. Tokini Peterside, the founder of Art X Lagos which was launched in 2016, begun the event as a business bet on the growing number of Nigerian and African collectors and a cultural investment in the city, which she recognizes continues to have a negative reputation.

> We hope to redeem some of that image by providing a good reason for people to come to Lagos. It may have challenges, but it's a pretty exciting place.[14]

Art X, a glamorous affair West Africa Style, focuses on displaying and promoting established and emerging talents from across Africa and the diaspora. In doing so it helps reverse the flow of information and experiences, bringing the leading contemporary art institutions to Nigeria—from the Tate Modern, Xeitx MOCAA, the National Museum of African Art at the Smithsonian, the Art Institute of Chicago and Centre Pompidoi[15]—to experience a different, vibrant, and unbelievably talented side of Lagos and the broader West African world.

Similarly, 'Ake Arts and Book Festival', established seven years ago by writer and educator Lola Shoneyin, aims to bring together African writers, thinkers, and artists, to celebrate, develop, and promote creativity in the African continent. Like all the festivals discussed in this paper, the festival is put on by local authors, thinkers, and change agents and is aimed primarily at local participation—i.e. Nigerian and African creatives and communities. Each year since its inception the festival has grappled with some of the most challenging issues that Nigeria or Nigerians have to grapple with, including important issues of identity; the 2020 theme of 'Black Magic' is thus described:

> Whilst envisioning a proud and powerful resurgent identity, we shall explore the expansion of black imagination and black consciousness. AkeFest2020 will be an unapologetic reclamation of cosmologies, mythologies and belief systems that have sustained Africa and her Diaspora through millennia of disruption and change. We also seek to celebrate the magic of black people as a locus for interrogating cultural memory, as well as notions of black excellence, resilience and resistance.[16]

This 'envisioning', 'reclaiming', and 'celebrating' actively challenges narratives of deficit and despair.

The 2018 theme 'Fantastical Futures' specifically focused on the ideal future of Africa, explicitly asking people to explore the possibilities of different futures. Shoneyian, who is also the director of Ake Festival, explained,

[14] Available at https://www.nytimes.com/2019/02/08/arts/design/lagos-nigeria-art-x-art.html.
[15] Available at https://artxlagos.com/about/.
[16] Available at https://www.akefestival.org/theme/.

> I believe we need to have lots of conversations about the Africa that we want, but not in the spiritual sense of 'speaking it into being'. I'm looking at the practicalities, where two or three thinkers get together and talk about the Africa they desire and imagine. In having those conversations, they can start fine-tuning that vision.[17]

Thus the organizers aimed to challenge thinkers on various aspects of the continent's future with over fifty panels, films, book talks, art exhibitions, and performances on everything from being 'queer' in Africa; entertainment, education, and technology in mother tongue; 'black britishness' and the influence of the diaspora; music as a vehicle for change; whether Africa is really open for business; the intricacies of Afropolitanism; divinity and spirituality; and Understanding Afrofuturism and the Black Panther phenomena. What is particularly important from a 'development industry' lens is that the conversations are never limited to the creatives, with a range of political leaders—from vice presidents to governors to traditional leaders—and thinkers always part of the panels or focused events.

These alternative and disruptive local and global narratives are as essential to people's wellbeing, the development of positive identities, and for the next generation's capacity to aspire to a different future for themselves and their communities. An integral part of the Ake festival each year is taking authors and their books out to hundreds of schoolchildren as part of their outreach programme, with the explicit aim of promoting a different imagined future. Presenting the possibilities of a more empowered future is particularly important for Nigeria's young people. If you have never met a Nigerian author or read books in which Nigerians had a myriad of lives, it may be hard to imagine the possibilities beyond those around you—which may derive from living in a poor household and experiencing a barely functioning school environment. The festival makes sure there are as many Nigerian authors as any others at the festival, and explicitly focuses on African literature, key to their aim 'to develop, promote and celebrate creativity on the African continent'.

The IME[18] Nepal Literature Festival has been running for a similar time to Ake with similar aims—to provide a 'forum for fostering pluralities of thought and ideals of tolerance and inclusiveness',[19] seen as key for a country recovering from a war driven by exclusion and socio-economic divides. While IME founders wanted to

[17] Available at https://johannesburgreviewofbooks.com/2018/11/05/we-need-to-have-lots-of-conversations-about-the-africa-we-want-an-interview-with-lola-shoneyin-founder-of-the-ake-festival/.

[18] The International Money Express (IME) Group is the title sponsor of the festival. Established in 2001, the IME Group is one of the leading business conglomerates in Nepal, with investments in remittance, banking and financing services, automobiles, energy industries, communication technology, tourism and other services. The group prides itself in giving back to society through its support to non-profit initiatives.

[19] Available at http://nepalliteraturefestival.com/about-us/about-festival/.

put their home city and country's writers on the map globally, they also wanted to create a space for discussion and sharing locally.

> You need a community to thrive even if you are more of an introvert like many writers. You need to be able to see what is possible and reflect on where you come from. Events like the Nepal Literature Festival provide a platform to create and grow such a community and to hopefully inspire [the] next generation to come join.
>
> Nepali writer

Both Ake and IME Nepal Literature Festival include political and economic writers as well as authors of fiction; both focus on issues of national, political, and economic interest, as well as more traditional literary themes. And both hold public debates with political leaders and leading thinkers. As such they provide invaluable insights into various local perspectives on current debates. Invariably more insightful than the donor driven policy dialogue that is a common tool for engaging on specific topics with various stakeholders, such platforms would provide development partners with insights and information on all sorts of issues pertinent to their engagement in each country. Such discussions both reflect and challenge the dominant development discourses, but importantly they insist on the importance of bringing local representations and local voices to the discussions of change.

The Power of 'Contemporary' Framing

> I am not an African Artist or a Nigerian Artist. I am just a Contemporary Artist. Everyone is always looking to the 'traditional' in Africans as if we are still in the dark ages. It is a way of keeping us in our box.
>
> Nigerian visual artist

All of the festivals discussed in this chapter deliberately situate themselves within the contemporary arts space. As such they have very different aims, audiences, and conversations than many of the more localized festivals I have been to in either country. While I do not imagine that many of those involved subscribe to the crude juxtaposition of traditional vs contemporary, the very positioning of a piece of work or an event as 'contemporary' stands in contrast to much western framing of both Nigerian and Nepali art and culture as 'traditional'.

The idea of 'contemporary' in the arts world is inherently linked to modernism (and postmodernism), projecting a current, forward-facing, globally connected perspective of creativity, even where a particular piece or event involves a reflection on the past. The label and claim of the contemporary art scene in a place like

Nigeria—with its ratings near the bottom of most development indexes—is a direct challenge to the linear model of development that measures 'progress' along certain measurable, predominantly economic indicators.

Frustration with the 'traditional' framing of local artistic practice and outputs is particularly felt by those working in the various artistic communities in Nigeria. This is in part because the framing is often so derogatory and linked to a long history of dispossession, colonization, and race-based prejudice, and in part because the growing sophistication of the arts scene in the country is more actively demanding respect on the global stage. It is fair to say that, far from portraying traditional painting from some imagined remote village, major Lagos arts events are known for their high glamour and high-end price points. Art X, in its fourth year—'of comparable scale to the Africa-focused contemporary art fairs 1-54 (held in London, New York and Marrakesh) and AKAA, in Paris'[20]—is attracting an increasing number of international collectors.[21]

Although the festival modality tends to focus less on the market than the Art X art fair, the Nigerian arts festivals—such as *Ake, Lagos Arts and Book Festival, Lagos Photo*—nonetheless keep some of the glamour and international connectedness in common with their more commercial counterpart. The constantly connected and circling Nigerian diaspora, along with their friends and entourage, provides the scene with a continuous sense of motion and dynamism. Equally challenging to western categorization is the seamless engagement between what in western framing are dubbed traditional social structures, leaders, and ways of being and high modernity that Nigeria can straddle. Many of my artist friends and leading names in the arts world hold important titles or positions in their local villages or communities; many move seamlessly between what others might deem inherently different worlds.

While it is common for those in the arts scene to reject labels such as 'African' or even 'Nigeran' literature or art, this does not mean that the rich history and culture of the country and the region does not inform its artistic narrative. Indeed, as in most places, much Nigerian art and literature draws on local stories, beliefs, mythologies, and experiences. But what I was told time and again by artists and those working in the arts sector was that they rejected how African art is too often framed, located, and understood in the contemporary art world. As one curator explained,

> the issue we have with the label of 'traditional' is not about rejecting our traditions, it is about rejecting others labelling and categorizing our lives and our expressions in ways that seem hierarchical and somehow negative. All cultures

[20] Mitter (2019).
[21] Mitter (2019).

> have traditions that their artists draw on, but that is not what that label is seeking to communicate.
>
> Nigerian curator

In Nepal, a similar 'traditional' framing is often used to romanticize the uniqueness and authenticity of Nepalese artisanship, which can be useful for the Nepalese arts market (discussed below) but is inherently confining of what is deemed to be authentic Nepali arts. It also risks tipping Nepali artists into the 'craft' framing that is equally undermining of artistic expression, uniqueness, not to mention the economic value of their work.

> As long as you are painting deities or other traditional motives you might make a living in the tourist trade. Even those trying to move away from or challenging these traditions often continue to use such motives in their works so that they are somehow legible to the viewers as Nepali.
>
> Nepali artist and gallery owner

This reflection shows how various elements of the development discourse can also actively shape artistic practice, along with the market forces and commoditization of art discussed below. When the arts community actively challenges linear or confining narratives, they are in turn often challenging the dominant development discourse of progress. The critique of western framing of 'tradition', and the embracing of various traditions noted above, does not mean that Nigerians and Nepalis don't challenge certain traditions themselves; they just do so on their own terms.

In *Photo Kathmandu* 2019, the organizers deliberately placed several exhibitions challenging discriminatory social norms in and around the old town of Patan, full of temples, monasteries, traditional architecture, and seemingly continuous rounds of cultural and religious festivals. To see the exhibition one needed to walk through many of the small lanes and squares in the old historical and deeply cultural parts of the city, where daily worship at small family and neighbourhood Hindu and Buddhist temples and shires is part of everyday life, and the old people sit out in the sun or under traditional pagodas passing time with neighbours. In these spaces and ongoing lives, the festival team inserted life-sized images speaking to exclusion and discrimination in powerful, visual ways. For example, the *Where Love is Illegal* exhibition[22] displayed moving images of LGBTQI+ couples from around the world on large standing displays in and around a series of old alleys and squares; the stories of the couples were printed in Nepali and English in large

[22] Led by photographer Robin Hammond, the work documented and captured the personal testimonies of the LGBTQI+ community around the world. Those who participated in this global storytelling campaign chose how they wanted to pose, what to wear, and how to present themselves. Available at http://www.photoktm.com/exhibition/where-love-is-illegal/.

font in one side of the stands. In a square nearby, images of a young women covered with red paint, red material, or with red-dots covering her face presented a testament to a young women's struggles with social norms and menstration taboos in Nepali society. In yet other laneways, *The Public Life of Women: A Feminist Memory Project* displayed historical pictures of women in public life in the most important parts of the old town of Patan, actively bringing them into the public gaze. But the exhibitions also brought people into these areas of deep history, culture, and artistic value; the aim was an exchange, not a rejection of tradition, but an effort to bring together the 'contemporary' with all its multifaceted layers and contradictions.

Deliberation and Contestation on Value, Politics, and Identity

> Artist don't belong to a class. They are social commentators. They are everyman.
>
> Visual arts from Lagos

The creative class drives agendas in ways that international donors or development agencies only ever scrap the sides of; these are their agendas and their communities, after all. This does not mean creative communities are not susceptible to co-option and commodification; indeed, one of the dangers of encouraging development partners in Nigeria and Nepal to pay attention to these spaces is how quickly they can start to influence the focus or scope of debate. Neither does it mean that the creative class itself does not play to the market and to where they feel they will have reputational and economic success, which in turn often necessitates speaking to particular interests, aesthetics, or norms. After all, creatives themselves are a product of their societies, cultures, and imaginings, and—like festivals—while drawing on local content and experiences, contemporary artists often look outwards both to their collectors or buyers and to what they perceive as their global community.

> Of course I want my art to sell. Of course I would love my work displayed one day in the Tate Modern or the Museum of Modern Art. Which artist doesn't aspire to that? My first international exhibition changed my life and changed the way people at home and abroad saw my work.
>
> Nigerian artist

But while the creative classes are part of the broader social context, they also posit themselves as challengers of the status quo—as norm changers and those that push the boundaries of possibility. While often supported by wealthy patrons and dependent on middle class intellectuals, they embody a mobility ethic. They are the trend and fashion setters. This gives them an influence well beyond their own circles, and festivals—themselves promoted as spaces of innovation and chance—provide a platform for self-identified change agents to promote new or alternative ways of seeing things.

Spaces for Engagement, Exchange, and Contestation

Perry et al. (2020: 611) argue that festivals should be seen as part of a new cultural heritage regime, promoting the interface between tangible heritage of place and intangible heritage—as the 'entanglement' of different relationships, agendas and properties:

> Critically it is in the entanglement between tangible and intangible heritage properties, mediated in and through space and place, that the essence of the festival experience can be grasped.

As noted above, Photo Kathmandu and Lagos Photo use the city landscape both as a stage and as part of the broader socio-political conversation the organizers are trying to promote. Photo Kathmandu's explicit aim is to promote this engagement: "'Photo Kathmandu" endeavors to create conversations between the city, its public, its past, and its dreams and aspirations'.[23] Lagos Photo aims to influence a more international and regional dialogue on African experience and identities—it does this in part by 'large-scale outdoor prints displayed throughout the city with the aim of reclaiming public spaces and engaging the general public with multi-faceted stories of Africa'.[24] At their core these festivals are about creating space for different conversations to be had, for different understanding to be developed.

According to Perry et al. (2020), understanding festivals as symbolic domains of shared cultural practices highlights their role in promoting cultural heritage. Given that cultural heritage has some acceptance as a valid value within development discourse, defining festivals as key sites for protecting and promoting cultural heritage—even contemporary arts festivals—may help bring their relevance for development practice into view.

One thing that continuously strikes me about such festivals in both Nigeria and Nepal is how communities are constantly grappling with multilayered identities, pluralist cultural heritages, and non-linear processes of change. It is not just western concepts of history and development that are inherently linear, but also our understandings of the processes of change that we believe we can influence through the practice of development. Equally, cultural heritage within development discourse is often understood in static and historical terms, rather than as

[23] Available at http://www.photoktm.com/about.
[24] Available at https://www.lagosphotofestival.com/festival-information.

part of living, changing communities. Arts festivals, in contrast, tend to throw up the messiness of the lived world, the pluralistic nature of identities and communities, the ever-evolving nature of cultural heritages, and the often-inherent conflicts in the development project itself. As such, they offer amazing opportunities for cross cultural learning.

> You development people always seem to be trying to fix or solve something, but I always wonder what the thing you are trying to fix is. There seems to be a focus more on money than meaning. Certainly seems to be a lot of focus on roads, without necessarily knowing where you want to go.
>
> Nigerian author

Where Politicians Play: Understanding the Power of Cultural Discourse

The framing of contemporary festivals as places of open debate and the sharing of ideas seems to open up space for political discussion in ways that more political or public interest events never manage. They are viewed as somehow a-political, even when they convey clear political content. As noted above, in some ways their power lies in the aim to spark a conversation rather than communicate a defined message; they tend not to set up dichotomized political debates, are generally not linked to political parties, and rather tend to focus on the value of ideas and debate itself. At the same time, politicians seem willing to accept invitations to such events in 'fashionable' and trend-setting spaces and even play by their rules.

An anecdote perhaps best conveys this. Sitting in the artist lounge at Ake Festival across the lunch table from the governor of a powerful, oil rich state in Nigeria, I was stunned by the openness and reflection that was rarely present at formal meetings or the ongoing donor/government policy dialogues that are a central part of development practice. I had met the governor on quite a number of occasions in my role at the World Bank. In these meetings, often surrounded by advisors of various kinds, we were both deeply ensconced in our socio-political roles. While clearly he was aware of the power and influence of various cultural activists and commentators at the table at Ake, this was different. This was a conversation framed as if on a level playing field, among intellectual equals, discussing their perspectives on the state of Nigeria and its future.

At the time, this governor was at the centre of a major power play within Nigerian politics—both within his own state and at the national level—and like many of his contemporaries, he was plagued with ongoing corruption scandals. And yet here he was on the other side of the country chatting to a bunch of writers about the way corruption was understood and what might lead to change in its various forms. He discussed openly what he thought should be distinctions between various forms of rent sharing, where 'things still get done', versus what he saw as abject theft. It was a conversation about some of the real challenges of being in power in the context where many rules and regulations don't apply or are not enforced, and where there are clear expectations that politicians will distribute power and wealth in certain ways. It was a frank discussion about whether change was possible is such a distorted economic context. It was a conversation that development practitioners should, but rarely could, have with their political partners. It was striking. In a context plagued by the 'resource curse', where economic diversification has shrivelled, and economic and political power is so deeply entwined, ideas become one of the only available sources of countervailing power. These people had influence and he knew it; not the usual sort of influence in Nigeria garnered by money and political networks, but the influence of ideas.

A not dissimilar similar dynamic is often at play in the Nepal Contemporary Arts scene. Nearly all arts events I have attended in Nepal have been officiated by a senior politician or civil servants. Along with the families of past rulers, these are the people in Nepal with money and influence in a society that is deeply hierarchical and until relatively recently still largely feudal. On the one hand, artists and writers rely on these upper-class patrons for their promotion and livelihoods; on the other, they are often challenging the norms and structures that keep these people in power. While it is a complex relationship, it oftentimes provides space of mutual understanding, exchange, and even change. There are very few other spaces that I have seen in Nepal where people from different castes, ethnicities, and class come together as seeming equals to discuss important aspects of Nepali life.

> As a writer I have been able to cultivate different relationships than I did as a journalist. Journalists are seen as political or untrustworthy or something. Writers, like artists, belong to a different class. I still work as a journalist. We all wear different hats. I suppose I have realized more and more that people I used to criticize a lot also have different hats.
>
> Nepali writer

What has become clear to me as I have listened to and spoken to a range of politicians or political elites who have attended or participated in various contemporary arts and cultural festivals or events that I attended during my time both in Nigeria and more recently in Nepal is their deep concern with their historical legacy, and indeed their deep concern for their countries' cultural legacy. Their concern about legacies and how their biographies were or might be written turns out to be a key incentive that we as development practitioners rarely would think about.

And it is important to note that this is not just politicians with relatively benign histories—this included all sorts of politicians accused of all sorts of human rights and corruption charges. All still wanted the opportunity to tell something of their side of the story and most still care what people think. And most still want their people and communities to be celebrated.

Understanding 'Value' in Development

Arts and culture, I have been told often by my colleagues, is not something we can expect poor people to care about and is really not a development issue. Poor people need food, education, health care, and infrastructure, and poor countries need economic growth, and then perhaps they might be able to think about arts and culture. But in places like Nepal and Nigeria, where art and culture is so visually evident wherever you look—from brightly coloured wall murals or complex architectural styles, to intricately woven or died cloths, baskets, and mats, to amazingly colourful local religious or cultural festivals filled with dance, theatre, and music—this perception of what people need or what is important to them seems extremely limited.

To understand this seeming blind spot in development discourse requires acknowledging that the dominant narrative values some things over others. For example, while there many be value in the of individual rights, the priveleging of this perspective within development discourse may fuel critiques of community or collective practices and belief systems without examining alternative values they may also bring. Too often when an indigenous group defend certain practices framed as 'traditional',, the individuals are deemed to have internalized their oppression with limited efforts to understand the perceived values of those practices to the group. But more than this, acknowledging and valuing these alternative narratives means giving up control of the storytelling itself, which is perhaps an even harder ask of an industry premised on one-way support and learning and an evolutionary concept of progress.

As noted, as the bringer of aid and knowledge, development agencies usually have focus on the myriad ways that a community is in 'deficit', and on how our interventions will help address these deficits. This preoccupation assumes that we know what the menu of problems are and in turn have a menu of solutions, and ultimately that we are all heading along the same path. Besides limiting our ability to see the various capacities that do exist in a particular context, or indeed that possible different values might be at play, this approach excludes altogether the possibility of a completely different story of development. Values of course can apparently be reduced to personal preferences within an instrumental economic model. But however distributive or equitable such an economic model might be, they are inherently limited by the questions being asked. Important elements of our interconnectedness and our identities, and the various cultural events that allow people to express, perform, and share various elements of their interconnectedness, get lost.

Creative industries, except when they are seen as a drivers of economic growth, are rarely part of the industry's menu for development. And yet it is exactly within these industries where new possibilities emerge.

Market Relations, Livelihood Strategies, and Promotion

While much of this chapter is on the aspects of festivals and creative communities that the development industry rarely engages with, it would be remiss not to mention the economic importance of festivals for many in the arts industry and the growing focus on cultural industries as a driver of growth in development strategies. As Patrick Kabanda highlights in his contribution (Chapter 12 in this volume), the arts contribute substantially to developing country economies and as such should be taken more seriously by development organizations. A musician himself, Kabanda argued in his (2018) book on the subject that the creative sectors of countries provide both economic and social value in a way that promotes meaningful development.[25]

Since 2008, a series of reports on the 'Creative Economy' have been put out by various UN agencies, promoting the role various 'creative industries' play in economic growth strategies.[26] This is the part of 'Arts and Culture' that the development model understands, an industry that can drive economic urban economies and arguably promote broader business innovation. Importantly from a social development perspective, the creative industry tends to promote jobs and lead to more distributive economic growth.

In many parts of the world festivals are seen as a useful strategy for city promotion and the arts as an important part of the urban economy. Festivals provide a platform for sales, for the development of new market links, and are often an important link in an arts value chain. Ake and the IME Nepal Literary Festivals, for example run bookstores throughout the festival where local and international publishers have stalls. Importantly, international publishers are increasingly sending people to these events to talent scout and/or negotiate with local publishing groups.

In Nigeria, bookshops were scarce. While I was living there, there were two small independent shops in the capital Abuja, and a scattering more in the large, bustling Lagos. There were of course numerous bookstalls at airports or attached to supermarkets selling American self-help books and every version imaginable of 'how to make your millions'. So while books were available, quality literature and

[25] Kabanda (2018).
[26] See for example, UNCTAD and UNDP (2008) and UNESCO and UNDP (2013).

more importantly stories written by Nigerians about Nigerians were extremely hard to come by. It was not uncommon for Nigerian friends to ask me to bring back from one of my overseas trips a range of books by Nigerian authors; on one occasion I even handed over a book I was reading by a Nigerian author to a young woman on a plane who looked at it longingly as I went to put it away. While a number of small, independent publishing houses in Nigeria do what they can, it continues to be easier to order books by Nigerian authors outside of the country. Literature festivals, with their vibrant bookstalls, were an exception to this. In festivals like Ake and Lagos Arts and Book fair, people were not only able to stock up on Nigerian literature; publishing companies with authors from around the continent were represented. It was not uncommon to see people walking away from these stalls with boxes of books, with the sales injecting critical cashflow back into the small publishing houses.

Similarly, visual arts festivals create opportunities for artists to promote their work and to network with art writers, critics, and gallerists, although also with potential buyers and collectors. Exhibition profiles and exposure clearly feed directly into an artist's profile and the contingent market value of their work, whether they sell work at the festival or not. Globally situated festivals such as Art X Lagos or the Kathmandu Triennale are also frequented by international institutions and galleries who pick up artists to represent in other countries or internally.

Festivals are also often linked to cultural tourism. As noted above, both Photo Kathmandu and Lagos Photo focused in part on the promotion of the city spaces and their embedded cultural histories and communities. Promotors of the Kathmandu Trienale and ArtX Lagos talk about putting these events on people's cultural calendars; the events are often deliberately timed to fit with other such events in the region to encourage extended cultural tours.

De Beukelaer and O'Connor (2016) argue that unlike the 'Culture and Development' movement of the 1990s, which never really gained traction in mainstream development discourse, the creative economies were easily and quickly taken up within the development industry. There is a constant tension between the commercial aspects of festivals and their cultural value. Several researchers have argued that the conceptualization of festivals as marketing events for cities can risk their commoditization and the reproduction of sameness.[27] Others argue that the promotion of the 'creative economy' is about transforming cultural value into economic value.[28] In his examination of the cultural economy of cities Scott (2000) identified a growing tension between an understanding of culture as grounded in place and culture as non-place based globalized events and experiences.[29] However in my experience, this dichotomized notion ignores both the constantly

[27] Quinn (2005).
[28] De Beukelaer and O'Connor (2016).
[29] Scott (2000).

evolving nature of culture in all its forms and the discursive nature of change. It also fails to recognize that the arts can provide economic benefits without necessarily or automatically being undermined by this fact. The tension between these two sides of a festival in part fuels the intersecting dialogues, the coming together of different viewpoints, and both the promotion and the critique of various ideas. Further, as one of my Nigerian published friends told me, in the modern world it is difficult to spread these ideas or new stories without the marketing and promotion tools, and without the sales that drive the publication runs and the efforts to expand the audience. As De Beukelaer and O'Connor (2016) argue, the creative economy brand 'gets "culture" to the negotiating table with the powerful economic, technology and development Ministries in a way that the "culture and development" debate never managed to do'.[30]

Reimaging Development

If anything provides hope for the future of both Nigeria and Nepal it is the ever-present and courageous creative class: people that build on extremely rich histories of art, music, performance, and literature while locating themselves solidly in the contemporary space. If development is at least in part about having a meaningful and empowered life, it is fair to say that empowerment is intrinsically linked to being able to tell your own story and represent your own ideas and identity, and for those stories, representations, and identities to be valued. While the creative classes don't shy away from the devastating everyday realities that plague ordinary Nigerians or Nepalese, these realities are embedded in contexts where resistance and resilience are ever present, where experience in all its forms is given voice and valued, where amazing characters can and do learn, develop, and succeed, and where positive change can and indeed does happen.

The arts, in any society, reflect, communicate, and are conduits of meaning and value. They are vehicles through which people understand their lives, the lives of others, and the never-ending changes and struggles that human existence entails. This understanding is central to many of our philosophical, theological, and contemplative traditions. Similarly, the quest to understand identity and meaning in our cultures and societies is a core part of many social sciences. It is therefore interesting to reflect on why such a fundamental part of any given society is not at the centrer of the development project.

[30] De Beukelaer and O'Connor (2016: 30).

Conclusion

Contemporary Arts Festivals provide spaces for people to put their voices, ideas, and creations out into the world, and provide a platform for them to be discussed, contested, understood, and transformed. They are consciously both local and global, both context specific and universal, expressing specific histories and traditions in a contemporary world; as such, they reach across the dichotomized notions of development discourse while challenging more linear notions of progress. The festivals discussed in this chapter present opportunities to hear and engage with these ideas and debates, but alas the 'professional' development community—especially international agencies and donors—is rarely present or listening. It is true that there are a few international organizations such as the British Council, Alliance Francaise, Goethe Institute, and the Prince Klaus Foundation who do actively support the arts in countries like Nepal and Nigeria. Yet these arts programmes remain disconnected from mainstream development activities, expressed in terms of cross-country diplomacy and cultural exchange.

It is hard to not wonder whether such palpable expressions of identity, perspective, and imagination are too challenging for the developmental, imperial gaze—that such expressions of empowerment present an inherent challenge to the way development practice structures relationships between 'donor' organizations and beneficiaries, between those with 'limited capacity' or various needs and deficits, and those with the apparent 'technical capacity' and resources to fill those needs. Or perhaps whether we have forgotten the point of development in the first place, too busy building roads without knowing where we are going.

An engagement with the vibrant and vocal creatives in any given country is one way to start a new conversation about what inclusive, culturally embedded development can and should look like. To be willing to rethink our narratives and our assumed goods, and to be really present and listening as a development 'partner', the assumptions would have to change; a reciprocal pedagogy is required, a conversation has to be started. Contemporary Arts festivals provide spaces to join conversations which can drive new ways to engage in development imaginings and practice.

Acknowledgements

This chapter is based on observations at a number of festivals over the four years that I lived in Nigeria from 2010–14 during which time I compiled over fifty interviews with Nigerian festival directors, visual artists, writers, photographers, gallery owners, curators, and art critics, plus my experience over the last two and a half years in Nepal and a similar set of interviews with a smaller group of ten gallery owners, curators, and artists. The views expressed in this chapter are those of the author alone, and should not be attributed to the World Bank, its executive directors, or the countries they represent.

References

Appadurai, A. (2004) 'The capacity to aspire: Culture and the terms of recognition', in Vijayendra Rao and Michael Walton (eds) *Culture and Public Action*. Palo Alto, CA: Stanford University Press, pp. 59–84.

Bayly, C.A. (2004) *The Birth of the Modern World 1780–1914: Global Connections and Comparisons*. Oxford: Blackwell.

Bayly, C.A. (2018) *Remaking the Modern World 1900–2015: Global Connections and Comparisons*. Oxford: Wiley Blackwell.

De Beukelaer, C. and J. O'Connor (2016) 'The creative economy and the development agenda: The use and abuse of 'Fast Policy', in P. Stupples and K. Teaiwa (eds) *Contemporary Perspectives on Art and International Development*. London: Taylor & Francis, pp.24—47.

Escobar, A. (1995) *Encountering Development: Making and Unmaking of the Third World*. Princeton, NJ: Princeton University Press.

Kabanda, P. (2018) *The Creative Wealth of Nations: Can the Arts Advance Development?* Cambridge: Cambridge University Press.

Mbengue, M. Seyni (1973) *Cultural Policy in Senegal*. Paris: UNESCO.

Mitter, S. (2019) 'Lagos, city of hustle, builds an art "ecosystem"', *New York Times*, February 8, available at https://www.nytimes.com/2019/02/08/arts/design/lagos-nigeria-art-x-art.html.

Perry, B., L. Ager, and R. Sitas (2020) 'Cultural heritage entanglements: Festivals as integrative sites for sustainable urban development', *International Journal of Heritage Studies* 26(6): 603–18.

Quinn, B. (2005) 'Arts festivals and the city', *Urban Studies* 42(5/6): 927–43.

Scott, A.J. (2000) *The Cultural Economy of Cities*, London: Sage.

Stupples, P. and K. Teaiwa (eds) (2016) *Contemporary Perspectives on Art and International Development*. London: Taylor & Francis.

UNCTAD and UNDP (2008) *Creative Economy Report 2008: The Challenge of Assessing the Creative Economy. Towards Informed Policy Making*. Geneva: UNCTAD, United Nations.

UNESCO and UNDP (2013) *Creative Economy Report 2013*. Paris and New York: UNESCO and UNDP.

Zubikova, A. (2017) 'Resource curse: Case study of Nigeria', paper presented at the Proceedings of 8th Economics and Finance Conference, International Institute of Social and Economic Sciences, London, 29th—31st May 2017, pp. 258—269.

11

Who Consumes?

How the Represented Respond to Popular Representations of Development

Sophie Harman

Introduction

Research on popular representations of development and the visual or 'aesthetic turn' in international relations has highlighted the utility of the arts as a method of explaining and understanding complex ideas, facilitating more pluralist methods of research, and developing a 'sympathetic imagination' within different publics (Bleiker, 2012; Shapiro, 2013; Lewis et al., 2014a: 4). Popular representations of development and global politics have been read and expressed through art (Ingram, 2011), music, literature, photography (Bleiker and Kay, 2007; Campbell, 2007), and film (Lewis et al., 2014b; Shah, 2014). The intended impact can be educational or to promote change, but often a unifying aspect has been affect: to affect the emotion, thoughts, or experience of the audience engaging in such representations. However, the impact of the representation upon audience tends to be assumed or based on the 'other' audience rather than the subject of the representation. As Bowman argues (Chapter 3 in this volume), this can lead to an uncomfortable disconnect between the different stories that are told. This is a key gap in engagement with popular representations of development: to think about representations is not only to think about the subject of the representation but how the represented view themselves and the representation.

This chapter argues that consumption of popular representations of development is as important as production. How popular representations are consumed is critical to assessing the authenticity of the representation and how it depicts certain aspects of poverty and international development: if the represented do not find it engaging or reflective of their experience then the popular representation could have flawed claims to authenticity. In addition, a focus on consumption is important in recognizing and expanding the universal appeal and interest in popular representations of international development. Popular representations should not just be material drawn from the Global South for consumption in the Global North. For such representations to be popular, they should have global appeal to a

Sophie Harman, *Who Consumes?*. In: *New Mediums, Better Messages?*.
Edited by David Lewis, Dennis Rodgers, and Michael Woolcock, Oxford University Press.
 DOI: 10.1093/oso/9780198858751.003.0012

wide variety of audiences. This will lead to greater engagement, involvement, and potential production of such popular representations from diverse sources around the world. Fundamentally, issues surrounding popular representations of development have to consider not only issues or who speaks, who is represented and who benefits in the production, but also who consumes.

The chapter begins to explore how the subject of popular representations of development respond to and consume such representations. It does so by considering the responses to the feature film *Pili* by the cast members and community in which the film is set. It starts by foregrounding its analysis of consumption and response by the represented with an overview of the three main issues of debate around popular representations of development. Second, the chapter then sets out the background to the production of *Pili* as a form of co-produced research between an academic, film crew, and women drawn from rural Pwani in Tanzania. Third, the chapter explores the reaction to and impact of the film on the women in the film. This section draws on aspects of understanding response in film theory. Fourth, the chapter reviews how different audiences in the local community read and responded to the film. The chapter then draws together its main conclusions with regard to the importance of impact and response of the represented.

Three Issues with Popular Representations of Development

The potential of popular representations to resonate with diverse and broad audiences is the main aspect of its growing appeal to practitioners and researchers working in international development. However, the appeal is also accompanied by a set of concerns as to the wider politics and ethics of such representations. Popular representations of development are not separate from the wider politics and processes of international development, and in many ways present a microcosm of debate over inequalities and power in the development process. With regard to popular representations of development, this debate can mainly be summarized as: who is able to speak; who or what is represented; and who benefits.

The first issue—who is able to speak—points to a wider concern as to the relationship between people living in poverty and those who seek to address or understand such poverty. This is often crudely depicted between a Global North and Global South divide or between low-income and high-income states: the poor live in the Global South as recipients of aid, and those who provide aid or direct international development strategies live in the Global North (Therien, 1999; Hulme, 2010). Actors in the Global North are seen to have the platform to speak on issues of international development that rob or silence the voices of those living in the Global South or poverty (Chowdhry and Nair, 2002: 15). With regard to popular representations of development this refers to how people living in poverty or the 'subject' of international development projects are included in the representation and who is able to create the representation. People living in poverty may have their voice and images excluded, ignored, silenced, misrepresented, homogenized, universalized, or appropriated through various representational forms. For example, in a documentary people living in poverty may be the visual subject but spoken of by an academic expert rather than speaking themselves; or in a photography exhibition their image may be used but presented in a different context that does not represent their experience. The visual images of development can mislead, stereotype, and homogenize populations of communities, regions, states, and even continents through saturating media and visual outlets with similar images of poverty and extreme need rather than representing the broad swathe of difference that exists within these populations. Compounding such issues are inequalities in who is able to produce the popular representation through funding and training for different outputs, and the networks and finance to make such representations public. Asymmetries in wealth, education, and exhibition opportunities often result in people from high- or middle-income countries being in a position to define who is able to speak and how in popular representations. While the poor may speak or represent themselves, they do so in a structure that has been framed and established by another (Harman, 2019).

The second issue—who or what is represented—relates to what the popular representation of development is really about: the subject of the representation or the person that created it. During colonial rule, colonial rulers used low- and middle-income countries as a means in which to make sense of their own statehood (Mbembe, 2001). As scholars such as Amoore (2007) argue, visual representations of global politics continue to shape how people make sense of themselves and sovereign statehood. Combining the visual and low- and middle-income countries, representations of development are less about the subject of the representation but more about how the producer of the representation makes sense of themselves. As Lewis et al. (2014b) argue films that focus on international development are often more about the person that made the film engaging in their own consciousness, than the subject matter itself. The debate here therefore advances the wider questions of who tells the story to consider what the actual issue being represented is, how this may be skewed towards a particular subjectivity, for example through the white/male/western/imperial/colonial gaze, and that the subject of the representation is really the power and relationship between the producer and those they seek to represent (Harman, 2019).

The final issue—who benefits—questions the ethical dilemmas of popular representations. The initial ethical dilemma is over consent: whether a person consents to be represented, how they give informed consent, and how that consent is given once the representation is in the public domain. The secondary dilemma relates to who benefits from the representation and who is at potential risk. Benefits and risks can be financial, employment-based, and social. Financial and employment benefits and risks are generally straightforward: who gains or loses employment or career advancement; who makes money or loses money. The social is more complex as it can relate to who uses the representation for wider leverage in different social contexts (e.g. for political power, claims to expertise) and can also have negative outcomes (e.g. stigma, assumptions of new wealth). Underpinning the ethical dilemma of who benefits is the concern that popular representations can lead to exploitation, notably of producers of the representation using the subject for their own financial, social, and career gain at the expense of the subject's financial, social, and career loss.

Thinking and engaging with these three issues are central to both understanding and engaging in popular representations of development. Critical reflection on such issues has led to wider emphasis on the importance of co-production of popular representations, highlighting work from low- and middle-income, and non-western or English-speaking states, and the potential of education and training for the represented to fully represent themselves at every stage of the production process. These reflections are important for addressing the three debates, particularly with regard to how popular representations are produced. How representations are consumed has been subject to less attention or reflection. Consumption is only addressed through understandings of how such resources are used in teaching (Harriss, 2014), how academics read popular representations (Shapiro, 2009), or how such representations have historically been used as part of colonial rule or behaviour change and education programmes (Diawara, 1992). Less attention has been made to how such representations are engaged and consumed by the subject of contemporary representations. Consumption is an important component of understanding popular representations of development both at an instrumental level (measuring impact, affect, and potential change) and because it is a key factor for marking the efficacy and authenticity of the representation. It is not enough to assess the representation through critical academic engagement or the view of audiences outside of the subject matter to assess the representation, as in many respects the average viewer trusts what they see or hear in popular discourse. Key to understanding popular representations of development is to engage how the represented themselves view or interpret the representation. Interpretation of the representation by the represented furthers our understanding and provides a greater test of authenticity in response to the three debates: who is able to speak; who or what is represented; and who benefits. This chapter explores how this can be done and how it furthers our understanding of popular representations of development.

Film as Popular Representation: *Pili*

The popular representation of development that this chapter is interested in is the feature film *Pili*. *Pili* is an eighty-three minutes feature length drama about the everyday risk of HIV/AIDS in Tanzania based on the stories of the cast of women who act in the film. Set over three days the audience follows the lead character 'Pili' as she tries to secure a loan for a much sought-after market stall. Desperate to get out of working in the fields for less than US$2 a day and have a more stable income for her and her two children, Pili has been saving money but needs to borrow more from a micro-lending group. As Pili tries to get the money, she faces a number of difficult decisions and compromises, while at the time struggling to keep her HIV positive status a secret from her children, friends, and the community. Despite the narrative style, the content of the film draws on a number of themes within international development and politics: gender and HIV, health systems, infrastructure, micro-lending, bureaucracy, informal labour, social reproduction, temporality, and community health workers (Harman, 2019). The aim in writing *Pili* was to create a universal story that anyone in the world could relate to—the desire to create a stable life and income for you and your family—without necessarily having an interest in HIV/AIDS or international development. The decision to make a narrative feature rather than a documentary was twofold. First, to provide a character and story for the women in the film to hide behind so as to protect their identity in the community in which they live. The second was to secure a wide audience beyond the core demographic of viewer that would want to watch a development documentary. One film-maker at the 2015 Global Health Film Festival depicted the target audience for development documentaries as Claire who lives in North London, has two children, a job in the public sector, who reads the *Guardian* newspaper and sometimes the *MailOnline* as a guilty pleasure. For *Pili,* the aim was to secure an audience that included Claire as well as a broad cross section of the population in Europe, North America, and crucially, East Africa where drama-based films are more popular with audiences than documentaries (Harman, 2019).

The intention behind making the film was to make the stories and lives of women living with HIV/AIDS visible, to challenge the aesthetic of HIV/AIDS on film, and to provide a means of co-producing research in a way that the represented could represent themselves (Harman, 2016, 2018, 2019). The co-production element of the project was critical to addressing issues of representation and authenticity: not necessarily in a way in which such problems can easily be addressed, but in a way that explores the 'messy politics' of doing this kind of research (Desai, 2007; Harman, 2018, 2019). The co-production was between an academic working in the field of international relations, a UK and Tanzanian film crew, and a group of women mainly drawn from the rural town of Miono in Pwani, Tanzania. The cast of Tanzanian women involved in the project saw the value of participation in using their stories as a way of helping people in a similar situation so that they know they are not alone, and for informing people about their lives and the everyday experiences of HIV/AIDS. In addition, they received a regular daily income for participating in the project and at least one meal a day (but most often two—lunch and breakfast and/or dinner depending on the time of the shoot) and were aware that any profit made by the film would go back to the community for the women to draw on. For the crew, the value of being involved in the film despite the low pay for the work was the opportunity to make a feature (a key marker of success for early career film-makers) and for the UK crew to travel to Tanzania and work with the community in Miono. The value for me as an academic researcher was to explore film as a method of co-produced research, to think of different ways to make conspicuously invisible women visible, and communicate my work to non-academic audiences.

Co-production took place in the pre-production and production of the film (see Harman 2019 for a detailed explanation of the production). During pre-production, Director Leanne Welham and I met with over eighty women individually and in groups to hear their stories. We then took these stories and identified the main themes and key points arising from them: most of the women were a 'left one' or single parent; nearly all of the women had children, some were grandmothers; most of the women were HIV positive and had experienced some form of stigma—either their own self-stigma or from the community; the majority living in the more rural towns and villages worked in the *shamba* or the fields; some had lived in the local area all of their lives but a good number had also moved around with family; most women were Muslim and faith was an important structure in their lives; and all of the women wanted to secure a small amount of money to set up their own business. These key parts of their lives, my knowledge of the global politics of HIV/AIDS, and Director Welham's understanding of narrative were combined to make the story and key characters for the film.

The story was then tested with groups of women in Bagamoyo and Miono for authenticity and believability, and audience interest. Welham and I sketched out the story; once tested with the women and refined, Welham then wrote the screenplay. The screenplay was written in English and then translated into Swahili. However, during production it became clear that a number of the women in the film had only basic literacy and struggled with the script. The screenplay was therefore a guide for the crew, and the cast improvised much of the narrative that appears in the film. The language of the film is Swahili with English subtitles.

Casting of the main characters happened during pre-production. With the exception of one trained actor who plays the character 'Mahela' all of the cast were drawn from the groups of women that contributed to the story of the film and the locations where the film was shot: Miono, Makole, and Bagamoyo. The main casting took place following an acting workshop in Miono with all other roles cast one week before production, or on the same day for extras and minor parts. Existing members of the cast would recommend people for particular roles or input on ideas for whom to cast, with the final decision made by Director Welham in consultation with me as the producer. All cast, including any extras, were fully briefed about the ethics and risks of participating in the project and signed or thumb stamped standard university consent forms and were able to withdraw from the project at any point. Around 65 per cent of the main cast were known to be HIV positive and with the exception of Nkwabi Elias Ng'angasamala who played 'Mahela', only one person had acted in community theatre and the rest of the cast had never acted before.

The main production of *Pili* took place over six weeks; one week of final preparation to finalize locations, ethics checks, and additional workshops with the cast; and a five-week main shoot. A number of issues arose during the period of the shoot around co-production and an unfortunate series of events with a corrupt member of the Tanzanian crew and local authorities (Harman, 2016, 2018, 2019). The production finished on time, within budget, and with exit meetings with each of the main cast so as to explain what would happen next with the project. Post-production—the edit, colouring, sound edit, score, and sound mix—all took place in the UK. This was the only part of the project into which the women in Tanzania had no direct input. However, with the exception of one major change that was not directly related to the story and lives of the women but the structure of the narrative, the film was cut as close to the original story and screenplay as possible. This was both for issues of authenticity in the story the film would tell and because of practical reasons that—given the budget and time to shoot the film—there was little space for extra footage.

Pili was completed in September 2016 to make the deadline for submission to the Sundance International Film Festival. The main route for securing an audience for a film is selection and premiere at a notable film festival where the film is viewed by a number of buyers and distributors. The film is then hopefully bought and distributed usually for a short theatrical release and then online. *Pili* was submitted to a number of A-list festivals via British Council Film. British Council Film screened the film to selectors from Sundance, Berlinale, Venice, and Cannes who all showed an interest and shortlisted the film (including in competition for *Un Certain Regard* at Cannes) but did not finally choose *Pili* for selection. The process of festival selection took one year, with *Pili* being selected for its premiere at the Dinard British Film Festival in September 2017 that led to a UK distribution and international sales deal (Harman, 2019). In the interim the film was shown at a private screening to cast, crew, and selected invitees in September 2016 and to the cast and community in which the film was shot in October 2016.

Pili was released in UK cinemas and toured around Tanzania in partnership with the US Embassy in 2018, and screened as part of film festivals and specialist partnership events with UNAIDS and Cine ONU and STOP AIDS. The film was well received by film critics in *Time Out*, *Total Film*, *The Telegraph*, and *Metro*, and was nominated for the 2019 BAFTA for Outstanding Debut by a writer, director, or producer. *The Guardian* film critic Peter Bradshaw suggested the film was shot with 'compassionate and remarkable boldness' (Bradshaw, 2018) and Pamela Hutchinson suggested the film 'transforms a simple tale into a substantial film. It's a very moving story, if far from melodramatic—knotty moral quandaries such as these are the stuff of stimulating drama' (Hutchinson, 2018). Screened in partnership with the US Embassy and the National Council of People Living with HIV (NACOPHA) across Tanzania, part of World AIDS Day events in Geneva with Cine ONU, and alongside STOP AIDS's #itaintover campaign, *Pili* has been used to reach a diverse set of audiences around the world. However, what is important here is not how general audiences and film critics assess the representation of the everyday lives of women living with HIV/AIDS, but what the women themselves think of the representation. The co-production of the film attempted to address one of the key problems of popular representation of development: who represents whom and who can speak for the poor. What is equally important is who is able to assess whether the first criterion was met. Non-participant viewers, non-governmental organizations (NGOs), art critics, and academics often make these assessments. The voice that is left out is the participant and subject of the representation. To make a project that seeks to involve people and provide the space for them to represent themselves requires co-production both in the process of making the representation and in the final assessment and analysis of the representation.

Responding to *Pili*: How the Represented Consume the Representation

Film studies make two distinctions when considering response to film: the singular spectator concerned with what happens in the viewing of the film and the collective audience that can be shaped by marketing and mass media (Phillips, 2011). While mass media can shape expectations (reviews, critic opinions), knowledge of what to expect (trailers, interviews), the collective experience of film viewing can engender different reactions. For example, collective laughter can make the individual feel they are part of the audience as they also found something funny, or have an adverse reaction because they did not see what was funny. This is an example of cognitive processing of response as outlined by Phillips (2011); here the audience may make similar meaning (can see that the narrative is supposed to be funny) but have different affects (laughter or aversion). Either reaction is a collective experience and contributes to the notion of films as 'moments of experience' (Dudley, 1998). For authors such as Barthes (1977), films only come into being through their reading by an audience. The singular spectator in contrast refers to the individual relationship to the film that can trigger different readings and reactions that can change with repeated views or watching different films (Phillips, 2011). As Hall and Whannel (1964: 78) argue, film is a physical medium in that 'the experience of watching a film makes a direct impact on us ... the film, which we feel so directly and immediately, can often by-pass some of the social and cultural barriers that cut off audiences from material in the more traditional arts'.

This section considers the singular and the collective audience response to *Pili* by first concentrating on the cast of the film and its singular response, and second the collective audience response from the wider communities in Miono and Makole where the film was shot. *Pili* was screened to the communities and cast members of Miono and Makole in October 2016. The first screening took place on the secondary school playing field in Miono and the second, smaller screening in one of the larger homes used as a set for the character 'Cecilia' in Makole. Both screenings involved a mobile cinema set up by a production and events company from Dar es Salaam. The final estimated audience for the Miono screening was approximately 500 people, the smaller Makole audience was thirty people. As the section demonstrates, the personal narrative of the film means the singular is very much situated within the collective response, as the self-awareness of the cast and their position in society provoked a public response to the film that distanced them from the personal narrative of the main story. Both the singular and collective audience response from the cast and communities in which the story is based and acted out is a crucial component for assessing the outcome of a co-produced project and the authenticity of the representation.

The Cast Response

The women involved in the production of the film first saw *Pili* at the large screening in Miono. This was also the first time I had seen the cast members since the wrap of the main production six months earlier. I did not give any of the cast or Tanzanian crew members advance notice of the screening because of threatening behaviour from one of the ex-crew members and the risk he posed to my safety (see Harman, 2016, 2019 for further details); therefore the days before the first screening involved my travelling around Miono hearing my name called and to then see a cast member running towards me with their arms outstretched. This was a completely different relationship compared to during the main production where I was seen as the main *bossi* of the project. During the screenings I was treated more as an old friend: I was told I had put on weight; I was asked to share news of all of the UK crew members; and was told about all of the happenings in Miono over the past six months: bad harvest; one cast member's new home was taking shape and needed a new roof; another cast member had remarried and was therefore no longer drinking alcohol and generally trying to behave herself (we all agreed this was a shame and doubted how long the new 'good' behaviour would last). In general things were mostly unchanged in Miono; *shamba* work was hard, money was tight and bad when a child needed a new uniform or a roof leaked. There was a sense that the cast and their families were more interested in hearing about how everyone was than what the final film looked like. There was a discussion about having a smaller cast screening before the public screening but it was jointly decided that it might be better to wait for the collective audience experience. For me, this was so that they would not get nervous in front of the audience or potentially become overwhelmed on seeing the final product. For them, this was from a sense of excitement of watching the film together with their friends, family, and neighbours.

Response studies in film theory suggest individual spectator and audience responses to film draws on four components of the self: the *social self* who responds to a film or makes meaning from it in a way as to those of a similar ideological persuasion; the *cultural self* who uses intertextual references (for example films they have seen before) to make sense of it; the *private self* who might draw on their own experience or memories to make sense of the film; and the *desiring self* that brings conscious and unconscious meaning to the film that does not directly draw on the film's content or 'surface' (Phillips, 2011). The response of the cast to the screening of *Pili* complicates this response given their involvement in the film's production and the personal narratives from which the story of the film is drawn. It was expected that the *private self* and the *desiring self* would come to shape the main cast's response and meaning from the film as it was these two elements of the self that defined and shaped the narrative of the film. In practice, the cast's public response to the film was to draw on the *social self* while downplaying the *private self* and *desiring self* to the wider audience. The cast acutely understood their position in the community, the community's reaction or ability to make meaning from the film, and thus their *social self*. They were therefore keen to disassociate publicly from their personal *private self* response to the screening. The film engaged the *private self* of the cast but in being acutely aware of the *social self*, the cast continued to perform for the screening and responded to the film's content on this basis. The *social self* was performed at the outset of the screening with each of the women standing up to introduce themselves, the part they played, and to reiterate they were playing a role, not themselves; they then reiterated this at the end of the film.

The *social self* also pertains to the context of the screening within the wider politics of international development and representation outlined above. Both public screenings took place in the communities in which the film is set; therefore the majority of the audience would have seen the crew around the area during production, and were thus aware that the film is a collaboration with outsiders from the community, from the capital Dar es Salaam and larger town of Bagamoyo, and 'mzungus' or white people from Europe. For the cast members involved in the project this awareness was even more acute and may have shaped how they thought they should react to the film. The expectation may have been that they would like the film. This expectation was based on the fact that the film was drawn from their stories and they were involved in it. When shown work that is complete to a broad audience the expectation is to like and support that work as a means of gaining broader interest and audience and safeguarding your professional and community reputation. Compounding such social expectations around the screening of the film is the potential benefits of the film to the community. Should the film make a profit, such a profit will be returned to the community: the onus was therefore not only on me to manage expectations as the producer and project lead but for the women in the film to manage expectations as to what they were able to achieve for the community by participating in the film. The screening of the film and the role of the *social self* in understanding audience reaction can therefore not be separated from the wider context of the local politics of development: co-production of projects as a source of future investment or revenue, and the impetus for liking or being positive about the project as a success. The results or success imperative and the potential for sustainable income played out at the micro level here reflect wider trends in macro level development projects operating at the national and global scale.

Masking the *private self* response to the film on account of an understanding of the *social self* demonstrates how the film resonated with the real lives of the cast and community in which the film is based. The distancing of the cast from the public *private self* response suggests the film was effective in representing their lives and the authenticity of their everyday experience. The *private self* was displayed through their recognition of the connectivity and authenticity of the story that meant the audience could potentially misunderstand the narrative as the women playing themselves rather than a character. The *private self* was only displayed in the privacy of the main shoot itself, with particular scenes—when 'Pili' reveals her HIV status to the micro-lending group, when 'Cecilia' tries to get 'Pili' to confide in her—leading to clear displays of emotion from some of the cast. The *private self* was engaged by the cast to deliver their performances in the film, but consciously disassociated from their public response to the final output.

The only evidence of the *cultural self* in response to the film was made with regard to the nature of the film: some of the cast thought it was too dark in parts, and less colourful than some of the *Bongo Flava* films they watch. The response to the film itself produced a standard 'mzuri sana'—very fine/very good—which is a positive Swahili response to a number of questions. Some of the women and audience members reflected on their favourite characters, who tended to be the lead character 'Pili', the gossip 'Ana', or 'Pili's' son 'Ibrahim'. Audience members particularly liked the moment in the film when 'Pili' and 'Ibrahim' danced together and he suggested he could look after her. It was expected that none of the women would be effusive in their praise for the film, because this would be out of character, and none would be negative towards the film, as they wanted me to make it a success that made money and perhaps please me and my perceived expectations. The only benchmark of positive feedback was the desire of some of the cast to watch it again and from two of the children in the film who danced, laughed, and suggested their photograph was taken to recognize their star role.

My conversations with the cast following the Miono screening suggested they were happy with the story and the representation and for the story of *Pili* to be made visible; but it was made clear that their key aim for the project post-production was to make money from it (Harman, 2019). The cultural and wider impact potential of the film was discussed with regard to what would happen next with the film and the audiences around the world that we hoped to get for the film. The response of the women was it was good that these stories would get out into the world, to help people understand how they are living their lives, and the importance of living positively as someone living with HIV/AIDS. They also expressed an interest and hope to travel to the UK as part of the film's promotion and screenings, stating they wanted to see where the UK crew members lived and to meet their family and friends. The interest in the cultural impact of the film was much more micro in how they could relate to different individuals and people, rather than a macro scale of difference of large audiences in various countries around the world. The response of the women was both an endorsement of the initial project aims—to make their stories visible and co-produce research—but also an acute reminder of their needs, aims, and ambitions for the project—to make money. The film was not principally assessed on story or representation for the women, but the instrumental abilities of the film to make them money. The response of the cast to the film therefore drew more on the *social self*—awareness of their own position in the community and how the film represented both their lives and the community—and the *desiring self*—their shared aspiration with *Pili* to make money to get out of the fields and start a business; for *Pili* this was a market stall, for the real cast members this was ensuring the film was a financial success.

The Community Response

The collective audience response can be understood by looking at the collective reaction to aspects of the film as it plays, followed by smaller group discussions about the content of the film once it has finished. The smaller discussions combine the collective audience narrative—how individuals shape their views and ideas to fit with the wider group dynamic and interpretation—and the spectator narrative by asking individuals questions directly. This section is based on the collective audience response at the two screenings, with a more concentrated understanding of the spectator/audience dynamic in the smaller Makole screening of thirty people. Assessing the spectator/audience dynamic in the Miono screening was more difficult because of the large number of people in attendance, how the audience grew throughout the screening, and how people rapidly dispersed once the film had ended.

What the audience at Miono does suggest is interest in a film such as *Pili*. At the beginning of the Miono screening there was a large crowd of approximately 250 people, however, as the screening went on the numbers doubled with schoolchildren leaving classes to join the viewing, buses and motorbikes arriving at the playing fields bringing more people who had heard something was happening, and people wandering over to see what was going on. The large audience who attended and remained at the screening until the end of the film most likely suggests a curiosity to see what is happening in the small town in which cinema screenings are rare, or at best an interest in seeing the places and people they know on screen. However, the number of people who watched the film to completion also indicates an interest in films of this kind: drama based on social realism that draws on auteur cinema and themes of international development. The interest in the content of the film was particularly high among some of the older schoolchildren: at the end of the screening a number of the students approached a member of the cinema crew to ask if they could see the film again and if I could visit their school the next day to talk to them more about the issues and themes within the film. The final marker of interest was evident in the smaller Makole screening where one audience member recorded the entire film on her phone. The recording was either for her to watch again or share with friends or to reproduce somehow and bootleg the film; all three options suggest she saw took an interest either for herself or the potential wider audience it could reach.

The unexpected and most evident audience reaction to the film in Miono was laughter. The audience laughed at the intentional funny moments in the film: the slapstick and gossip of the character 'Ana'. 'Ana' was written as providing light relief in the film and was inspired by a number of peer educators I had met. Peer educators work for free in care and treatment clinics, provide peer to peer support for people living with HIV/AIDS and community education, and also help with clerical support to clinics' medical staff. On meeting a number of peer educators it had always struck me that one of the benefits of the job was not only helping people and the stature of such a position in the community, but that it was also a position to get good gossip from the community. The actor who plays 'Ana' agreed with this depiction and improvised care and concern interspersed with gossip and nosiness in her portrayal of the character. Her portrayal clearly resonated with the audience, whose laughter was the result of not only the comedic performance but the ability of the character to connect with the audience: everyone knew an 'Ana'. The position of 'Ana' and the role of gossip in the community were picked up in comments on the film made by the local doctor from the care and treatment centre. The doctor's response was a formal statement that, as perhaps to be expected, focused on the educational elements of the film for people living with HIV/AIDS, but also highlighted the community element:

> The film has got various educational aspects. The message of adherence was strong. The importance of checking your CD4 and staying on top of your illness was very powerful. The importance of community was emphasised which

reflects the reality of living in villages. I was pleased to see that the message of living positively was emphasised.

The other major source of laughter was during the more tense scenes, particularly those between 'Mahela' and 'Pili'. When 'Mahela' propositions 'Pili' the audience responded with a mix of laughter and cheers. This was initially surprising to me as my own experience of watching this scene was of quiet tension and discomfort; until I realized that the laughter was a part of the collective tension of watching such a scene. The collective laughter was nervous laughter in processing and sharing something uncomfortable but familiar. The cheering was either because the audience supported the actions of the characters or was to trivialize or make light of what was being depicted. The vocal responses to tense scenes were a form of collective audience sense-making of the issues and themes depicted in the film and brought to the fore in hard to watch moments. The laughter and cheers provided a collective outlet for such tension and was evidence of discomfort and engagement with what was shown.

What was striking about the laughter was not how it jarred with my own discomfort around the scene but how it differed with audience reactions to screenings of the film at the Dinard British Film Festival a year later. At the *Pili* screenings in Dinard, the audience was completely silent during this scene. Looking around the room at audience members, people looked tense and concerned watching it. What was less striking was the similar response from audiences about the content of the scene and the proposition, with audiences making similar suggestions to the Tanzanian 'it happens'. Such acknowledgment tended to come from audience members who stated they had experience living or working in rural Africa or were aware of issues around gender and international development. Other Dinard audience members wanted to know what was happening in the lives of the cast members and what they thought of the film. The audience expressed not only an interest in how the film was made and film-making in Africa, but a connection with the characters in the film. One audience member, a film producer, approached me to tell me he initially did not want to attend one of the screenings 'as I have seen these films before', but was impressed that it was not another development film about poor Africans.

In this regard, one of the main differences about *Pili* in contrast to other representations of international development such as Bowman's *Aid, NGOs ... with you always* (see Chapter 3, this volume), is the absence of the international from the film itself. There are no NGOs, no 'spaces of aid' such as four-wheeled drive vehicles or gated compounds (Smirl, 2015), and only a fleeting glimpse of white people in the film. It is this absence of the physical representation of the international that appealed to these specific Dinard audiences. The response from select members of the 1,507 people who watched *Pili* during the festival was drawn from their *cultural* and *social self*, regarding both their expectations as to what a film set in Africa about a poor woman would be like, and their own interest in these stories and lives. What was notable was how the film resonated with male audience members in equal ways to female members; it was male audience members who asked the most questions during the Q&A sessions, and stopped me to talk about the film in detail. This recognition and resonance with audience members led to *Pili* winning the Hitchcock Audience Award and receiving Special Mention by the festival jury for the way the screenplay was devised (Grater, 2017).

The laughter was evident in the Miono large group screening but less so in the smaller, more intimate Makole screening. The smaller group gave more scope for group and individual conversation about the film. When asked what the audience members did not like about the film they tended to focus on the character of 'Mahela' rather than the film itself. When asked about the film the general response was *mzuri*/fine or nice. The crew that had set up the mobile cinema made the initial responses to the film: they wanted to know why some scenes were so dark and were concerned that it would impact on the film being selected for a major film festival. They then wanted to know what happened to 'Mahela'; this provoked a wider discussion among the group as to who was responsible for the risky behaviour depicted in the film: 'Pili' or 'Mahela'. A number of male respondents thought it was important to include the proposition scene as 'it happens' in the community and women often had to navigate such issues. As one respondent suggested when asked if 'Pili' was in the wrong in how she managed the proposition, 'what choice did she have?'

To engage the predominantly female members of the audience, I asked them direct questions about the decisions Pili makes in the film. This prompted a discussion on the everyday risky encounters women face and the politics of negotiating such encounters when one had to balance health, the health of others against financial gain, and the future for their children. One respondent was particularly interested in the portrayal of self-stigma; as someone who had self-stigmatized when they were first identified as HIV positive, they thought the film was important in showing people were not alone, should not be afraid of their status, and should ask for help. The issue of anti-stigma seemed to resonate with a large number of the group, particularly the members of the group who volunteered as peer educators. Again, the response to these issues in the film tended to be short 'it happens', 'it is a problem', or 'the community need to be educated' with regards to issues of stigma around HIV/AIDS, single motherhood, and gender relations.

Conclusion

This chapter has explored the response to a feature film about the everyday risk of HIV/AIDS by the cast and community that are the subject of the film. In so doing it has argued that the consumption and response of popular representations of development by the people who are meant to be represented is central to assessing the politics of authenticity of the subject matter and the universality of such representations. Cast and community responses to watching *Pili* highlight the continued relevance of who is able to speak; who or what is represented; and who benefits beyond the production process. The responses show that the social and community context in which the representation is based shapes the reaction and meaning attributed to a film. In this case such context and response suggested the film resonated with audiences as depicting issues that are prominent in the community and could be misunderstood as real events. It is imperative that those represented are afforded the opportunity to speak for themselves, particularly in their immediate social contexts, so as to minimize unintended risk or loss as a consequence of their participation. However, similar to the production of popular representations, these responses took place within a defined social–political context. To ignore the subject of the film or the represented is to ignore the most important audience and reinforce crude divides between the Global South as subjects for content and the Global North as the producers and consumers of such content. Popular representations of development cannot claim to be authentic or represent everyday lives if those to whose lives it relates do not want to watch it. The final issue to consider when exploring popular representations of development is therefore not only who can speak, but also who consumes.

Acknowledgements

This project was funded by an AXA Insurance Outlook Award on the Everyday Risk of HIV/AIDS. Thanks to Ansity Noel, Kieran Read, and Duncan Skelton for additional help in recording audience feedback at the two Pwani screenings.

References

Amoore, L. (2007) 'Vigilant visualities: The watchful politics of the War on Terror', *Security Dialogue* 38(2): 215–32.

Barthes, R. (1977) *Image-Music-Text*. London: Fontana.

Bleiker, R. (2012) *Aesthetics and World Politics*. London: Palgrave.

Bleiker, R. and A. Kay (2007) 'Representing HIV/AIDS in Africa: Pluralist photography and local empowerment', *International Studies Quarterly* 51(1): 139–63.

Bradshaw, P. (2018) '*Pili* review – Hard lives and tough choices in rural Tanzania', *The Guardian*, 11 October 2018.

Campbell, D. (2007) 'Geopolitics and visuality: Sighting the Darfur conflict', *Political Geography* 26: 357–82.

Chowdhry, G. and S. Nair (2002) 'Introduction: Power in a postcolonial world: Race, gender and class in international relations', in G. Chowdhry and S. Nair (eds)

Power, Postcolonialism, and International Relations: Reading Race, Gender and Class. London: Routledge, pp. 1–32.

Desai, M. (2007) 'The messy relationship between feminisms and globalizations', *Gender and Society* 21(6): 797–803.

Diawara, M. (1992) *African Cinema: Politics and Culture.* Bloomington, IN: Indiana University Press.

Dudley, A. (1998) 'Film and History', in J. Hill and P. C. Gibson (eds) *The Oxford Guide to Film Studies.* Oxford: Oxford University Press, pp. 176–89.

Grater, T. (2017) "'God's Own Country", "Daphne" win top prizes in Dinard', *Screen Daily*, available at https://www.screendaily.com/news/gods-own-country-daphne-win-top-prizes-in-dinard-/5122876.article.

Hall, S. and P. Whannel (1964) *The Popular Arts.* London: Hutchinson Educational.

Harman, S. (2016) 'Film as research method in African politics and international relations: Reading and writing HIV/AIDS in Tanzania', *African Affairs* 115(461): 733–50.

Harman, S. (2018) 'Making the invisible visible in international relations: Film, co-produced research, and transnational feminism', *European Journal of International Relations* 24(4): 791–813.

Harman, S. (2019) *Seeing Politics: Film, Visual Method, and International Relations.* Montreal, QC: McGill-Queens University Press.

Harris, J. (2014) 'Notes on teaching international studies with novels: *Hard Times, Half of a Yellow Sun*, and *The Quiet American*', in D. Lewis, D. Rodgers, and M. Woolcock (eds) *Popular Representations of Development: Insights from Novels, Films, Television, and Social Media.* New York: Routledge, pp. 38–52.

Hulme, D. (2010) *Global Poverty: How Global Governance is Failing the Poor.* London: Routledge.

Hutchinson, P. (2018) 'Pili', *Sight and Sound*, 28(11), November.

Ingram, A. (2011) 'Making geopolitics otherwise: artistic interventions in global political space', *The Geographic Journal* 177(3): 218–22.

Lewis, D., D. Rodgers, and M. Woolcock (2014a) 'Introduction: Popular representations of development', in D. Lewis, D. Rodgers, and M. Woolcock (eds) *Popular Representations of Development: Insights from Novels, Films, Television, and Social Media.* New York: Routledge, pp. 1–15.

Lewis, D., D. Rodgers, and M. Woolcock (2014b) 'The projection of development: Cinematic representation as an(other) source of authoritative knowledge?', in D. Lewis, D. Rodgers, and M. Woolcock (eds) *Popular Representations of Development: Insights from Novels, Films, Television, and Social Media.* New York: Routledge, pp. 113–30.

Mbembe, A. (2001) *On the Postcolony.* Berkeley, CA: University of California Press.

Phillips, P. (2011) 'Spectator, audience and response', in J. Nelme (ed.) *Introduction to Film Studies.* London and New York: Routledge, pp. 113–41.

Shah, E. (2014) 'Affective histories: Imagining poverty in popular Indian cinema', in D. Lewis, D. Rodgers, and M. Woolcock (eds) *Popular Representations of Development: Insights from Novels, Films, Television, and Social Media.* New York: Routledge, pp. 131–47.

Shapiro, M.J. (2009) *Cinematic Geopolitics.* London: Routledge.

Shapiro, M.J. (2013) *Studies in Trans-disciplinary Method: After the Aesthetic Turn.* London: Routledge.

Smirl, L. (2015) *Spaces of Aid: How Cars, Compounds, and Hotels Shape Humanitarianism.* London: Zed Books.

Therien, J.-P. (1999) 'Beyond the North-South divide: The two tales of world poverty', *Third World Quarterly* 20(4): 723–42.

12

The Arts in the Economy and the Economy in the Arts

Patrick Kabanda

Introduction

The circumstances that prompted the missive are unknown, but almost three decades ago the iconoclastic economist John Kenneth Galbraith—who once said that 'the only function of economic forecasting is to make astrology look respectable'[1]—penned a passionate letter to Mr Walsh, a staffer at the Boston Museum of Fine Arts. In it he posited that:

> the arts, no one should doubt, are for the enjoyment and enrichment of life. But there is another dimension insufficiently recognized. That is their contribution to economic life and well-being. For after production comes design; with economic development things must not only work well; they must look well. And after material wants are satisfied there must be artistic enjoyment. From this also comes economic advance and economic reward.[2]

Citing Italy in modern times as an example, Galbraith hailed this European nation as a world leader not only in aspects of design production, but also in cultural tourism that attracts visitors from around the world, and he ended his letter suggesting that 'from this the lesson: we certainly support the arts for their own sake. We also do so because of their indispensable contribution to the higher stages of economic life'.[3]

Despite such a weighty endorsement, conceptualizing the ways in which the arts and culture have contributed to human progress has long been a marginal endeavour in development. If development is about enhancing human welfare, however, then the approach to promoting it cannot remain largely technical, no matter how useful such tools might be for addressing certain kinds of problems. Centring development on human beings involves accommodating the kinds of lives people

[1] The Economist (2016).
[2] Holt, ed. (2017: 572).
[3] Holt, ed. (2017: 572).

Patrick Kabanda, *The Arts in the Economy and the Economy in the Arts*. In: *New Mediums, Better Messages?*.
Edited by David Lewis, Dennis Rodgers, and Michael Woolcock, Oxford University Press.
DOI: 10.1093/oso/9780198858751.003.0013

live and value on a daily basis,[4] including the stories they tell, which are conveyed using a wide array of cultural mediums. Those stories are often manifested most powerfully in the arts and popular culture, an area that, despite its historical neglect, is steadfastly kindling interest, in particular in relation to the way that the so-called 'creative economy' can contribute to meaningful development if done in an inclusive manner.

Because development tends to be largely understood in material terms, the immediate economic value of artistic expressions is often neither seen nor understood.[5] The arts are often the first subject to be cut in schools when budgets need to be trimmed, and creative students are repeatedly told not to major in the arts lest they become 'starving artists'. Such thinking ignores the fact that many important ideas tend to be interdisciplinary (Robinson, 2001), that playful creative expression is responsible for many of the central ideas that have shaped our modern world (Johnson, 2016, 2017), and that the arts can greatly enrich people's everyday lives (Sen, 2001). This is perhaps why many creative initiatives tend to grow outside of government policy (see below).

The human development approach rightly asserts that holistic development is 'about expanding the richness of human life, rather than simply the richness of the economy in which human beings live' (UNDP, n.d.). To this end, the arts certainly play a central role in enriching the lives of people everywhere and may be especially salient—as others in this volume have noted[6]—for those whose voices cannot be expressed or experienced in more conventional forms, whether because of such isssues as illiteracy, inability to speak the national (or locally dominant) language, or political suppression. The arts also matter intrinsically; enjoying them does not have to serve an instrumental purpose. But for the purposes of influencing development policy and practice, it surely helps to have compelling examples of how the creative arts have indeed contributed instrumentally to development outcomes—which is the central focus of this chapter.

This chapter is structured as follows. We begin with a quick overview of the notion of the creative economy and estimates from around the world of its material contribution to national economic life. From there we venture to countries on three different continents—Zambia, Colombia, the Philippines—to examine particular cases where the arts have actively and uniquely contributed to the attainment of tangible development outcomes. My claim is not that these cases are 'representative' of such efforts elsewhere—the creative arts, almost by definition, are as varied as the diverse contexts from whence they come—but that they provide instructive insights into the ways in which policy can support, rather than

[4] For more on this, for example, see Sen, 2000.

[5] As former World Bank Senior Vice President and Chief Economist Kaushik Basu once put it, 'there are purists who shirk at the mention of art and commerce in one breath' (Basu, 2011: 75; see also Kabanda, 2018: 204).

[6] See also Lewis et al. (2014).

undermine or ignore, a vitally important source of meaning, expression, and revenue for billions of poor people. The discussion ends with some specific policy options, touching on such areas as funding, intellectual property, and data collection.

The Creative Economy and Its Material Contribution to Development

What is the creative economy? According to the United Nations Educational, Scientific and Cultural Organization (UNESCO), 'The cultural and creative industries are those that combine the creation, production and commercialization of creative contents that are intangible and of a cultural nature. These contents are usually protected by Copyright and can take the form of a good or a service. Besides all artistic and cultural production, they include architecture and advertising'.[7] In terms of numbers, the exact size of the creative economy is not easy to determine, but some credible estimates have nonetheless been made. Howkins (2001), for example, estimated that in 2000 the creative economy was worth US$2.2 trillion worldwide. For Howkins, who in 2001 was deemed to have popularized the very term 'creative economy', this US$2.2 trillion was not static but rather growing at a rate of 5 per cent per annum. From the arts to science and technology, he also applied the term to fifteen industries, meaning that even such items as toys, games, and research and development (R&D) are embraced here. All the same, 'while recognizing cultural activities and processes as the core of a powerful new economy', the creative economy, he argued, 'is also concerned with manifestations of creativity in domains that would not be understood as "cultural"'.[8]

Consider also Nigeria, home of the 'Nollywood' movie industry, which saw its gross domestic product (GDP) in 2013 jump from ₦42.4 trillion to ₦80.2 trillion (more than US$500 billion) overnight, a change that came about largely because the country retired its old approach to accounting. The new approach meant including, for the first time, fast-growing parts of the economy such as mobile telephony and the movie industries.[9] That same year, the US Bureau of Economic Analysis announced that it had created a new category called 'intellectual property products'. This category incorporated expenditures for R&D and for so-called 'artistic originals', entertainment, and literary works. These entries became treated as fixed investment, itemized together with software expenditures (BEA, 2013).

[7] UN (2010); Buitrago Restrepo and Duque Márquez (2013: 37); UNDP and UNESCO (2013); Kabanda (2018: 225–8). See the same sources for other definitions. For a definition of creative work see Kabanda (2015: 4).

[8] Howkins (2001), as cited in UNDP and UNESCO (2013: 19–20); see also Kabanda (2018: 28).

[9] The Economist (2014); see also Kabanda (2018: 16).

That change made the US economy about 3 per cent, or US$400 billion, larger than was previously thought (Imasogie and Kobylarz, 2013).[10]

With respect to international trade, the exchange of creative goods and services 'totaled a record of $547513 millions of dollars in 2012, as compared to $302058 million in 2003', according to a 2015 report by the United Nations Conference on Trade and Development (UNCTAD), an increase primarily led by Asia, and China in particular. Between 2011 and 2012, however, several countries reported a decline in data, 'due to changes in methodologies related to the transition to [a new] version in which many countries did not report data at the time', as UNCTAD explains. UNCTAD's updates and corrections are certainly welcome (UNCTAD, 2015: vii, 1) but it must be remembered that the expansion here may not just be growth alone; it could also be because more countries are reporting their data.[11] In any case, even without debating the nature of jobs in the creative economy, the numbers here are unlikely to capture the true size of the sector. That caveat is important to remember because for one thing most creative or cultural sectors are informal, appearing nowhere in official statistics, even as they clearly do contribute to the economy.

The need to include the arts and culture in development accounting instigated, in 2008, the first of the UN Creative Economy reports (with the second UNCTAD Creative Economy Outlook and Country Profile report (2018) being the most recent of these as of this writing).[12] A separate 2013 report published by UNDP and UNESCO noted that 'the creative economy is the fount, metaphorically speaking, of a new "economy of creativity," whose benefits go far beyond the economic realm alone' (UNDP and UNESCO, 2013: 15). This arts-inclusive approach has also inspired publications such as the author's own book, *The Creative Wealth of Nations* (Kabanda, 2018), which champions the application of arts to promote meaningful development. To see what this activity looks like in practice, the next subsections of this chapter outline three country case studies: the emergence of a domestic film industry in Zambia; the creation of public bonds to support creative industries in Colombia; and the use of the arts to promote awareness of mental health issues in the Philippines. It must be noted that these various contributions—monetary and non-monetary, instrumental and non-instrumental—are not static; as Galbraith's letter (above) shows, these aspects can be deeply complementary, interacting in a dynamic fashion.[13]

[10] See also Kabanda (2018: 16).

[11] See also UNCTAD (2018).

[12] Available at https://unctad.org/en/pages/PublicationWebflyer.aspx?publicationid=2328.

[13] See Kabanda (2015) and Holt, ed. (2017: 572), for example. The monetary and non-monetary can also be seen as direct and indirect.

'Growing the Film Industry' in Zambia

A new kind of creative industry is emerging in Zambia,[14] inspired by Nigeria's Nollywood, which in recent years has emerged as the world's second-largest movie producer in terms of number of films made. After agriculture, Nollywood is now apparently considered the largest employer in Nigeria; excluding pirates, it is estimated to employ more than 1 million people and to officially generate, on average, some US$600 million annually for Nigeria's economy.[15] In the early 2000s, Nollywood movies were just known as Nigeria's home videos; as they became popularized at first via video-cassette traded across Africa, however, that has changed—they have become more and more popular, and now are available on satellite and cable television, not to mention streaming services.[16]

That these movies normally deal with African themes for Africans by Africans no doubt makes them appealing to Africans. But in Zambia there is something else that was initially associated with Nollywood—the budget, as things currently stand, is small, with sources putting the cost at making a movie somewhere between US$15,000 and US$30,000 or US$25,000 and US$70,000.[17] Notwithstanding changes in cost, the ability to work with small budgets and makeshift arrangements seems to have fuelled the kind of ingenuity needed to deal with obstacles: in Zambia, as in Nigeria, local film-makers have learned not to count the walls but how to climb them.[18] The walls range from working with shoestring budgets to dealing with short production timeframes; they climb them not only to make a living from their creative instincts, but also to tell their own stories.

In 2016, the journalist Norimitsu Onishi (who helped coin the term Nollywood) reported that local Zambian film-makers were found shooting a family melodrama in the town of Kitwe in Nollywood style: the budget was US$7,000, the endeavour took about ten days, and the studio was a private home. If we appreciate that this home was hardly an African state house, or that a feature film can cost more than US$70 million to make in Hollywood style, then we can recognize, with the German expert on African popular culture Matthias Krings, that Nollywood has 'created a model for movie production in other African nations' (Onishi, 2016).[19]

Whether Krings's observation is a recent phenomenon or not is another story. What is clear is that trade in creative goods and services is not just a luxury, or exclusively for the rich nations. Countries like Zambia also have vibrant stories

[14] Lumbe (2018).
[15] Oh (2014), as cited in Kingsley (2017); see also Kabanda (2018: 84) and Moudio 2013).
[16] Onishi (2016), as cited in Kabanda (2018: 84).
[17] Nsehe (2011) and Omanufeme (2016), as cited in Kabanda (2018: 84).
[18] Comment by Nigerian film producer Bond Emeruwa, as cited in Kabanda (2018) and *This is Nollywood* (2007).
[19] See also Kabanda (2018: 85).

to tell, unique creative arts, and extraordinary creative abilities that can be a viable source of income; Zambians can make a living from the creations of their minds. Such small-scale creative trade is often neglected in national accounting; but as is often the case, local artists and entrepreneurs[20] are not waiting for governments and development agencies to act—the film-makers in Kitwe were found making a product, a movie burned on a DVD, to be sold both nationally and in neighbouring countries (Onishi, 2016).

Creative trade of this type and scale raises the question whether such a medium should become a focus for the Zambian government over other art forms. The Zambian government has considered promotion of the creative sector before, but its focus was not just film. For example, as a member of the African, Caribbean and Pacific Group of States (ACP), the country was the subject of a 2011 report called 'Strengthening the Creative Industries for Development in Zambia', the first in a series of policy-oriented reports prepared as part of UNCTAD's pilot project involvement with five ACP countries. The project was funded by the Ninth European Development Fund of the European Commission as part of the ACP cultural industries support programme. Implemented between 2008 and 2011 by the International Labor Organization (ILO), UNCTAD, and UNESCO, it also received institutional support from ACP's Secretariat (UN, 2011: xvii, 1). The project's objective was in line with what the Kitwe film-making episode exemplifies: expanding trade and employment in the creative sector.

In the familiar aspects of international trade, Zambia might be better known for its copper and cobalt exports. But Zambia has a long history of being active in the film industry, with the Zambian actor and historian Henry B. J. Phiri noting that the country's film sector dates back to the 1970s, during which its most famous production was the 1979 release of the British film *Touch of the Sun*. Considered to be the first Zambian-produced full-length feature film, *Touch of the Sun* featured the celebrated Zambian actor Edwin Manda, who seemingly remains the most recognized name of all Zambians who took part in the film (Lumbe, 2018).[21] Almost four decades later, in 2018, the Zambian–Welsh director Rungano Nyoni's *I Am Not a Witch*, a satire about misogyny, brought Zambian cinema back to the global spotlight. Although Nyoni acknowledges that her much-acclaimed debut is not 'a savior of Zambian cinema', its global acclaim may open doors for more Zambian film-makers; and it has also elicited some much-needed government support. Shot in 2016 in Lusaka, Zambia's capital, *I Am Not a Witch* had its own Nollywoodian overtures: it took just six weeks to shoot and featured non-professional local actors (Obenson, 2018), though details of the budget are not stated in the

[20] Onishi (2016); see also Kabanda (2018: esp. ch. 4). Surely, as the Nobel economist George Akerlof points out, 'All individuals and all communities live by the stories they tell and by the music they produce' (Akerlof, 2018).

[21] Other names include Patrick Shumba Mutukwa who appeared in the celebrated film *Black Panther* (see Lumbe, 2018 for details).

present citations. Nonetheless, Nyoni, who hoped to film a story in more familiar territory in Wales and whose transnational identity is likely to have influenced her film-making approach, 'instead found herself in Zambia, making a low-budget film that ticks all the wrong boxes for first-time filmmakers, working with multiple nationalities, animals, amateurs and children in a country with little in the way of infrastructure for doing so' (Wise, 2018).

Given the infancy of the film industry in Zambia and the paucity of associated official statistics, it is unclear how many people the film industry employs, how fragmented it is, and exactly how much the entire creative sector contributes to the nation's economy. Even so, in 2015 the industry was said to be worth some US$350,000 per annum (about 4.5 million Zambian kwacha). And although such firms as M-Net's Zambezi Magic channel and Super Shine Investments are picking up interest in distributing the films, most of the distribution is done on the streets by local producers themselves, selling their DVDs for about US$2 a copy (Mwizabi, 2015). Whatever the case, since creative work is rife with intellectual (or rather creative) and monetary exploitation, what matters most might be not the sector's size or growth rate per se but whether the benefits, including monetary gains, are shared fairly with those who are active in the industry, especially in an age where inequality is escalating at an alarming rate.

This issue, which even plagues industries like Hollywood, is especially critical in Zambia. As Gethsemane Mwizabi writes, 'Zambia's emerging filmmakers, constrained by limited budgets, often use their homes and neighbourhoods as locations, and cast family members, neighbours and friends as actors' (Mwizabi, 2015). If we consider such concepts as trade in value added,[22] everyone and everything Zambian involved—including the creative mediums, and even the landscape that can be mapped as a geographical indication—are what make the films innately Zambian. Indeed, one could argue that the home-made character of these movies cannot be decoupled from them; it gives them relevance and meaning, it gives them value and power, and it makes them a cultural force that supports areas like branding, social integration, and cultural diversity—areas that convey authenticity and meaning beyond whatever monetary contribution they may or may not make to formal measures of economic growth.

In 2018, Zambia's Minister of Information and Broadcasting Services at that time, Dora Siliya, stated that 'the film industry has the potential to effectively contribute to the growth of the economy if properly harnessed' (Lusaka Times, 2018). Properly harnessing such growth might mean, above all, building cross-cutting infrastructure, as well as legislating a viable film policy, augmenting film training programmes, and attending and hosting international film festivals.[23] Creative endeavours like movie production certainly do not work in a vacuum; they interact closely with other areas, including tourism and education, music, fashion

[22] See Kabanda (2018: esp. 85–7).
[23] For more on the proposals, see UN, 2011.

and design, media, and information technology and trade. What is more, they entail developing legal frameworks that guarantee fair intellectual property rights for local artists.

If Zambia can appreciate what happened in Kitwe, creating movies for sale in Zambia and abroad means that creative mediums like film-making need a prominent place in Zambia's Vision 2030[24]. Moreover, it should not surprise anyone that Zambia's National Arts Council was pleased that Nyoni 'produced an indigenous Zambian story, told by indigenous Zambian actors, with an indigenous Zambian language (Bemba) taking center stage in the film' (Obenson, 2018). In our current moment, where indigenous languages are dying at an alarming rate, such indigenous productions have never been more relevant. With active government support there may be more of such films to come.

Harvesting 'Orange Bonds' in Colombia

In recent years, the Republic of Colombia, a country known as the 'gateway to South America' and perhaps even better known for its coffee,[25] has decided to tap into its equally fertile creative soil to grow the world's first-ever 'orange bonds'. It has done so with the full support of President Ivan Duque Márquez, who has promoted it as part of a broader national development strategy. If the more familiar green bonds are earmarked to fund climate and environmental projects,[26] orange bonds are earmarked to fund creative and cultural projects, used specifically to finance areas such as literature, visual media, and the performing arts. (More generally, cultural and creative tourism also qualify.) Promoting the arts using bonds in this way is historically unique,[27] and Colombia's move may show that 'orange bonds' could potentially enable vastly larger sums of investment monies to flow into creative industries than ever before.

Orange bonds are so named because, according to Buitrago Restrepo and Duque Márquez (2013: 42), culture, creativity, and identity are often associated with the colour orange, which has its own longstanding history. Ancient Egyptian artists, for example, used the orange arsenic sulphur realgar to render hieroglyphic decorations of their pharaohs' tombs in antiquity; the Hindus place orange chakra on the belly to represent an individual's centre of creative power; Native Americans associate orange with leadership and learning; and for Peru's Túpac Katari, orange represents society and culture. Drawing on such cases, Buitrago Restrepo

[24] For more about Vision 2030, see Embassy of the Republic of Zambia (n.d.). See also Republic of Zambia (2017).

[25] In 2011, UNESCO inscribed Colombia's coffee cultural landscape Eje Cafetero a World Heritage Site. The country is among the top five largest coffee producers in the world. See Department for International Trade (2018) for an overview of Colombia's geography, economy, and other aspects.

[26] See also the related story by Anderson et al. (2019).

[27] See Cummans (2014) for an insightful overview of the history of bonds.

and Duque Márquez (2013: 42–5) decided to label the cultural and creative economy The Orange Economy, doing so, they said, because it otherwise 'lacks a brand identity'; hence the bold title of their 2013 book, *The Orange Economy: An Infinite Opportunity.*

Orange bonds are administered in Colombia by Bancóldex, a state-owned development bank created in 1992 with a mandate to promote business growth and foreign trade as part of a larger plan to open up Colombia's economy (Bancóldex, 2018a).[28] Dubbed 'the entrepreneurs' bank', Bancóldex offers entrepreneurs both financial and non-financial services 'focused on knowledge and information fixed on understanding the needs of Colombian companies' (Bancóldex, n.d.). In 2018, according to the general shareholders' meeting report, Bancóldex disbursed a record COP$4.81 trillion (about US$1.27 billion[29]), which represents a growth rate of 37 per cent; as of this writing it is the highest rate registered in the bank's history (Bancóldex, 2018b: 3).

Another record in the bank's history may have been set on 29 November 2018—the day Bancóldex made the first issuance of the orange bonds 'worth COP$400,000 million (approximately US$125,000)' (Bancóldex, 2019a: 9)..[30] This project received technical assistance from the Inter-American Development Bank. As one observer noted, President Duque 'isn't pushing the Orange Economy just to promote the arts—he wants to lessen the Colombian economy's dependence on things like oil' (Sonneland, 2018); even so, the appetite for orange bonds on auction day was clearly not small: bids were received from over 320 investors, more than doubling the initial investor forecast, with the minimum bid around US$3,100. According to Juliana Martínez Hernández, Bancóldex's head of the creative economy, and her colleagues, Bancóldex currently has three to four active bonds. The maturity dates are two to three years, and the bonds are local so far, in that they are bought and sold only in Colombia. (Although foreigners can buy the bonds, they have to go through local brokers, as do local investors.[31])

As a tool for social and economic development in Colombia, the orange economy is intended not only to finance but also to refinance initiatives in Colombia that meet one of these three orange categories:[32]

[28] For related information about the bank, see Ocampo and Arias (2018: 189–94).

[29] Aproximate figure according to the current exchange rate (but this may certainly flactuate).

[30] Juliana Martínez Hernández, personal communication, 5 September 2019. Other sources (for example, Sonneland, 2018 and Gudmundsson, 2018) provide various figures. All the same, the debút of this intitaive genereted much interest.

[31] Juliana Martínez Hernández et al., personal communication, 5 September 2019. See also Gudmundsson 2018. On the difference between a bond 'dealer' and bond 'broker', see Thau (2011: 12).

[32] Funds from orange bonds shall not finance or refinance projects that meet one or more of the following categories: projects that previously received Bancóldex funds provided by international development banks and other sources; projects that may not meet what the Ministry of Culture defines as orange tourism; and projects that may elude environmental concerns (Bancóldex, 2019: 8–9).

i. *Conventional Cultural Industries.* Examples include books and the printing industry (though it remains unclear whether a novel and an economics textbook count equally); audiovisuals such as films and movie theaters; and radio and recorded music dubbed as phonographic (Bancóldex, 2019b: 6).
ii. *Functional Creations, New Media, and Software.* Examples include software content and design, such as video games and industrial products; adverting; and news and information services (Bancóldex, 2019b: 7).
iii. *Arts and Heritage.* The largest category thus far, examples here range from visual and performing arts to tourism and 'tangible and intangible heritage'. Curiously, alongside such entries as crafts, archeological sites, traditional knowledge, festivals and carnivals, culturally specific food production is also included under this umbrella (Bancóldex, 2019b: 8), thereby enabling gastronomy and UNESCO's world heritage sites like Eje Cafetero, Colombia's Coffee Triangle, to link cultural tourism with the orange economy.

In aggregate matters, President Duque's goal is to have the Orange Economy contribute at least around 6 per cent to Colombia's GDP by 2027,[33] doubling its current contribution of about 3.3 per cent and thereby 'putting it roughly on par with the manufacturing industry'.[34] But as Buitrago Restrepo, who was in September 2019 named Vice Minister for Creativity and the Orange Economy and thereafter served briefly as Minister of Culture (from January 2021 to June 2021), notes, 'As with any projections, the issue is always timing'. Indeed, if the timing works here, the aim is to reach at least 10 per cent by 2030, or shortly thereafter. Nonetheless, if anything, the coronavirus outbreak, which affected global economic and social order in unforgiving proportions, may complicate realizing goals based on pre-COVID-19 projections. On the other hand, it can certainly be argued that the pandemic has provided an opportunity to build greener and more inclusive economies that, among other things, would call for huge investment in such areas as the arts and parks, given their immense contributions to people's holistic well-being. Whatever the case, Buitrago Restrepo believes that, as a society, Colombians need to set their goals high if they are serious about transitioning their economy. As he points out, the creative economy contributes about 10–11 per cent to the GDP of the United States.[35] In simple maths, if we calculate this using Colombia's 2018 GDP of more than US$330 billion (World Bank, n.d.a), then the 6 per cent goal would be about US$19 billion, and the 10 per cent about US$33 billion—a handsome figure,

[33] Felipe Buitrago Restrepo, personal communication, 11 September 2019.
[34] Sonneland (2018) and LatinAmerican Post (2018); see also Beer (2019). Since many creative activities are informal, the current contribution of the creative sector to Colombia's GDP might be well over 3.3 per cent (and it is just not counted in official statistics). This is the case in many countries; moreover, if one considers such concepts as trade in value-added, then it is almost certainly so.
[35] Felipe Buitrago Restrepo, personal communication, September 11, 2019.

larger than the 2018 GDP of Zambia, which stood at around $26.3 billion (World Bank, n.d.c).

As previously noted, however, growth should not be for growth's sake. For Buitrago Restrepo, the idea is to create about 700,000 direct and 300,000 indirect jobs. In a country with a population of about 50 million (World Bank, n.d.a) that might seem relatively small, but since all jobs are not created equal, this point merits attention: the types of jobs created in the orange sector tend to be greener and more enjoyable than jobs in traditional manufacturing sectors (Throsby, 2010: 40).[36] Thus the funds from the orange bonds are not only about access to formal credit, diversifying 'sources of resources' and improving investment prospects; they are also aligned with the Sustainable Development Goals (Bancóldex, 2019b: 9). Target 8.3 under Goal 8 is particularly apropos: 'Promote development-oriented policies that support productive activities, decent job creation, entrepreneurship, creativity and innovation, and encourage the formalization and growth of micro-, small- and medium-sized enterprises, including through access to financial services' (UN, n.d.).

Such a target anchors the orange funds selection process and evaluation. Beyond examples of activities or interventions arising from these orange bonds, perhaps the most important aspect is that the very issuing of these types of bond is in itself a concrete intervention, placing investment in cultural initiatives in the same financial space as (say) oil refineries. Just as such investment is likely to bear fruit later, the specific orange economy outcomes are also likely to be harvested later as Colombia seeks to meet the 2030 Sustainable Development Goals.[37] But since the creative sector is cross-cutting, two immediate concrete activities of note include: (a) the passage of Law No. 1834 in 2017, better known as The Orange Economy Law, a creation of the Ministry of Culture's National Council of the Orange Economy, which seeks to centre its policies on 'information, institutions, infrastructure, integration, inclusion, inspiration and industry' (van Schaick, 2019); and (b) the establishment of agreements like the Colombia–Japan permanent orange working group, whose goal is to advance common interests in trade, investment, and cooperation in the creative sector (Moss, 2019).[38]

Such ventures are not without their own risks. For President Duque, who upon assuming office in 2018 promised not to let the orange economy grow in an 'untamed manner' (like a wild bush), his promise could satisfy the following objective: Orange funds should absolutely be available for social issues that may not raise GDP or job numbers immediately, but are nonetheless important in the overall application of meaningful development. But why? Creative sectors are not immune from tending to grow in an ad hoc manner, fuelling elite capture, entertaining

[36] See also Kabanda (2018: 20).

[37] See *Colombia Crea 2030 Strategy* (Republic of Colombia, n.d.)

[38] The bilateral trade between Japan and Colombia reached over US$799 million in the first half of 2019. That figure includes US$217.5 million in exports (Moss, 2019).

exploitation of different sorts, and widening income inequality. And since trickle-down economics does not always trickle down as promised, the clamant desire to focus on GDP and job growth could imply that even such well-meaning initiatives as the orange bonds might succumb to the temptation of elevating numbers at the expense of the quality of the outcome.

In any case, bonds have a propensity to fluctuate in price due to changes in interest rates. Technically speaking, this is known as 'interest rate risk' or 'market risk'. As such, 'all bonds are subject to interest rate risk, regardless of the issuer or the credit rating or whether the bond is "insured" or "guaranteed,"' as Annette Thau (2011: 25–6) has argued. Therefore, how exactly the orange bonds initiative will play out will take time to tell. But arguably the political, intellectual, and practical leadership in Colombia is there, and it could inspire others grappling to identify innovative ways to fund cultural initiatives. What is more, if diversity that includes all ethnic groups across the territory—involving everyone from the Amazon and San Andrés to the Pacific and Guainía—is the most important aspect to promote equity, as Colombia's former Minister of Culture Carmen Inés Vásquez Camacho has said,[39] then Colombia's approach could be the new orange deal that inspires inclusive development across the world.

Using the Arts to Promote Mental Health in the Philippines

Worldwide, it is estimated that some 970 million people in 2017 had a mental disorder or substance abuse problem. Anxiety disorder, estimated to affect about 4 per cent of the global population, was highest on the list (Ritchie and Roser, 2018). Yet nearly 'half the world's population lives in countries where, on average, there is one psychiatrist to serve 200,000 or more people; other mental health care providers who are trained in the use of psychosocial interventions are even scarcer' (WHO, 2013: 8).[40] Globally, 'annual spending on mental health is less than US$2 per person and less than US$0.25 per person in low-income countries, with 67 per cent of these financial resources allocated to stand-alone mental hospitals, despite their association with poor health outcomes and human rights violations' (WHO, 2013: 7–8).[41] Hence the quality of care 'tends to vary between the inadequate and the shocking. Treatment remains predominantly based in large psychiatric institutions, which can absorb a huge share of all mental health spending'.[42]

[39] Carmen Vásquez, personal communication, Eighth Inter-American Meeting of Ministers of Culture and Highest Appropriate Authorities, 20 September 2019, Bridgetown, Barbados.
[40] See also Kabanda, 2018: 181).
[41] See also Kabanda, 2018: 177.
[42] WHO-AIMS (2006), as cited in EIU (2016: 38).

In the Philippines, that share is up to 95 per cent.[43] The psychiatric care infrastructure, moreover, is concentrated in Manila, with few mental health specialists in rural areas (EIU, 2016: 40). The Philippines has 'the highest number of depressed people in Southeast Asia', writes Sara Soliven de Guzman (2018), noting that 'the National Statistics Office reported that mental illness is the third most common form of disability in the country. Records show a high number of cases among the youth'. Indeed, according to a 2003 study by the Department of Health, the ninth leading cause of death among Filipinos aged between 20 and 24 years is intentional self-harm. The WHO's 2011 Global School-Based Health Survey reports that 'in the Philippines, 16 per cent of students between 13–15 years old have ... seriously considered attempting suicide while 13 per cent have actually attempted suicide one or more times during the past year' (Department of Health, 2018; see also Senate of the Philippines, 2018).

The arts can potentially play a promising role in elevating human welfare generally, but in alleviating mental illness in particular, which is increasingly prevalent in both poor and rich countries. If there cannot be genuine physical health without sound mental health, there can also be no genuine mental health without sound mental health awareness. The latter is what inspired the creation of the Julia Buencamino Project to foster mental health awareness in the Philippines. The project was started in 2016 following the suicide of a teenager named Julia Louise Centenera Buencamino in her Quezon City home in 2015. The youngest of four children, Julia was the daughter of the actor Nonie Buencamino and actress Shamaine Centenera-Buencamino. Following in her parents' Roscian footsteps, Julia was an actress who became better known as Amelia 'Aimee' Chua in the 2015 Philippine TV series called *Oh My G!* (PeoplePill, n.d.), a series in which her father also appeared.

Determined to do something about a problem that was now not just a statistic but a family tragedy, Julia's parents founded the project in her name. And as artists from a long lineage of artists, it was only natural that they would use their talents to promote mental health awareness. In 2018 they participated in that year's Festival of Arts and Ideas organized by the Cultural Center of the Philippines (CCP).[44] The Festival programme, it said, 'engages artistic expression to create awareness and hold conversations on issues concerning mental health conditions'. It would

[43] WHO-AIMS (2006), as cited in EIU (2016: 38).

[44] This was a three-day affair focusing on mental health, and the budget for it was a little over ₱1 million (over US$19,000) met by CCP. In many ways, however, the Julia Buencamino Project relies on its founders to operate. In some cases, they have operated on as little as ₱50,000 to ₱100,000 (about US$1,000–US$2,000), and while they have received some donations from concerned individuals, the total since the project began is only about ₱100,000 (US$2,000) as of this writing—so they also have to rely on pro bono services from artists and venue and equipment providers. Accordingly, although they may get public grants, as Julia's mother Shamaine Centenera-Buencamino said, this is 'civic work' for all of them. The audience is admitted free of charge, however, so this makes it easy to ask artists to perform for free (Shamaine Centenera-Buencamino, personal communication, 17 October 2019).

help participants express their struggles through interactive arts activity, with the hope of helping them cope with their mental strife by discovering new interests and acquiring new skills, while gaining support from the arts community (CCP, 2018).

Julia also wrote poetry, and her poem 'When my mask shatters / and you see how broken I really am, / will you still love me?' became not only a headline but also the centrepiece of the Festival. Indeed, as Julia's mother, who directed the Festival, said,

> Julia's poem speaks of the fear that most people struggling with mental health suffer—the fear that they won't be accepted and loved. That is why we need to talk about mental health. Mental health affects everyone. Mental health problems need to be talked about. The Festival is not just to increase awareness, but to hold conversations to understand and help manage these mental conditions.
>
> (CCP, 2018)

In 2018, conversations about managing mental health conditions were held at various venues of the CCP, 'the premiere showcase of the arts in the Philippines' (CCP, 2018, (n.d.a, n.d.b). A government agency founded in 1969, CCP works under the National Commission for Culture and the Arts (NCCA), and its vision provides thus: 'Art matters in the life of every Filipino' (CCP, n.d.a). Meeting that vision in the Philippines, which has a population of over 100 million people (World Bank, n.d.b), is certainly no small task though some preliminary steps have been taken to create a fully-fledged ministry or Department of Culture.[45] Given that such proposals normally take time to materialize it is difficult to bank on them. For the Julia Buencamino Project, however, immediate action has meant providing participants with an array of activities.

Besides showing short films on mental health, the activities at the 2018 Festival included workshops on 'Cultivating Attunement, Inner Composure, and Resilience through Arts'; learning to play the ukulele; and immersion in 'Poetreat', a medium that employs 'the power of poetry in helping people recognize difficult emotions and express them through literary means'. The Festival culminated with 'Will You Still Love Me?', a performance featuring mental health poetry readings interpreted with leaps of dance as well as video testimonials and a forum (CCP, 2018).

In sum, the 2018 Festival's objective, according to Julia's mother, was three-pronged: First, the workshops were 'designed to teach participants skills to practice

[45] The proposal was mentioned when the author was in Manila to present a paper entitled 'Beat by Bit' at the 2018 International Conference on Cultural Statistics and Creative Economy, sponsored by NCCA. See 'An Act Establishing the Department of Culture, Appropriating Funds Therefore, and For Other Purposes' (Escudero, 2019). As of this writing, NCCA is the Philippine government's official cultural agency, based in the Office of the President.

the arts as a way to improve the mind and manage stress'. Second, the film screenings were intended to 'give viewers more information on different mental conditions as well as an opportunity to ask psychologists questions to understand mental illness more'. And third, the performances were to 'allow audiences to empathize with those who suffer and to continue fighting mental illness by living inspired lives' (CCP, 2018).[46]

Some Implications for Development Policy

The cases cited above—promoting film production in Zambia, issuing public bonds to support creative industries in Colombia, and using the arts to address mental health issues in the Philippines—suggest at least five practical areas in which active support from policymakers could go a long way towards both supporting the arts for their intrinsic value and enhancing their capacity to contribute to human well-being and national prosperity.

Delisting Arts Equipment as 'Luxury Goods'

In numerous countries, items like video equipment and cameras have been subject to luxury taxes. This tends to frustrate artists, producers, and creative entrepreneurs, most of whom can ill-afford high prices. Recognizing this problem, the UNCTAD Zambian report recommended the removal of such equipment from the Zambia luxury import list (UN, 2011: 30–1). Some items in this domain may well be justified but given that many artistic endeavours run on shoestring budgets, it is worth making an exception on these duties for creative artists. Until these countries start making their own recoding equipment, luxury duties may only narrow the entrepreneurial space for artists and entrepreneurs. Many potential investors in familiar industries are offered tax incentives in the name of luring them to invest in a given area; creative artists should expect nothing less.

Protecting Intellectual Property for Development

Intellectual property is one of the most contested issues in development. What should be done, for example, when it is estimated that Nollywood loses 50 per

[46] There were around 500 people who attended this event. But this figure excludes those who viewed the exhibit. And since the event was held in the lobby near the 'little theater', theatregoers accessed it during intermission. That CNN Philippines also made a TV feature makes it likely that the programme reached a bigger audience (Shamaine Centenera-Buencamino, personal communication, 17 October 2019).

cent of its revenue from piracy? The Trade-Related Aspect of Intellectual Property (TRIPS) treaty certainly has its shortcomings, yet from Zambia to Colombia there is surely a great need to consider how protecting intellectual property can work for (rather than against) local artists and creative businesses, instead of just favouring global corporate interests. Given the knowledge gap here, education remains one of the most primary interventions, ranging from teaching about intellectual property in educational and judicial systems, as Taiwan has done,[47] to teaching artists about copyright. Moreover, many countries need to identify how income from locally attuned intellectual property provisions can be collected and distributed fairly. This is critical because some abusers here may not be poor students but instead big firms and producers.[48]

Find Creative Ways to Fund the Creative Arts

Colombia's example shows that the government can play a major role in finding ways to fund cultural projects (even though it remains to be seen if the momentum to promote cultural financing will last after Duque is out of office and how truly inclusive it be). Whether governments get their monies from bonds or lotteries or taxes on such things as soft and hard drinks, for a number of ministers of culture, their primary lament is inadequate funding. Strategically, one way to correct this is to repeatedly and publicly contrast how much countries spend on their military and their cultural industries (for instance, in GDP percentages). This will require a shift in mindsets, but since the connection of the arts to the economy is cross-cutting, there must be better coordination of funds across ministries of finance, tourism, trade and investments, education, and foreign affairs, health, social development and economic planning, and so forth. Since budget fights are not uncommon, a constructive way forward may be to explore how a cultural agency can access funds from the trade ministry to promote trade and investments in creative work.

Equitable private and nonprofit funding as well as public and private partnerships are also options. Their application, however, should not eliminate serious public investments for inclusive cultural initiatives from consideration. And here, via frameworks such as south-to-south cooperation, countries in the so-called 'Global South'[49] have much to learn from each other in finding innovative ways of funding—this might include tackling issues of domestic resource mobilization, tax evasion, and the like. There is also a need to explore ways to create (something like) an International Fund for Culture, whose mandate would be to finance

[47] See the Taiwan Intellectual Property Training Academy (n.d.), available at www.tipa.org.tw/ep1.asp.
[48] See Faris, 2013; Kabanda, 2018: esp. 94–111.
[49] There is an impassationed debate against the usage of this term, but that is a topic for another day.

cultural activities. Ideas informing its design and operation could be drawn from frameworks such as those underpinning Muhammad Yunus's social business innovation[50] or Brazil's Social Service of Commerce (SESC). The latter, a leading arts funder with US$600 million a year to spend, is a 'private, nonprofit entity whose role is enshrined in the national Constitution'. SESC 'derives its budget from a 1.5 per cent payroll tax imposed on and collected by Brazilian companies'.[51] The creation of such a fund should not mean that organizations like the World Bank and regional banks take a back seat; they also need to earnestly explore ways in which cultural funding can be realized.

Applying the Arts to Underfunded Development Issues

Mental health issues are also vastly underfunded across the world, but in the first instance the arts can at least help to promote greater awareness. Discussing such issues may be a taboo in many cultures but avoiding the problem altogether does not solve it. Initiatives such as the Julia Buencamino Project deserve wider attention and application if they are not to remain ad hoc endeavours. The arts themselves can also be therapeutic: in addition to schools and community centres, more health agencies should consider how the arts can help people suffering from mental disorders. Globally, the WHO can do much more to examine how nations might tap into their creative wealth to promote mental health—at present, even in its 'comprehensive mental health action plan 2013–2020', the arts and healing are mentioned nowhere.[52] There should also be greater cooperation between ministries of culture and ministries of health, but one can imagine potential synergies with other areas.

Expanding Data Collection

There is a clear need to improve the scope, accuracy, and curation of cultural statistics—one cannot ignore the reality that such numbers are needed to enhance the political standing of the arts in policy deliberations, and to demonstrate its material utility. Many cultural activities lose out due to lack of official numbers. Even as there are many arts attributes that cannot be measured, attempts to measure what can be measured are needed. One practical suggestion is the creation of

[50] A social business is a business with a mission to solve social issues. It is not a charity, however, although it does not function as a typical profit-maximizing business. As such, it 'might be defined as a *non-loss, non-dividend business*'. See Yunus (2007: ch. 2, esp. p. 24); also available at www.yunussb.com/about-us.

[51] That budget figure may have changed, since the reporting in 2012. See 'Brazil's Unique Culture Group Stays Busy Sharing the Wealth' (Rother, 2012).

[52] See also (Kabanda, 2018: ch. 8).

a 'Cultural Trade Index' and a 'Cultural Exchange Index'. The former would deal with how countries participate in international trade in creative goods and services; the latter would measure international cultural exchanges between nations (Kabanda, 2018: 217–20).

Conclusion

Their historical neglect notwithstanding, the arts and popular culture often tell people's stories in powerful ways, conveying and indeed themselves comprising the kinds of lives people have reason to cherish, even (or especially) in the midst of perpetual difficulties. These stories connect the cultural and economic domains, in so doing helping to explain why today increasing interest and support is being given to the creative economy and its contribution, actually and potentially, to inclusive development.

A stronger dose of that interest and support is badly needed—especially now as countries rebuild after the COVID-19 pandemic. This is because an arts-inclusive approach can provide multi-pronged benefits. Zambian moviemakers, as we have seen, are creating jobs in one of the most underfunded and under-recognized sectors yet in doing so they are also tackling some of the biggest issues in global development, such as promoting youth employment and economic diversification. Furthermore, besides telling their own stories and engaging in 'greener' jobs, the value of employing such creative mediums to promote social issues—from gender parity and indigenous languages to nation branding and public health—cannot be underestimated.

But if culture is underestimated so too is politics, broadly speaking. At a time when it is easy to despair about the capacity of governments to deliver even basic services to their citizens, let alone their willingness to sponsor the arts, Colombia's orange bonds should remind us of how political will can muster cultural financing and that genuine cultural investment can deliver returns that simultaneously tackle multiple challenges. As we saw in the Philippines, mental health is a multi-pronged problem and so money spent on the arts and mental health can generate cross-cutting benefits.

A common limiting factor when making a case for promoting the arts in development is the absence of data: neither supporters nor sceptics can reliably present an evidence-based argument. More and better data alone, however, are unlikely to get the arts adequately appreciated by the development community. What is also needed is persuasion from the heart as much as listening with the heart. Key actors in the case studies discussed here undoubtedly show that, in so doing they are perhaps echoing one of the twentieth century's most famous economists. In the preface to the First Annual Report of the Arts Council (1945–46)—among the final documents he wrote—the great economist John Maynard Keynes, also the founding chairman of the Arts Council of Great Britain, pondered a future in which

> the economic problem will take the back seat where it belongs, and that the arena of the heart and head will be occupied, or reoccupied, by our real problems—the problems of life and of human relations, of creation and behaviour and religion. And it happens that there is a subtle reason drawn from economic analysis why, in this case, faith may work. For if we consistently act on the optimistic hypothesis, this hypothesis will tend to be realised; whilst by acting on the pessimistic hypothesis we can keep ourselves for ever in the pit of want.[53]

The optimistic hypothesis can certainly help emancipate our imagination, liberating us from the pit and pity of want. And if imagination occupies our hearts and our heads, it can permit us to find ways to elevate meaningful development in meaningful ways. On that premise, as we see in Zambia, Colombia, and the Philippines, the arts can lead the way.

Many governments acknowledge that the creative and cultural industries have always been there, but never before has there been a desire to augment their contribution to development, as is the case now. Across the world, not just in the three countries considered here, what is needed is to have international organizations work with governments and the private sector to adequately promote creative sectors, recognizing them for what they are—authentic mediators and powerful conveyors of our 'real problems'.

References

Akerlof, G. (2018) 'Cover endorsement', in Patrick Kabanda. *The Creative Wealth of Nations.*. Cambridge: Cambridge University Press.

Anderson, J. T. Gartner, A. Mauroner, and J. Matthews (2019) 'Conservation finance takes off as the Netherlands issues one of the largest green bonds ever', World Resources Institute, June 21, available at www.wri.org/blog/2019/06/conservation-finance-takes-netherlands-issues-one-largest-green-bonds-ever.

Bancóldex (n.d.) 'About Bancóldex', available at www.bancoldex.com/about-bancoldex.

Bancóldex (2018a) 'History', July 18, available at www.bancoldex.com/about-bancoldex/history-916.

Bancóldex (2018b) *Report of the Board of Directors and the President to the General Shareholders Meeting 2018*. Bogotá: Bancóldex, available at www.bancoldex.com/sites/default/files/documentos/1._report_of_the_board_of_directors_and_the_president_2018.pdf.

[53] Keynes (1946).

Bancóldex (2019a) *First Orange Bonds Annual Report.* Bogotá: Bancóldex, available (in Spanish) at www.bancoldex.com/sites/default/files/bancoldex_-_reporte_de_bonos_naranja_2019.pdf.

Bancóldex (2019b) *Framework Bonos Naranja Bancóldex,* Updated August. Bogotá: Bancóldex, available at www.bancoldex.com/sites/default/files/bancoldex_framework_bono_naranja_actualizado_agosto_2019_definitivo_pdf.pdf..

Basu, K. (2011) *An Economist's Miscellany.* New Delhi: Oxford University Press.

BEA (Bureau of Economic Analysis) (2013) 'Changes to how the U.S. economy is measured roll out July 31', July 23, available at www.bea.gov/news/blog/2013-07-23/changes-how-us-economy-measured-roll-out-july-31.

Beer, J. (2019) 'Colombia wants to be known for its creative economy even more than its coffee', *Fast Company*, June 6, available at www.fastcompany.com/90367601/colombia-wants-to-be-known-for-its-creative-economy-even-more-than-its-coffee.

Buitrago Restrepo, P.F. and I. Duque Márquez (2013) *The Orange Economy: An Infinite Opportunity.* Washington, DC: Inter-American Development Bank, available at https://publications.iadb.org/en/orange-economy-infinite-opportunity.

CCP (Cultural Center of the Philippines) (n.d.a) 'About Us', available at https://culturalcenter.gov.ph/about-us/.

CCP (Cultural Center of the Philippines) (2018) 'Will You Still Love Me: Festival of Arts and Ideas', Press Release, November 21. (Also see www.clickthecity.com/events/e/35529/will-you-still-love-me-festival-of-arts-and-ideas.)

Cummans, J. (2014) 'A brief history of bond investing', October 1, available at http://bondfunds.com/education/a-brief-history-of-bond-investing/.

de Guzman, S.S. (2018) 'Mental health of Filipinos today', *Philippine Star*, August 27, under 'As a Matter of Fact', available at www.philstar.com/opinion/2018/08/27/1846128/mental-health-filipinos-today.

Department for International Trade (2018) 'Overseas Business Risk – Colombia', Government of the United Kingdom, updated November 12. Available at www.gov.uk/government/publications/overseas-business-risk-colombia/overseas-business-risk-colombia.

Department of Health (2018) 'Mental Health Program', Republic of the Philippines, available at. https://doh.gov.ph/national-mental-health-program.

The Economist (2014) 'How Nigeria's economy grew by 89 per cent overnight', April 7, available at www.economist.com/blogs/economist-explains/2014/04/economist-explains–2.

The Economist (2016) 'A Mean Feat', January 9, available at www.economist.com/finance-and-economics/2016/01/09/a-mean-feat.

EIU (Economist Intelligence Unit) (2016) 'Mental Health and Integration: Provision for Supporting People with Mental Illness: A Comparison of 15 Asia Pacific Countries', London: EIU, available at https://impact.economist.com/perspectives/sites/default/files/Mental_health_and_integration.pdf.

Embassy of the Republic of Zambia (n.d.) 'Trade and economy', available at www.zambiaembassy.org/page/trade-and-economy.

Escudero, E.G. (2019) Republic of the Philippines. House. 'An Act Establishing the Department of Culture, Appropriating Funds Therefore, and For Other Purposes' (Department of Culture Act of 2019). HR 21. 18th Cong., 1st sess., (July 1), available at www.congress.gov.ph/legisdocs/basic_18/HB00021.pdf.

Faris, S. (2013) 'Can a tribe sue for copyright? The Maasai want royalties for use of their name', Bloomberg Business, October 24, available at www.bloomberg.com/bw/articles/2013-10-24/africas-maasai-tribe-seek-royalties-for-commercial-use-of-their-name.

Gudmundsson, H. (2018) 'Colombia's Bancóldex to offer 300b pesos in orange bonds', S&P Global Market Intelligence, November 28, available at www.spglobal.com/marketintelligence/en/news-insights/trending/9witdmckuaqmbvnx0_wjow2.

Holt, R. P. F. (ed). (2017) *The Selected Letters of John Kenneth Galbraith*. Cambridge: Cambridge University Press.

Howkins, J. (2001) *The Creative Economy: How People Make Money from Ideas*. London: Penguin.

Imasogie, O. and T. J. Kobylarz (2013) 'Yes, Lady Gaga's songs contribute to GDP', *Wall Street Journal*, May 27, available at www.wsj.com/articles/SB10001424127887324767004578491452865597808.

Johnson, S. (2016) *Wonderland: How Play Made the Modern World*. New York: Riverhead Books.

Johnson, S. (2017) 'How play shapes the world', *1A* WAMU 88 and NPR. Hosted by Joshua Johnson, January 25, available at www.npr.org/2017/01/25/511670498/how-play-shapes-the-world.

Kabanda, P. (2015) 'Work as art: Links between creative work and human development', Background paper, Human Development Report 2015. New York: UNDP, available at http://hdr.undp.org/sites/default/files/kabanda_hdr_2015_final.pdf.

Kabanda, P. (2018) *The Creative Wealth of Nations: Can the Arts Advance Development?* Cambridge: Cambridge University Press.

Keynes, J.M. (1946) *First Annual Report of the Arts Council (1945–1946)*. London: Arts Council of Great Britain.

Kingsley, I. (2017) 'In the frame', *Accounting and Business*. Africa Edition, July/August, available at www.accaglobal.com/content/dam/ACCA_Global/Members/AB/2017/July-August/AB-AFR-July-2017.pdf#page=26.

LatinAmerican Post (2018) Editorial: 'Colombia: Is the orange economy the solution?', November 8, available at https://latinamericanpost.com/24427-colombia-is-the-orange-economy-the-solution.

Lewis, D., D. Rodgers, and M. Woolcock (eds) (2014) *Popular Representations of Development: Insights from Novels, Films, Television and Social Media*. London: Routledge, Taylor & Francis Group.

Lumbe, L. (2018) 'Growing the film industry', *Zambia Daily Mail*, April 28, available at www.daily-mail.co.zm/growing-the-film-industry.

Lusaka Times (2018) 'Government committed to supporting movie industry', November 18, available at www.lusakatimes.com/2018/11/18/government-committed-to-supporting-movie-industry.

Moss, L. (2019) 'Japan and Colombia agree to promote "Orange Economy" bilateral trade', *Finance Colombia*, September 5, available at www.financecolombia.com/japan-colombia-agree-to-promote-orange-economy-bilateral-trade.

Moudio, R. (2013) 'Nigeria's film industry: A potential gold mine?' *Africa Renewal* 24–25. May, available at www.un.org/africarenewal/sites/www.un.org.africarenewal/files/Africa-Renewal-May-2013-en.pdf#page=24.

Mwizabi, G. (2015) 'A starring role for Zambian stories' *Mail & Guardian*, October 16, available at https://mg.co.za/article/2015-10-16-starring-role-for-zambian-stories/.

Nsehe, M. (2011) 'Hollywood, meet Nollywood', Forbes, April 19, available at www.forbes.com/sites/mfonobongnsehe/2011/04/19/hollywood-meet-nollywood.

Obenson, T. (2018) '"I am not a witch": How a satire about misogyny is transforming Zambia's film industry', IndieWire, September 17, available at www.indiewire.com/2018/09/i-am-not-a-witch-rungano-nyoni-interview-zambia-1201999906/.

Ocampo, J. Antonio and P. Arias (2018) 'Colombia's system of national development banks', in S. Griffith-Jones and J. Antonio Ocampo (eds) *The Future of National Development Banks.*, Oxford: Oxford University Press, available at http://dx.doi.org/10.1093/oso/9780198827948.003.0007.

Oh, E. (2014) *Nigeria's Film Industry: Nollywood Looks to Expand Globally.* Washington, DC: United States International Trade Commission, October, available at www.usitc.gov/publications/332/erick_oh_nigerias_film_industry.pdf.

Omanufeme, S. (2016) 'Runaway success', *Finance and Development*, June, available at www.imf.org/external/pubs/ft/fandd/2016/06/omanufeme.htm.

Onishi, N. (2016) 'Nigeria's booming film industry redefines African life', *New York Times*, February 18, available at www.nytimes.com/2016/02/19/world/africa/with-a-boom-before-the-cameras-nigeria-redefines-african-life.html.

PeoplePill (n.d.) 'Julia Buencamino', https://peoplepill.com/people/julia-buencamino.

Republic of Colombia (n.d.) 'Colombia Crea 2030 Strategy', Bogotá.

Republic of Zambia (2017) 'Report of the Committee on Media, Information and Communication Technologies for the Second Session of the Twelfth National Assembly. Appointed on Thursday, 21st September 2017', Lusaka: National Assembly of Zambia, available .at www.parliament.gov.zm/sites/default/files/documents/committee_reports/Media_report_main.pdf.

Ritchie, H. and M. Roser (2018) 'Mental health', Our World in Data. First published April, available at https://ourworldindata.org/mental-health.

Robinson, K. (2001) *Out of Our Minds: Learning to be Creative.* Chichester, UK: Capstone.

Rother, L. (2012) 'Brazil's unique culture group stays busy sharing the wealth', *New York Times*, March 27, available at www.nytimes.com/2012/03/27/arts/brazils-leading-arts-financing-group-shares-the-wealth.html.

Sen, A. (2000) *Development as Freedom.* New York: Anchor Books.

Sen, A. (2001) 'Preface', in *Workshop on the Development of the Music Industry in Africa'.* Development Economics Research Group on International Trade, June 20–21. Washington, DC: World Bank.

Senate of the Philippines (2018) 'Hontiveros lauds signing of Mental Health Law, says 'Help is finally here'', July 21, available at https://legacy.senate.gov.ph/press_release/2018/0621_hontiveros1.asp.

Sonneland, H.K. (2018) 'Explainer: What is Colombia's orange economy?' Americas Society/Council of the Americas, December 4, available at www.as-coa.org/articles/explainer-what-colombias-orange-economy..

Thau, A. (2011) *The Bond Book: Everything Investors Need to Know About Treasuries, Municipals, GNMAs, Corporates, Zeros, Bond Funds, Money Market Funds, and More* (3rd edn). New York: McGraw-Hill.

This Is Nollywood (2007) Directed by Franco Sacchi, available at www.thisisnollywood.com/film.htm.

Throsby, D. (2010) *The Economics of Cultural Policy.* New York: Cambridge University Press.

TIPA (Taiwan Intellectual Property Training Academy) (n.d.) 'About TIPA', available at www.tipa.org.tw/ep1.asp.

UN (United Nations) (2010) *Creative Economy Report 2010: A Feasible Development Option*. New York and Geneva: UNDP and UNCTAD, available at https://unctad.org/system/files/official-document/ditctab20103_en.pdf.

UN (United Nations) (2011) *Strengthening the Creative Industries for Development in Zambia*. New York and Geneva: UN, available at https://unctad.org/en/Docs/ditctab20091_en.pdf.

UN (United Nations) (n.d.) 'Goal 8', Department of Economic and Social Affairs, Sustainable Development, available at https://sdgs.un.org/goals/goal8.

UNCTAD (United Nations Conference on Trade and Development) (2015) *Creative Economy Outlook and Country Profiles: Trends in International Trade in Creative Industries*. Geneva: United Nations, available at https://unctad.org/system/files/official-document/webditcted2016d5_en.pdf.

UNCTAD (United Nations Conference on Trade and Development) (2018) *Creative Economy Outlook: Trends in International Trade in Creative Industries 2002–2015; Country Profiles 2005–2014*. Geneva: United Nations, available at https://unctad.org/en/PublicationsLibrary/ditcted2018d3_en.pdf.

UNDP (United Nations Development Programme) (n.d.) *What is Human Development?* available at http://hdr.undp.org/en/content/what-human-development.

UNDP (United Nations Development Programme)) and UNESCO (2013) *Creative Economy Report 2013 Special Edition: Widening Local Development Pathways*. New York and Paris: UNDP and UNESCO, available at www.unesco.org/culture/pdf/creative-economy-report-2013.pdf.

van Schaick, H. (2019) 'Colombia's efforts to harness the prospects of its emerging orange economy', Oxford Business Group, April 8, available at https://oxfordbusinessgroup.com/blog/harry-van-schaick/roundtables/colombia%E2%80%99s-efforts-harness-prospects-its-emerging-orange-economy.

WHO (World Health Organization) (2013) *Mental Health Action Plan 2013–2020*. Geneva: WHO, available at www.who.int/mental_health/publications/action_plan/en.

WHO-AIMS (2006) *WHO-AIMS Report on Mental Health System in The Philippines*. Geneva and Manila: WHO and Department of Health, Manila, The Philippines, available at www.who.int/mental_health/evidence/philippines_who_aims_report.pdf.

Wise, D. (2018) '"I Am Not a Witch" director Rungano Nyoni worked with non-professionals overseas on "super-ambitious" Zambian fairy tale', Deadline, February 16, https://deadline.com/2018/02/i-am-not-a-witch-rungano-nyoni-baftas-interview-news-1202291631/.

World Bank (n.d.a) 'Colombia', available at https://data.worldbank.org/country/colombia.

World Bank (n.d.b) 'Philippines', available at https://data.worldbank.org/country/Philippines.

World Bank (n.d. c) 'Zambia', available at https://data.worldbank.org/country/zambia.

Yunus, M. with K. Weber (2007) *Creating a World without Poverty: Social Business and the Future of Capitalism*. New York: Public Affairs.

Index